2
3

Joe Fagan

Joe Fagan

Reluctant Champion

The Authorised Biography

Andrew Fagan and Mark Platt

Aurum

First published 2011 by
Aurum Press Limited
7 Greenland Street
London NW1 0ND
www.aurumpress.co.uk

A catalogue record for this book is available from the British Library.

ISBN 978 1 84513 550 8

10 9 8 7 6 5 4 3 2 1
2015 2014 2013 2012 2011

Typeset by Eclipse, Chelmsford, Essex

Printed and bound in Great Britain by
the MPG Books Group

This book is dedicated to Joe's wife Lil, who sadly passed away during the course of its production, and to the thirty-nine victims of the Heysel Stadium Disaster

CONTENTS

FOREWORD

JOE FAGAN, TO me, is without doubt one of the most important figures in the history of Liverpool Football Club. In fact, I'd go further than that. He was the top man, the glue that held everything together during the most glory-laden period of Liverpool Football Club's illustrious existence. A legend in the truest sense of the word.

And when I say this I certainly don't intend any disrespect to the memory and achievements of those other two renowned Anfield sages, Bill Shankly and Bob Paisley. Far from it. I have nothing but the utmost respect and admiration for what they achieved.

They are up there in the highest echelons of Kop folklore and deservedly lauded for the roles they played in making this club the worldwide institution it is today. Take a walk around Anfield on any given day and you're reminded of their contribution everywhere you look. Rightly so.

But in my eyes Joe was the best. Respected like no other but given the least praise. When the legends of Liverpool are discussed it saddens me that his name is too often conspicuous by its absence.

Then again, knowing Joe as I did, he wouldn't want it any other way. That's how he was: unassuming and as down-to-earth as they come, his only concern being the good of the club. Men like him, and indeed everyone else in the Bootroom for that matter, weren't in it for personal gain or glory.

However, as with Bill and Bob, what he did for this club should never be forgotten. Recognition for what he achieved is long overdue and hopefully this book will redress the balance.

His Liverpool career spanned twenty-seven years. That's over a quarter of century of unstinting loyalty to the Reds' cause, during which time he played such a highly significant but unsung role in Liverpool's transformation from Second Division also-rans to Kings of Europe.

I first got to know Joe back in the mid-1960s when I joined Liverpool as a teenaged apprentice, and until the sad day when he passed away in July 2001 he never changed. From day one he became my mentor in football, a father-figure I looked up to and I know many of the other lads felt exactly the same way about him.

I learned so much from him. He was a massive influence not only on my football career but my life in general. A truly fantastic man, as honest as the day is long and as straight as they come, he had an aura that commanded respect. When he spoke you listened and his word was final. If you had a problem it would be Joe you went to: quiet, understanding and approachable Joe. No wonder he was given the nickname 'Uncle Joe'.

You won't hear many bad words said about him but, of course, he had his off days. Nobody is perfect. There'd be days when he'd moan and groan with the best of them and woe betide anyone who got on the wrong side of him. He was most definitely no soft touch.

Everything he did, though, was done in the best interests of Liverpool Football Club. Apart from his family, Liverpool was his life and his dedication to the cause knew no bounds. Loyalty to the Liver Bird was etched in his psyche, while his knowledge of the game was second to none. On the training pitch he wasn't one for fancy phrases or tactical analysis. 'Just go out and play,' was his catchphrase. Together with his fellow Bootroom disciples he preached simplicity. That was the secret.

His coaching credentials alone were enough to see legendary status bestowed upon him. But what followed when he reluctantly agreed to step out of the shadows and take over as manager was the stuff of which dreams are made. Three trophies in one season. His first season. What a remarkable achievement that was.

And it couldn't have happened to a nicer man. There wasn't one person in football who would have begrudged him that success. Given all those years he'd worked quietly behind the scenes, he'd more than earned his moment of fame.

The cynics said he'd simply inherited the Treble-winning team from Bob Paisley. That he had the easiest job in football. What a load of rubbish. If anything, following in the footsteps of a man who'd won nineteen major trophies in nine years, was an unwinnable task.

It was typical of Joe that he answered his critics in the best possible fashion. Yet life in the spotlight didn't rest easy on his sturdy Scouse shoulders, and for him to bow out in such tragic circumstances, just twelve months after the glory of Rome, was awful. He didn't deserve that. Nobody did.

Heysel cast a shadow over his retirement but it shouldn't be allowed to cloud a truly outstanding career in football. There's a famous image of me consoling him as we made our way across the tarmac on our return to Speke airport. It was an emotional moment and one that still lingers in the memory whenever people talk about Joe.

Me? I prefer to remember the good times. And there were plenty of them. Too many to mention or remember. When I shut my eyes, though, I can still see that infectious smile, feel his warmth and hear those footballing words of wisdom.

I'm glad Joe had the chance to prove his worth as manager. He's gone down in history as the first manager to win three trophies in one season and that can never be taken away from him.

For me, though, his best work was done when Shanks and Bob were in the hot seat. If they were around today they'd be first to tell you that football is a team game and without the help and dedication of their tried and trusted backroom lieutenants the success and fame they enjoyed wouldn't have been possible.

I was privileged and honoured to have been just a small part of this team. To Joe I have a lot to thank for that because I believe he had a say in my own elevation to the revered ranks of the Bootroom.

Everyone played their part, men like Reuben (Bennett), Ronnie (Moran), Tom (Saunders), Geoff (Twentyman) and John (Bennison). But, above all, Joe Fagan was the rock. He was there through it all and I honestly believe he was the one person the club could not have done without during this time. Without him I'm not sure the success would have continued for as long as it did.

If it hadn't have been for Joe's brief but successful spell as manager then maybe this book would never have been written. That would have been a crying shame because if anyone's story deserves to be told it's his.

If he was still with us now he'd wonder what all the fuss was about. 'I was only doing my job,' he'd say with typical modesty. But what a job he did.

Simply the best.

To me, that's what Joe Fagan was.

Roy Evans
Liverpool
August 2011

NO ORDINARY JOE

Anfield
Saturday, 26 December, 1981
Liverpool 1, Manchester City 3

CHRISTMAS ENDED EARLY for the red half of Merseyside those thirty years ago. Little more than twenty-four hours after eagerly ripping the wrapping off their presents, 37,929 pairs of feet shuffled home through the cold and dark streets around Anfield. They had just witnessed Liverpool Football Club, reigning champions of Europe, the pre-eminent team in England for a decade, embarrassed in their own backyard. And not for the first time that season. The atmosphere was as gloomy as the leaden sky. Out of sight an almost apologetic-looking Manchester City were packing up and preparing to head home weighed down with gifts. The Christmas visitors from the other end of the East Lancs Road had taken full advantage of their hosts' generosity and the increasing number of individual lapses from Liverpool players.

Bob Paisley's team completed the calendar year of 1981 in an almost unthinkable twelfth position in Division One. City were the third team to leave Anfield with maximum points. The aura of invincibility that had surrounded the famous old stadium for so long was beginning to slip. In his Monday morning match report, the *Daily Post*'s Nick Hilton wrote: 'They looked ordinary – at times downright ragged and City plundered their disorganised ranks with efficiency if not style.' Since the early days of Bill Shankly in the late 1950s, Liverpool had been on a consistently upward spiral and had established themselves as the most successful club in England. Now evidence was building that the once great empire was beginning to crumble. Liverpool may have won their third European Cup seven months earlier, but they had finished the 1980–81 season a disappointing fifth in the League, nine points behind champions Aston Villa. 'There were plenty of murmurings about the beginning of the end of Liverpool's dynasty on Saturday,' added Hilton, 'and the statistics back them up.' As those Liverpool supporters trudged home on Boxing Day in 1981, the cold turkey waiting for their suppers looked, at that moment, like a metaphor for the club's future.

Inside Anfield, a short walk down the corridor from the dressing-rooms, Joe Fagan sat quietly in the hallowed Bootroom. The Liverpool assistant manager had just discussed the latest debacle with his trusted colleagues. He opened his well-thumbed diary for 1981 and settled down to record his private thoughts. 'Dismal,' he wrote. 'Not up to the standard we require. I would say two blokes in our team are playing to their ability, the rest? No.' He put his pen down, sat back wearily and reflected on the significance of the day's events. Were these the final days of the great bastion he had helped to build under Shankly and Paisley? It had been a fantastic run but, realistically, Joe knew it could not last forever. Was this the sad but inevitable end of Liverpool's greatest period of success?

Joe Fagan, for one, would not stand by and watch the curtain fall on the golden era. Immediately his thoughts shifted to finding the solution. What could be done? The players were good enough, that much was clear. Their poor form, he felt certain, was down to psychological issues more than lack of talent. Was there a need to massage some egos? Should they simply knuckle down, work a little harder in training and wait for things to get back to normal? Both were techniques that had worked in the past and would work again. This time, though, Joe decided something a little out of the ordinary was required. He was not given to ranting and raving, but things had gone too far. Twelfth in the table? Liverpool? Not good enough. The players had Sunday off to be with their families, but when they returned Joe was determined to sort them out.

On Monday morning the Anfield dressing-room was packed with some of the finest and most successful players in English football history. There were Kenny Dalglish, Graeme Souness, Ian Rush, Alan Hansen and Bruce Grobbelaar. No less conspicuous were Mark Lawrenson, Phil Neal, Ronnie Whelan, Craig Johnston, Alan Kennedy, Sammy Lee and Phil Thompson. Great players all. But here they were shifting uncomfortably in the wooden bench seats as Bob Paisley handed over the floor to his unusually serious-looking assistant. Joe stepped forward and let rip. He was wild with fury. He tore into the players individually and he tore into them as a team. He criticised their performances, their attitudes, their application and their professionalism. Nothing was left unsaid. The message was loud and very clear: 'This is Liverpool, there are certain expectations and right now they are not being met.' Joe had decided that the players were having too many meetings, spending too much time discussing their own individual problems and the problems of the team. He demanded instead that they took responsibility. There would be no more looking around at each other. It was time to look in the mirror.

The effect of the tirade was enormous. Joe's default setting was an easy grin. His anger was a rarely used weapon. That made it all the more potent. The players were taken aback. This was not a normal dressing-room dressing-down, this was a major event. As the players emerged on to the Anfield pitch to train – the Melwood training ground being frozen – Joe knew he had rattled them. He knew they would be asking some tough questions of themselves. They had needed recalibrating, reminding of the values that had got them to the top. Yelling and making a scene was not part of the job Joe relished. But it was what Liverpool Football Club needed at that moment, so it was what he had done.

The next match was a tricky third-round FA Cup tie at much-fancied Swansea, who were going well under the leadership of former Liverpool talisman John Toshack. Many predicted that this would be a watershed moment. A time for the obituary writers. Liverpool, the wounded giant, would be cut down by the hungry, upstart Welshmen. Not quite. A rejuvenated Liverpool won 4–0. Three days later they beat West Ham United 3–0 in the League at Anfield. The tide had turned. Over the course of the next four and a half months Bob Paisley's team rode a wave of exceptional form all the way to glory in the League Cup and, amazingly, the League title, too. Liverpool were back. And so was Joe Fagan's smile.

Joe's part in the turnaround of the 1981–82 season was typical of his contribution to Liverpool during twenty-seven years at the club. Something needed to be done, so he did it. His skill was being able, unerringly, to select the correct means to right the ship. Usually a more subtle response than bawling and screaming would be used, but the principle was the same. Joe would simply not allow the club to deviate from the path studded with success.

Every morning, almost without fail, he could be spotted making his way along Utting Avenue, crossing the junction of Priory Road and continuing his journey up Arkles Lane, alongside Stanley Park, in the direction of Anfield. In winter months, with his trademark flat cap and sheepskin coat, he was easily recognisable. Passers-by would acknowledge him with a nod of the head and a polite hello, to which he would reply in kind. He could have been anyone: a regular guy out for a morning stroll to the local newsagents to pick up the papers or a pint of milk. But this was no ordinary Joe. This was Joe Fagan: reluctant hero, original Treble-winning manager and Liverpool FC legend.

It is amazing to think, three decades on, that during his entire Liverpool career and beyond, Joe lived in the same modest three-bedroom house just a few hundred yards from the place he worked. Nowadays, a sprawling mansion out in the suburbs would be the norm. Or a multi-million pound property high up on the Wirral peninsula. Or somewhere along the coast towards Southport. Wherever, it would be guarded by electric gates and a mile-long driveway so a fleet of chauffeur-driven top-of-the-range cars could be parked comfortably.

Joe, however, would have been unimpressed by such luxuries and was more than happy with his lot in life. He was a man of simple pleasures. He enjoyed a drop of Scotch, no doubt poured from the never-ending supply of gallon bottles awarded to the 'Manager of the Month' and stored in the Bootroom. And he would drag on any number of cigarettes during the course of a day, a habit that earned him the nickname Smokin' Joe. But that was the height of deca-dence in his eyes. Family holidays usually consisted of a week away at a caravan in Anglesey. Even then he would often return home early if duty called. He once thought about moving house but quickly changed his mind. After all, there was nothing wrong with the house he already had.

To Joe, working for Liverpool was the best job in the world and he appreciated every minute of it. 'One day I might have to go out and get a proper job,' he would often remark. 'That's the way he felt about his role at Liverpool,' says son Stephen. 'He felt privileged to work there and fully appreciated that he was in a fortunate position. Going to work was never a chore.' Since Matt McQueen, who lived within earshot of the Kop in a terraced house on Kemlyn Road while in charge during the 1920s, it is doubtful if any manager has lived closer to his football club than Joe. The fact that he was more than happy to live among the fans is testament to his unassuming, down-to-earth nature. But it also offers an explanation why, beyond the confines of Anfield, he is the forgotten man of a significant part of Liverpool's history.

The great Bill Shankly, who arrived at the club in 1959, was the catalyst who transformed Liverpool from Second Division also-rans to champions. Of that there can be no doubt. However, the creation of Liverpool as a famed giant of European football was certainly a team effort. Statistics do not begin to tell the whole story, but they can illustrate a point: Joe joined the Liverpool coaching staff in 1958 and by the time he left in 1985, the club had won twenty-two major trophies. Ten times they had been crowned champions of England, four times champions of Europe.

Shankly's Liverpool career has been widely heralded, and rightly so. His successor, Bob Paisley, unrivalled in collecting trophies as a Liverpool manager, has also been well studied and acclaimed. Joe was already there when Shankly's revolution started. Initially charged with developing young talent in the reserves, he worked behind the scenes under various job titles for quarter of a century before eventually following in the illustrious footsteps of the two Anfield behemoths. His tenure as manager was brief, ending tragically at Heysel. But during a remarkable first season in charge he surpassed all expectations, and led Liverpool to an unprecedented Treble. A similar feat would later see another manager knighted, yet Joe's achievements continue to be overlooked.

His relative anonymity is understandable: inevitably the manager attracts all of the attention afforded to off-field staff at a football club, and he was Liverpool manager for only two seasons. Joe never courted publicity and kept as low a profile as possible, so that when he ascended the Anfield throne he was unknown to the outside world. Inside Anfield, though, his value was clear, and so were his many and crucial contributions to Liverpool's success. He was not only an original member of the famous Bootroom, he is widely credited as being the man who created it.

Inevitably, Joe's presence and influence, day in, day out over such a long period meant the club as a whole absorbed his approach. As a result, his character and personality closely resemble what football enthusiasts would refer to as 'The Liverpool Way', a phrase now firmly embedded in the football lexicon. The feeling exists that employees of the club and the supporters should behave in a certain way, that they should somehow be different to those of other teams. The 'Liverpool Way' of doing things is understated, private, dignified, strong, principled and consistent. And as Alan Hansen acknowledges: 'Every aspect of Joe's character reflected what Liverpool were all about.'

Joe's time at Anfield spanned a period of great change. The success of The Beatles and Liverpool FC transformed the way the city was perceived by outsiders. Football, meanwhile, journeyed from popular game of the working class to multi-million-pound industry. Footballers themselves progressed from the standard short-back-and-sides to bubble perms and moustaches. Joe was there through it all, noting the changes, moving with the times when necessary, but never for a moment taking his eye off the ball.

During the 1950s and 1960s English clubs were seen as largely inferior to the best the Continent had to offer. But by the 1970s and 1980s English teams were regularly picking up the biggest European trophies. Liverpool were at the forefront of this progressive period. Through his training methods, professional approach and football philosophies, Joe was a key figure. The experience he amassed during a life in football was immense. Not many coaches could gauge the nature and severity of an injury just by watching a player run. Joe could. In dealing with the psychological side of football he had few rivals, constantly keeping his players just the right side of confident for maximum performance.

As a man Joe was humble, loyal and straightforward. He gave his best for others, and expected the same in return. During the research for this book, almost every former coach and player recounted their memories of Joe not only with fondness for the glory days but with great warmth for the man. Even when he had to deliver bad news, the players respected that he took no pleasure in delivering the message and recognised that he genuinely wished them the best. Unlike so many involved in football, he was not looking at others only in terms of what they could do for him. This level of respect and consideration was critical in fostering Liverpool's winning environment, an environment where people felt valued and comfortable.

The other key figures behind Liverpool's rise to the summit of European football, and the subsequent years of dominance, each possessed some of the traits Joe brought to the club. He took his lead from Shankly, worked with Paisley, Rueben Bennett, John

Bennison and Tom Saunders; men like Ronnie Moran and Roy Evans were his trusted lieutenants in later years. But in terms of possessing the whole package of skills needed to run a successful football club Joe may well have been a one-off. He was no miracle worker and he did not work alone. But what he did for Liverpool FC should not be underestimated. Roy Evans acknowledges: 'Bob or Shanks could have good days and bad days, but Joe was there every day, keeping the whole thing together. Without him I'm not sure where we would have finished. Bill and Bob would still have been great managers without Joe, but with him they had that vital somebody there maintaining that bottom line every day.'

The two great passions in Joe's life were football and family. In turn he was devoted husband, father, grandfather, coach and manager. Yet these two bedrocks of his life hardly ever entwined. While it is true that he ate, slept and breathed football, he very rarely took his work home with him. As dedicated as he was to Liverpool, he was always quick to return home to his 'other life', to have his tea or watch his sons play football on a Sunday. 'I also do a bit of gardening but not much. I've got a single track mind. When I'm in the house, I think about the family, and when I'm out I think about football,' he once commented. A visit to the Fagan family home offered few clues that the head of the household was one of the main men behind the phenomenal success of Liverpool Football Club. Mementos were kept hidden away and football was spoken about no more than in any other house across the city. To his five sons and one daughter, Joe was simply 'our dad', one who went to work in the morning and came home in the evening like any other. Joe thought of himself as an ordinary man. He tried to lead his life accordingly.

In truth, he would not have welcomed the attention a book about his career would have brought. Despite several approaches from publishers, he was never interested in producing an autobiography. Bringing attention to himself was not Joe's style. For him it was always about being part of a team. The diaries he kept, and upon which a large part of this book is based, were never intended for publication. 'It's just stuff I used to write down. Why would people want to read them?' would be his likely reaction if he was alive today. But the fact they have now been unearthed provides fresh insight into the machinations of Liverpool Football Club during the most successful era in their history. It also brings some long overdue recognition to one of football's great unsung figures.

The story of Joe Fagan is one that deserves to be told. It is a story of serious struggle, great happiness, glorious success and bitter sadness. It will take you to a bygone age, across Britain, Europe and beyond. But it starts, fittingly, in his native Liverpool.

Andrew Fagan and Mark Platt
August 2011

CHAPTER ONE

SCOTTIE

J OE FAGAN WAS born in Walton Hospital, Rice Lane, Liverpool, on 12 March, 1921, the first child to Mary and Patrick Fagan. Patrick was a labourer from Ireland while Mary was a born and bred Scouser of Irish descent. Liverpool had long been home to a large Irish population and the majority settled in and around the Scotland Road area of the city. Or plain old 'Scottie' as it is affectionately known by the city's citizens. The Fagans did likewise and young Joe was brought up within earshot of Anfield. Home was a lodging house on Smith Street at the north end of Scotland Road. From here a walk of less than a mile up Everton Valley and then Walton Breck Road would lead Joe to the gates of Liverpool Football Club's famous Spion Kop.

Life in Liverpool during the 1920s and 1930s was tough. Scotland Road, and its myriad of densely populated surrounding streets, was regarded as one of the most notorious slum areas of the city, with many of its inhabitants living below the poverty line. Unemployment was rife, housing conditions cramped and inhospitable. Children with holes in their shoes or even no shoes on their feet at all were a common sight. Pawn shops did a brisk trade as the poor were forced to make whatever sacrifices were necessary to clothe and feed their families. Despite these brutal hardships nothing could dampen the character of those who lived in the 'Scottie' enclave. To many it was a city within a city, a cultural melting pot that had not only welcomed the huge Irish influx but large swathes of immigrants from across Europe, notably Italy. With a pub on almost every corner it was a vibrant thoroughfare and referred to as the real heartbeat of Liverpool. Renowned for its friendliness and welcoming nature, front doors were always open and the common struggle fostered an endearing community spirit, the only divide being that of religion. The Fagan family, for their part, were Roman Catholics and though he never became a particularly religious man, Joe was baptised at Blessed Sacrament Church in Walton soon after his birth.

Like many of the housewives in 'Scottie,' Mary Fagan's life was centred on the drudgery of domestic chores. Joe's son Roger remembers his grandmother as: 'Typically downtrodden, always cleaning, cooking and mending clothes.' It was a difficult life and her plight was not helped by Patrick's recurring periods of absence from the family home. Described by the family as 'a bit of a rogue', Patrick's exact whereabouts are rather ambiguous and it is widely believed he found himself on the wrong side of the law on more than one occasion. When work as a labourer dried up, he became involved in the murky world of illicit gambling as a bookie's runner. Patrick would be out at all hours taking bets from punters in the local pubs. Always easily found and quite openly partaking in illegal activity, bookies' runners were often picked up by a police force struggling to find culprits for the more serious crimes committed in the area (this may explain some of Patrick's mysterious absences). Joe did have fond memories of his father taking him to the dog races and teaching him, with unerring accuracy, how to pick a winner. However, the pair's relationship inevitably suffered and Patrick's absence for the majority of the first thirteen years of Joe's life caused a good deal of resentment. The memory of effectively being abandoned by his father affected Joe's outlook on family life, and in later years he always took his responsibility to provide for and protect his family extremely seriously.

Young Joe was forced to grow up quickly and thanks, in particular, to the loving care of his mother, he did not veer from the straight and narrow. Joe's childhood was generally blessed with happiness and his love of football, which began almost as soon as he could walk, was always encouraged. With no father on hand, his Uncle Joe, Mary's brother, was an influential figure in Joe's formative years, a warm, caring man who was a constant source of support.

The close proximity of Anfield and Everton's Goodison Park meant football was a constant theme in the lives of those who lived around Scotland Road. Every Saturday swarms of supporters would make their way across the top of Smith Street and up Everton Valley towards the ground of whichever team was at home that day. Often Joe would join the throng, equally happy to enjoy the excitement and camaraderie on offer at Liverpool or Everton.

For Joe watching would never compare to playing, so he would take every opportunity to join in with the mass 'kick-abouts' which took place at all hours of the day on the wastelands of 'Scottie'. When there was no 'kick-about', Joe honed his skills on the cobbled streets with a ball made from waste paper. This he would kick against the gates of the timber yard at the foot of Everton Valley, on the site where aspiring local footballers now ply their trade on five-a-side pitches. Academically Joe was a bright pupil and, after attending Boaler Street and St Alphonsus primary schools, he passed his eleven-plus examination to win a scholarship at St Elizabeth's Central, then one of the few Catholic grammar schools in Liverpool, and situated on Breckfield Road South, just a short uphill walk from his home. He might have gone further with his education if his mind had not been so set on becoming a footballer.

Joe's ability with a ball at his feet, evident from an early age, flourished at secondary school. It was during his time at St Elizabeth's that he first showed his leadership qualities by captaining the school team to success in the *Daily Dispatch* Trophy, a competition run by the Lancashire Schools Football Association for teams across the North-West. It was a big achievement and whetted what would later become an insatiable appetite for silverware.

Joe's role in the success did not go unnoticed. In the 1934–35 season he was chosen to represent Liverpool Boys. To be regarded as one of the best eleven footballers in the city for his age was a tremendous honour, though it was a far from vintage campaign for the team: the end-of-season report noted that 'the 1934–35 City team has had only a mediocre year'. In the LSFA minute books a leading official, listed as Mr McSweeney, referred at some length to the apparent poor quality of the players and went on to explain that 'the expected points of finesse were lacking and the organisation during games was poor'. The real barometer of success at this level was how the team fared in the prestigious English Shield, which Liverpool had won on two previous occasions. It was the number one target of the Liverpool Schools FA at the start of every season and, with Joe in the team as centre-half, a 3–1 loss to Salford in an early round added to the foreboding sense of disappointment. So, too, would a surprise defeat at the hands of St Helens by the same scoreline in the Lancashire Cup, and a semi-final exit to Southport in the Merseyside Trophy. The one bright spot for Liverpool Boys that season was a 3–0 victory over Ormskirk on 29 November, 1934, at Goodison Park. As would be the case today, the opportunity for Joe to perform at such a grand setting was viewed as a real privilege. To cap an already unforgettable occasion he managed to add his name to the scoresheet. Joe also played his first game at Anfield that season and was on the winning side as Liverpool Schools defeated Bootle in the annual W.R. Williams Memorial match.

Though football was always his first love, Joe was almost as handy with his fists. It was quite common for boys to learn boxing in school at that time, and by all accounts Joe was a natural. On 'Scottie' Road, where gang culture was rife and street brawling commonplace, this toughness would have served him well. The family tell a story of him winning money at a local fair by knocking out the resident boxer and then successfully fighting numerous challengers who emerged from the crowd. Joe also excelled at cricket at St Elizabeth's and his all-round talent was rewarded with his school's Victor Ludorum, a trophy awarded to the pupil showing the most sporting prowess in each year. Where his penchant for sport came from no one knows as there was no history of athleticism in the family. Nor was it extended to Joe's younger brother, Frank, born in 1934. In spite of the 13-year age difference, the two Fagan siblings were extremely close. 'There was a great love between them,' says Joe's son Roger. Joe was the archetypal big brother who would look out for Frank and, as such, was viewed as the father figure they both lacked during Patrick's long periods away from home. With an expanding family, the Fagans moved four miles north of Smith Street to the more salubrious surrounds of 20 Amos Avenue, Litherland. At fourteen, Joe took on the responsibility of helping to support the family financially with his first serious job: a junior position at Sefton Tanning Yard brought home the princely sum of ten shillings (50p) a week. By this time Patrick had returned to being a constant presence at home but his relationship with Joe, now fast becoming an adult, would never properly recover from the years of absence.

Even as he became more closely acquainted with the realities of adult life, Joe's passion for sport never wavered. He remained a frequent visitor to both Anfield and Goodison, and though his father was a staunch Evertonian, Joe had no real preference for either team, which was quite unusual in Liverpool. Ever since Everton's acrimonious departure from Anfield in 1892, which resulted in an intense Merseyside rivalry, the city has been split into two distinct divides – red or blue. Wherever you go, be it in the street, on the factory floor, in the pub or in the school playground, there can be no escaping it. When strangers meet, the first question invariably asked is where their footballing allegiances lie. The nearest Joe came to stating a preference was when he suggested that Liverpool had 'a better boys' pen'.

Joe was still in nappies when Liverpool had last enjoyed success, as back-to-back League champions in the early 1920s. With the great Dixie Dean now leading their attack, Everton had become the dominant football force in the city during the 1930s. In 1927–28, Dean achieved immortality by scoring a phenomenal sixty League goals; in 1933, he was among the scorers at Wembley as Everton brought the FA Cup back to Merseyside for the first time in twenty-seven years. This was an era when the Cup was viewed as the most coveted prize in football and, like the impact Liverpool's miraculous Champions League triumph of 2005 had on the city, any impressionable local youngster with an interest in football could have been forgiven for becoming intoxicated by the 'magic of the Cup'. The day after they defeated Manchester City 3–0, Dean and his team-mates paraded the trophy past the top of Smith Street as the horse-drawn cavalcade made its way from the city centre to Goodison. Thousands lined the route to welcome home the victors, including a twelve-year-old schoolboy who, fifty-one years later, would also ride through the very same streets displaying the wares of his first season as Liverpool manager.

Though undoubtedly impressed, Joe did not become smitten with Dean's Everton. However, over at Anfield, where Joe was just as frequent a visitor, Liverpool were stuck on a downward spiral. As the country attempted to shake off the effects of the Great Depression, Liverpool were unable to escape the clutches of their own severe slump. Each Saturday evening the local *Football Echo*, the 'Pink' as it was commonly known because of the colour of its pages, would deliver further tales of woe for success-starved Liverpudlians. The League table printed on the front page would show their club firmly entrenched in the lower reaches of the First Division and on two occasions in the mid-1930s they only narrowly avoided relegation. But while Liverpool supporters could only look on in envy at the success enjoyed by their great rivals across Stanley Park, they too had heroes of their own: most notably the esteemed Irish goalkeeper Elisha Scott and South African centre-forward Gordon Hodgson, the club's all-time leading goalscorer until the late 1960s. Scott was so beloved at Anfield that a deluge of outraged letters to the local newspaper prevented the club selling him to Everton as his career began to slow in 1934. Players like Scott,

Hodgson and, of course, Dean, would leave their mark on all the football-mad youngsters in the city at this time and Joe was no different. As a defender he was also influenced by the likes of Everton's Warney Cresswell and Liverpool's Tom 'Tiny' Bradshaw. These footballers were far removed from today's 'superstars'. At his peak Dixie Dean earned £8 a week – a tidy wage but not enough to generate the kind of envy and bitterness we see from football supporters nowadays. The men Joe looked up to were easy for him to relate to: they lived in areas he knew well and came from similar backgrounds to his own. Years later, even as manager of Liverpool, Joe continued to live among the fans who watched his team. He could never understand those who saw footballers as somehow superior to everyone else.

As Joe grew older opportunities to watch football diminished because of his own playing career. By his mid-teens he was well known locally and described as 'the find' of the 1936–37 season. His signature was coveted by a host of the region's top amateur clubs and he was eventually signed by St Helens-based Earlestown Bohemians. Commonly known as 'The Bohs', Earlestown competed in the Liverpool County Combination, a strong league in which Liverpool and Everton both fielded their respective 'A' teams, alongside South Liverpool, Prescot Cables and Runcorn. Joe joined as a 16-year-old in August 1937 after impressing in a pre-season trial match. His talent shone through even in an 8–2 defeat. By his third game for the reserves he had become captain, and before the mid-point of the season had forced his way into the first team. He was instrumental in helping the Bohs finish fourth in the league and their first success in the prestigious George Mahon Cup. Joe's performance in the final, a 3–1 victory over Prescot BI, was described in the local press as 'brilliant', and he walked away with not only a winner's medal but also the accolade as man of the match. A local scribe said of him: 'The 17-year-old centre-half, only a youngster but full of pluck, determination and ideas, is perhaps the most constructive pivot the Bohemians have ever had.'

It was not long before his performances started attracting scouts from professional clubs. Among them were Liverpool and he was invited to Anfield for a trial. In charge of team affairs at Anfield at this time was George Kay, a dour Mancunian who had captained West Ham United in the famous White Horse FA Cup final of 1923, the first to be played at Wembley Stadium. He joined Liverpool from Southampton in 1936, inheriting from George Patterson a team in serious decline. He gradually began to turn the club's fortunes and, forever on the lookout for fresh talent, took a keen interest in the young triallists. According to family members and Liverpool FC historians, Kay liked what he saw in young Joe. A place on Liverpool's books was there if Joe decided he wanted it. It was an opportunity most young Scousers would have jumped at. But not 17-year-old Joe Fagan.

Even as a young man, Joe possessed an ability to see the bigger picture. Just as he would do years later as a coach and manager, he would not allow his heart to rule his head: he was certainly not one to be seduced by the romantic vision of running out for his hometown club. He was unconvinced that Liverpool would be the right move for him, believing that first-team opportunities would be limited. 'There was a feeling at that time that if a youngster joined his local club they would not think as much of him as they would an outsider,' Joe later explained. It was a justifiable claim, backed up by Liverpool's first-team squad list for the 1936–37 season just finished. Of the twenty-six players used during the campaign only three had been born locally – Alf Hanson, Jack Balmer and Syd Roberts; the following season the number in the squad fell to just two out of twenty-nine.

Of course, there is the counter-argument which suggests if a player is good enough their chance will come, as proved during that era by Eddie Spicer and Laurie Hughes. Both followed in Joe's footsteps by representing the City schoolboys side before joining their hometown club and going on to establish themselves as popular members of the successful post-War team. Had Joe also chosen to sign it is quite possible that he could have been even more of a Liverpool legend than he actually is.

But maybe he was deterred by the Anfield crowd's reputation for giving some of the home-grown players a hard time when results were not going well. Joe had seen and heard the abuse and vitriol regularly aimed at inside-forward Balmer who, despite racking up one hundred and ten goals in the red shirt, was often made a scapegoat and accused of a lack of appetite in the tackle.

Whatever Joe's reasoning, turning his back on Liverpool was a big risk, especially with no other offers on the table at this point. But he was to take a more unconventional, but ultimately equally rewarding route into Liverpudlian folklore. Such was the faith he had in his own ability, Joe decided to bide his time and wait for an opportunity to try his luck elsewhere. Manchester City and Manchester United soon expressed interest and he jumped at the offers to travel down the East Lancashire Road for trials. Both managers, Wilf Wild at Maine Road and Walter Crickmer at Old Trafford, were suitably impressed and both offered him a contract. Joe was torn between the two, but it was City's greater reputation and offer of £1 a week more that eventually swayed his decision. On 8 October, 1938, aged seventeen, Joe Fagan officially put pen to paper at Maine Road – his childhood ambition had been realised and a career in professional football was set to begin.

CHAPTER TWO

A LOYAL CITIZEN

D ESPITE BEING A division below neighbours United, Manchester City were generally perceived as the bigger of the two clubs in 1938. United had been champions twice during the early part of the century and, like City, had won one FA Cup. During the 1930s, however, they only narrowly escaped relegation to English football's third tier and suffered severe financial hardship that almost dragged them into bankruptcy. City, on the other hand, with their more modern stadium and bigger crowds, were considered a much more glamorous option for any aspiring young footballer. Arsenal may have been the dominant force in England during this decade, but City ran them a close second in terms of success, winning the FA Cup in 1934 and the League Championship as recently as 1936–37. However, they had suffered the indignity of demotion the following season: the first time in history that the reigning English champions had been relegated.

Compounding the misery for City fans in May 1938 was the fact that United passed them going in the opposite direction after securing promotion back to the top flight. No one knew it at the time but it was to signal the start of a turnaround in fortunes in which United would eventually usurp City. At the time of signing his first professional contract, though, Joe Fagan was adamant that he had made the right decision, and he never once regretted it.

Having scored more goals than any other team in the First Division during their relegation season, much of the blame for City's demise was placed on the defence in which Joe was now hoping to earn a position. Nevertheless, competition for places was intense, especially for a rookie teenager. With a team packed full of League and Cup winners, many of them fully-fledged internationals, patience was a virtue Joe needed in abundance. It was a sentiment he would later repeat on countless occasions to eager youngsters during the course of his coaching career. With men like Jackie Bray, Jack Percival and Les McDowall ahead of him in the pecking order it was never going to be easy to break through, but he simply knuckled down and got on with the job.

On and off the pitch, Joe adapted quickly to life in Manchester, a city that reminded him of Liverpool. Despite the great rivalry that has long existed between the two cities, the seeds of which were sown way back in the early days of the industrial revolution, Joe recognised the warmth of the honest, hard-working folk who lived at either end of the East Lancashire Road. He was made to feel very welcome in Manchester and at first lived in digs close to the ground. Former local resident Marjorie Cooper remembered: 'During the late 1930s he lived on my street opposite the ground. He used to come to our house and play cards with my parents. There was a woman who rented out a room to the club and she'd usually have three players in there. Joe was one of them and I think the other two were Albert Barr and Ray Freeman. It must have been pretty cramped with three players in one room, but that was pretty normal back then.'

Joe struck up early friendships with fellow young hopefuls George Smith and Billy Walsh, both of whom had recently joined the club. Joe's friendship with Fleetwood-born Smith and Dubliner Walsh would last a lifetime. Together, they progressed through the City ranks, often travelling to matches in a club car so old that Joe used to recall how they had to use bricks to hold the bonnet in place. In later years he would regularly holiday with Smith at Butlin's in

Skegness, while he kept in touch with Walsh long after their careers in football were over and even visited him in Australia during retirement.

It was not long after moving to Manchester that Joe met his future wife, Lillian Poke, a friend of Marjorie Cooper's and two years his senior, at a social club dance. Though Lil, who worked in a gentlemen's tie shop in the city centre, had no real interest in football she came from a large City-supporting family who lived very close to Maine Road. One of thirteen children, her father died at an early age but she enjoyed a lower middle-class upbringing and was acquainted with a family of local butchers, the Edwardses, who would later become synonymous with Manchester United. Lil took a strong dislike to one member of the Edwards clan and this led to her harbouring a firm loathing of all things Manchester United for the rest of her life. As on Merseyside the competition between Manchester's two clubs was intense and if Joe was not already aware of it, he quickly became indoctrinated into the City way of thinking thanks to Lil and her siblings.

They may have come from contrasting backgrounds, but Joe and Lil hit it off immediately. Lil remembered that on Saturday evenings after matches they would visit the cinema. However, regular attacks of cramp, bought on by sitting for long periods in such small seats, would force Joe to stand bolt upright in front of the projector and ruin the film for the rest of the audience. It may have put a stop to their trips to the cinema but it did not affect the relationship. Within two years of first setting eyes on each other they were married and had set up home in the shadow of Maine Road in a neat terraced house on Beveridge Street.

As the 1930s drew to a close, Joe's footballing future was also looking bright. He was making good progress at Manchester City, first in the 'A' and 'B' teams, then in the reserves, and was hoping to push for a first-team place before long. Like so many players of his generation, though, the Second World War would disrupt his burgeoning playing career. After just three games of the 1939–40 season, all League football was suspended, and would not return for seven years, wiping out the formative years of a generation of players.

Until the time came for his military service to begin, Joe continued to play whenever and wherever he could. City gave him permission to turn out in the Cheshire League for local non-League side Hyde United. With the Cheshire League not bound by the same Wartime restrictions imposed on the Football League, Joe was able to maintain his fitness in a competitive environment. Together with his close pal Billy Walsh, he made his debut for Hyde as a centre-back on 13 October, 1939, and played a significant part in a 2–1 win over Stalybridge Celtic. The *North Cheshire Herald* was full of praise for the new boys and reported: 'The outstanding player for Hyde was Walsh but Fagan, too, gave an attractive display in the pivotal position.'

Another debutant for Hyde that afternoon was winger Cyril Lawrence, formerly of Blackpool. Cyril lived in Salford and remembers travelling to matches on the tram with Joe. 'A smashing lad with a typical Scouse sense of humour,' he says of him. They were paid thirty shillings per game plus their travelling expenses and would often stop off at the White Lion public house in Market Square for 'a lemonade which the landlord, who was a Hyde director, would turn into a shandy'.

The standard may not have been as high as the Football League, but Joe continued to demonstrate his playing potential during his time at Hyde. With him in the team results improved immediately and the local press regularly reported that he had done a good job containing the opposition forwards. Other promising youngsters in the Hyde ranks around this time included Manchester United duo Charlie Mitten and Johnny Aston Senior, both of whom would win the FA Cup with United in 1948. With players of such quality success soon came Hyde's way. In May 1940 they triumphed in the Cheshire League East Section only to lose the two-legged play-off for the title against the winners of the West Section, Droylsden.

Joe played twenty-three league games for Hyde, plus a further three in the Cheshire Senior Cup, but by the start of the 1940–41 season he was back at City as they prepared to compete in the regionalised League North. Joe pulled on the famous sky blue shirt in a senior capacity for the first time on 14 August, 1940, in a charity match against an RAF XI at Maine Road, which City won 2–0. The following week he retained his place for the opening game in the North Regional League, a goalless draw at home to Everton. He played in the following four games, including a 4–1 derby victory over United played the day after German bombers had caused considerable damage and destruction by dropping high explosives on to densely populated areas of Liverpool. Fortunately, Joe's Liverpudlian family and friends escaped the brunt of these bombings, but Manchester also suffered from the night raids of the German Luftwaffe. In March 1941, Old Trafford was hit, forcing United to share Maine Road with City for the next eight years. Joe's participation in that Manchester derby was to be his last appearance in a City shirt until the War was over.

National service beckoned and, once again showing the tactical mind that was to serve him so well later in life, Joe opted to sign up voluntarily rather than wait to be called up. His reasoning was that if he volunteered he would have at least some element of choice over where he served; this would not be the case if he was called up. He opted for the Royal Navy, but the decision backfired spectacularly when he became seasick as soon as he left dry land. It was not long before he set sail for the Middle East where he served his country as a telegraphist on a minesweeping flotilla off the coast of Egypt. Unfortunately the sea-sickness never really abated and as a result he often referred to himself as 'the world's worst sailor!'

The experience of combat had a profound effect on Joe and it became part of his life he was reluctant to talk about in later years. Many of the men with whom he did his Navy training went on to serve aboard the ill-fated *HMS Hood* and never returned. Joe was acutely aware that this could easily have been his own fate. Countless footballers were killed in action during the War, one of the most high-profile being former Liverpool full-back and England captain Tom Cooper. Joe's future Manchester City team-mate George Smith was one of many who suffered injury: a gun-shot wound in South Africa resulted in the amputation of his left hand.

During the course of hostilities Joe fed his insatiable appetite for sport by playing football at every opportunity as well as resuming his interest in boxing. 'That's how he got his flat nose,' says Joe's youngest son Michael. 'He was a hard man, a really hard man. He was a good bare-knuckle fighter in the Navy and used to earn money from it. He was wiping the floor with everyone, winning all this cash until some officer got wind of it, went in the ring with him and pasted him everywhere, breaking his nose. The surgeon was supposed to fix his broken nose but instead took the bone out.'

When not fighting, Joe turned out for (and captained) the Alexandria Royal Navy, the Alexandria United Services and The Wanderers, a representative team for all servicemen in Egypt. On 19 November, 1944, the *Egyptian Gazette* reported that, 'with Fagan outstanding at centre-half', Alexandria United Services beat the Egyptian FA league representatives 1–0 at Bewsher Park, Moustafa. He made his Wanderers debut on 22 January, 1945, in a 7–0 thumping of the Cairo Egyptians. Joe replaced the captain of the team, Taffy Walters of Chester City, who was forced to sit it out with a cut head he sustained after being hit with a bat playing softball. The *Egyptian Mail* gave Joe a positive review, remarking: 'Fagan came into the team and gave a solid show under a big handicap.' Not only was the young defender making his debut in an unfamiliar team, he was also selected as captain, prompting the *Mail* to note: 'This surely must be a record for any man making his representative debut as an emergency player! It is a wonder he didn't have a rank bad show through sheer nerves.'

Other press reports were less favourable with Joe notably being given 'the run-around' by a tall, long-striding striker named Hariry representing the Egyptian FA XI. Joe survived that experience to keep his place in the Wanderers team for the victorious Chrystall Cup final against the Egyptian United Services in Pont de Kubbeh on 12 January, 1946. In a 2–0 win, Joe was praised as 'a grand stopper. He had the man-mountain Shal in his pocket for most of the game'. Joe returned to Britain to be demobbed days later and the *Egyptian Gazette* reported (perhaps harshly) that he had been forced to 'cry-off' from the Wanderers game the next weekend. However, they did note in an editorial piece covering the various players returning home, that finding a replacement for Fagan would be 'the biggest problem of the lot!'

When on leave, Joe had also represented Portsmouth, thanks to Fratton Park's close proximity to the Naval base. He also appeared for City against United in April 1944 and then managed to squeeze in another four appearances for them in the Football League North during the 1945–46 season, taking his total number of Wartime appearances for City to eleven. Standing at just over six feet tall, and weighing in at almost twelve stones, Joe established himself as a typical no-frills type of defender, more solid than spectacular, but good on the ground and commanding in the air. Despite his lack of first-team experience he was seen as very much part of City's post-War plans. Local Manchester journalist Eric Thornton commented that he was 'one of the strongest kickers of a dead ball I had ever seen, tough and never one to shirk a tackle'.

By the time competitive football resumed in 1946–47 Joe had become a father for the first time, with Lil giving birth to John in June 1945. He was now fully focused on forcing his way into a Manchester City side who were hoping to return to the top flight. With a squad including pre-War greats such as goalkeeper Frank Swift, Scottish inside-forward Alex Herd and captain Sam Barkas, City were among the favourites for promotion. They got off to a decent start, unbeaten in their first seven games, and Joe had to bide his time. However, there was a change of management in November when Wilf Wild, the man who signed him, reverted to his secretarial role and was replaced by City's captain of the 1930s, Sam Cowan. Cowan was a renowned motivator who it was hoped would bring fresh ideas on tactics and team selection. After leaving

Maine Road in 1935, Cowan wound down his career at Bradford City before accepting the player-manager role at Cheshire League side Mossley. In 1938 he joined the coaching staff at Brighton & Hove Albion and set up a physiotherapy business near the Goldstone Ground. However, the lure of the club where he had enjoyed so much success as a player was persuasive. Cowan took charge with City fifth in the table, just a point behind the four teams tied at the top. His arrival certainly had a positive effect as he immediately inspired them to a long unbeaten run.

Within a month of Cowan coming in, Joe finally made his official Manchester City debut, more than eight years after joining the club. He was nearly twenty-six. His big moment came on New Year's Day 1947 against Fulham at Maine Road, and according to Eric Thornton in the *Manchester Evening News* it was a long overdue call-up for a player who 'has been playing grand football with the reserves'. Joe lined up at right-half, taking the number four shirt from Albert Emptage, who moved across to left-half in place of the injured Walsh. Joe fully justified his selection by turning in a 'creditable performance' as City won comfortably 4–0.

It was an important victory as it took City back to the top of Division Two for the first time since the early weeks of the season. During this impressive run of form they would equal the club's all-time record of twenty-two league games unbeaten. Joe established himself as a regular in the side, most often deployed in his Navy position of centre-half, rather than right-half. He also received his first taste of playing in the FA Cup when Gateshead of Division Three North were despatched 3–0 at home in the third round. First Division Bolton Wanderers were overcome after a replay, but hopes of a prolonged run were vanquished emphatically by fellow promotion-chasers Birmingham City, who triumphed 5–0 at St Andrew's in round five, thus denying Joe the opportunity of a quarter-final tie at Liverpool.

City's success in the League attracted big crowds to Maine Road. Seven years without competitive football had whetted the appetite of football followers all over the country and it was no different in the Moss Side district of Manchester, where City boasted an average gate of more than thirty-seven thousand. But while it may have been boom time at the box office, it was not so lucrative for the players. With the maximum wage set at just £14 during the season, and £8 in the summer, the players threatened to strike and the row rumbled on throughout that inaugural post-War season. A harsh winter, which resulted in a record number of postponements, meant the season had to be extended, but City remained on course for their number one goal. Joe and his fellow defenders were in top form over Easter and throughout April, keeping four successive clean sheets. As the campaign entered May just a point was required to secure promotion.

As well as the goals from free-scoring front men Alex Herd, George Smith and, to a lesser extent in the second half of the season, Andy Black, a settled defence had been an equally key factor in City remaining at the top of the Second Division. But without the inspirational Frank Swift, who was in action at Hampden Park representing Great Britain in the so-called 'Match of the Century' against a Rest of the World XI, and the injured Les McDowall, a first League defeat since November, at home to Newcastle, caused the celebrations to be put on hold. It was a temporary setback and one that merely delayed the inevitable. Seven days later, in front of a heaving crowd of 67,672 at Maine Road, normal service was resumed. Swift was still absent, but McDowall returned alongside Joe at the back, and Herd scored the only goal to beat Burnley, their nearest challengers and the FA Cup finalists.

There were still five games to play and the extended season ran into June, but by then City, despite dropping points away to Bradford, Sheffield Wednesday and West Bromwich Albion, had done enough to clinch the Second Division title. Having made twenty appearances, Joe received his first medal in professional football. A memorable season was finally completed on 14 June when George Smith scored all five goals in a 5–1 demolition of Newport County.

*

Determined to build on this success, City officials were already looking to the future. Concerned that the squad was an ageing one – Joe was one of only four first-team regulars under the age of thirty – the board immediately sanctioned new investment. Wales international outside-left Roy Clarke was brought in for £10,000 from Cardiff City. A failed bid of £14,000 for Blackpool and England's Stan Mortensen was a sign of City's ambition. Other additions in time for the start of the 1947–48 season included Preston winger Jackie Wharton and Belfast Celtic's Eddie McMorran. However, manager Sam Cowan shocked everyone by announcing his resignation in June. When he took over initially an agreement had been reached that allowed him to spend part of each week in Brighton, where he continued to live, before travelling up to Manchester to prepare for matches. The constant commuting, however, was causing growing concern to the club's directors and in response to their pressure to move closer, Cowan resigned.

While a long-term replacement was sought, secretary Wilf Wild stepped back into the breach, an appointment that ensured minimal disruption ahead of the season. Cowan's resignation was a big disappointment for Joe: the manager had played a big part in his successful transition from the reserves. However, there was not much time for Manchester City's promising centre-back to dwell on the departure of his early mentor. Joe, despite his limited first-team experience, was now viewed as one of the mainstays in a team who had also said farewell to stalwart Sam Barkas during the summer. Joe's strong team ethic, loyalty to the cause and ever-ready smile made him a hugely popular figure with fans and team-mates alike. He clearly enjoyed himself during matches, and one newspaper noted that he seemed to play wearing 'a perpetual grin'. In October 1947 winger Billy Linacre joined the club from Chesterfield and he remembers Joe as 'a nice, straight guy, so dry that strangers might even think him sarcastic'.

Having established himself in the first team, Joe soon became firm friends with one of the greatest English goalkeepers of all time. Frank Swift was one of the few remaining members of City's

League and FA Cup-winning sides of the 1930s. At six foot tall, and with a finger-span of almost twelve inches, Swift was a larger-than-life character in more ways than one, and Joe looked up to him. They lived just around the corner from one another and, though there was an eight-year age difference, there was a mutual respect. Indeed, Swift affectionately bestowed on Joe the nickname 'Patsy', in reference to the popular Irish folk song Hallo Patsy Fagan.

According to one of the last surviving members of the City squad from that era, there was generally plenty of good-natured banter flying around the Maine Road dressing-room, and Joe was often at the heart of it. 'He loved to have a laugh and joke with the lads,' remembers Johnny Hart, a then up-and-coming youngster. He has never forgotten how he fell victim to a prank engineered by Joe. 'The club had a dog back then,' he recalls, 'and it could be pretty vicious, especially if someone blew it a raspberry, which is exactly what Joe did on this occasion when I was walking past the room where it was kept. Fortunately for me it was muzzled that day but it still managed to nick the skin on my hand. We laughed about it afterwards, but it was thanks to the likes of Joe that there was such a great team spirit back then.' Joe also had a ruthless competitive streak, as young Hart found to his cost. 'We used to play head tennis in the Maine Road car park after training. It was always me and Jackie Bray against Joe and big Swifty. Somehow we seemed to lose all the time and if we were ever winning they would insist the game continued so the result could be turned around,' he explains. 'This one day, I got a bit fed up of being on the losing side and gave Joe a bit of lip. Straight away I knew it was a mistake. He came bounding over the net and told me in no uncertain terms that because he was a more senior player, I should show a bit more respect. I was taken aback because he was normally such a quiet and likeable character.' Hart would go on to serve the club in a playing, coaching and management capacity for nearly three decades, but admits he was taught a valuable lesson that day, one that stood him in good stead for the rest of his career.

With Swift continuing to keep goal behind him, Joe was again a key figure in City's first season back in the top flight. They finished a respectable tenth, one place above reigning champions Liverpool. The season began with City winning a seven-goal thriller at home against well-fancied Wolverhampton Wanderers. At times during those early months they struggled for consistency and suffered some disappointing defeats, including two against Grimsby Town and Blackburn Rovers, who would both be relegated. Overall, though, they more than held their own.

In November 1947 Joe lined up against his future Anfield colleague Bob Paisley for the first time when Liverpool visited Maine Road. The game was played in such bad light that spectators 'could barely see the ball', and on treacherous ground it was reported that City's defence was 'as shaky as it could be'. Nevertheless, goals by McMorran and Smith ensured Joe came out on top in a 2–0 win. In the return fixture five months later he made his first professional appearance in front of the Kop. The two sides fought out a 1–1 draw, with Andy Black cancelling a tenth-minute opener from Joe's namesake Willie Fagan. Paisley again played, but it was Liverpool debutant Les Shannon, a late replacement for Albert Stubbins, who kept Joe occupied for most of the afternoon. According to the *Liverpool Echo*, Shannon, 'although on the frail side for a centre-forward, was giving Fagan plenty to think about'. But, 'despite starting off well, Liverpool were a trifle lucky' to escape without defeat.

Getting the better of the champions, albeit a team in steady decline, was a particular source of pride. However, another highlight was the first top-flight Manchester derby for more than a decade. Home advantage was City's on 20 September, 1947, though it did not count for much during the immediate post-War period as United were still playing their homes games at Maine Road. An all-ticket crowd of seventy-eight thousand brought the city to a near standstill, but as is often the case the ninety minutes of football did not quite live up to the hype. By sharing the spoils at least City maintained their one-point lead over United in the table. When the two sides met again late in the season Billy Linacre was on target in a 1–1 draw. City drew twice with eventual champions Arsenal that season and Joe's performances in those games (1–1 at Highbury and 0–0 at Maine Road) clearly made an impression on their captain Joe Mercer who, in later years, described him as 'a tough player, hard, but fair and a really good professional'. While Joe's primary job was to prevent goals being scored, he did on occasion venture up the other end, and on 25 October, 1947, he scored his first senior goal for the club, in a 1–1 draw at Burnley.

It was not until December 1947 that Sam Cowan's successor was finally revealed. It was a name and face familiar to Joe from his boyhood: the former Everton wing-half of the 1930s, Jock Thomson. As an FA Cup winner and League champion, Thomson had been a tough, highly-respected player in his day. However, like Cowan, he took over at Maine Road with little managerial experience, though he had been in the running to take over at Swansea just before. Such an appointment in the modern era would be greeted with howls of derision and some concern, but life at City carried on much as normal and the change in manager had no affect on Joe. Never one to hog the headlines – 'a solid player, more or less a plodder, but very dedicated', being Billy Linacre's assessment – Joe made a good impression on the new manager, remaining first-choice right-half and one of only two ever-presents in 1947–48.

The following season, despite the shock of conceding a goal after just seven seconds in their first home game, City made more encouraging progress. Joe cemented his reputation as one of the club's most reliable defenders by again figuring in every game. There was early disappointment in the FA Cup when City lost at Everton in the third round. However, on his next return to Merseyside, in April, Joe helped his team secure a crucial 1–0 win at Anfield to keep them in the pack chasing runaway leaders Portsmouth. With four games remaining, City even climbed to the lofty heights of third place. However, they had played more games than the majority of their closest rivals at that point and the title was never realistically within reach. They eventually had to settle for a still commendable seventh, their highest since the Championship-winning season of 1936–37.

*

In February 1949 Joe passed the 100-game milestone in a City shirt and was now an established senior figure at the club: the type young players coming through the ranks would look up to for inspiration and advice. Wearing number eight on the day Joe chalked up his century of appearances was a now 20-year-old Johnny Hart. Having made his first-team debut the previous season, Hart was enjoying his first prolonged run in the side and remembers how Joe had a big influence on him at this time. 'He was a determined bugger, dogged in everything he did and, in return, expected the same from those around him,' says Hart. 'But he understood what it was like to be a young player entering the first-team environment and how daunting an experience that can be. At every possible opportunity he'd be there offering words of encouragement, even though we played at opposite ends of the pitch. It was the same in the dressing-room, he was never afraid to say his piece if it was for the good of the team. From as far back as I can recall he had this air of authority about him and everybody listened.'

Hopes were high now that the club could kick on and challenge for honours. At twenty-eight, Joe was considered to be at the peak of his game, and he needed to be. The start of the 1949–50 season coincided with a goalkeeping crisis at Maine Road. With Swift having retired during the summer it was hoped that reserve goalkeeper Alec Thurlow would step up and fill the breach. But when he fell ill on the eve of the season Swift had to be persuaded to make a temporary return, which he did for the 3–3 draw with Aston Villa on the opening day. Due to his business interests as an executive for a Manchester catering firm, Swift was unable to travel long distances for away games and this meant City had to turn to 19-year-old plumber's assistant Ronnie Powell, who conceded twenty-two goals in twelve appearances.

Given the circumstances Joe could hardly have been blamed for any defensive uncertainties. But he acquitted himself well and such was his early-season form that when City travelled to Charlton in late August there was genuine talk about international recognition.

Indeed, among the thirty-one thousand crowd at The Valley that afternoon were members of the Football Association selection committee. With an England friendly against Ireland looming they were there to watch City captain Eric Westwood, but the *Manchester Evening News* suggested they were also assessing Joe for a possible call-up for the following summer's World Cup finals in Brazil. Joe managed to score only his second senior goal, a header, but it proved to be mere consolation in a 3–1 defeat. The selectors did not return for a second opinion and Joe was destined never to represent his country.

Much more impressive was his performance at Maine Road the following week when he helped shackle the formidable front line of champions Portsmouth as City recorded their first win of the season at the fourth attempt. It was a rare bright spot in an otherwise dismal campaign. With just two more victories before the end of November City plummeted. It was around this time that Joe's run of one hundred and twenty-three consecutive games came to an end. After appearing in the 3–0 defeat at Bolton on 19 November it was reported in the local press that Joe was on the injured list with no further explanation given. He was ruled out of the crucial home match against bottom-of-the-table Birmingham City on 26 November. Without him City recorded their best win of the season, 4–0. Jack Rigby, his replacement, had every reason to think he would retain his place, but the *Manchester Evening News* was of the opinion that: 'Fagan's return would strengthen a half-back line more promising than any since the season opened.' They could not have been more wrong. Joe duly returned to the team and City crashed to a 7–0 defeat by Derby County at the Baseball Ground. It was the club's worst League defeat since an 8–0 drubbing at Wolves in December 1933. Joe was one of five players – four of them defenders – who paid the price as wholesale changes were made for the following week's game.

For a two-week spell during the run-up to Christmas Joe was in and out of the team as City tried in vain to arrest an alarming slump. Reinforcements for the squad were constantly being sought, though not every new face met with universal approval. In October 1949 City caused a stir by signing former German paratrooper and prisoner of war Bert Trautmann. With the hostilities still fresh in everyone's mind the goalkeeper's arrival from St Helens Town was, not surprisingly, greeted with a lot of enmity from the fans. The fact that he conceded ten goals in two of his first three games did not help matters. However, he soon won them over and, in time, filled the void left by Swift and become a City legend in his own right.

Yet another defeat, away at Aston Villa on 17 December, meant City dropped into the relegation zone for the first time that season. Their position was fast becoming precarious. The seven-goal blip against Derby aside, it was in attack rather than defence that the real problems lay. Between mid-September and early April City went an incredible fourteen League games on the road without scoring. Several more players were signed during the season in an attempt to stop the rot, but no City player reached double figures for goals scored. Among those recruited to ease the striking burden were Sunderland centre-forward Ronnie Turnbull, winger Jimmy Allison from Falkirk and, in a last throw of the dice, former Wolves favourite Dennis Westcott.

The prospect of relegation was now becoming more and more likely and a 13-game run without a win, starting with a 1–0 defeat at Huddersfield on Boxing Day, helped seal their fate. On 25 March, 1950, Joe was a neutral spectator at Maine Road as his two home-town clubs, Liverpool and Everton, contested an all-Merseyside FA Cup semi-final. Future Bootroom colleague Bob Paisley was among the scorers as Liverpool reached their first Wembley final. However, by the end of a pulsating ninety minutes Joe's face was as long as that of the despondent Evertonians: League results elsewhere meant that City had fallen to the bottom of the table.

Two successive victories over Easter offered faint hopes of a revival. But following defeat at Wolves, the *Daily Express* reported: 'Last spasm of the Easter Soccer fiesta ended in an outsize hangover for Manchester City, bottom club of Division One. A three-goal defeat at Wolverhampton stifled their great comeback, so now

they're joint favourites with Birmingham and Charlton for relegation.' In the absence of Westwood, Joe captained City for the
first time at Molineux. Though the result dictated it was an occasion
he would rather forget, when he next led them out, away at title-
chasing Sunderland four days later, the outcome was much more
favourable as Oakes and Clarke scored in a surprise 2–1 win.

It was only a brief stay of execution, however. The following
Saturday, with Westwood back from injury, more than fifty-two
thousand City supporters roared on their favourites in the final
home game of the season, but a 2–2 draw with Derby left them
teetering on the brink. With two away games left to play,
Birmingham were already down, but third-from-bottom Charlton
could still be overhauled. However, on the day Liverpool lost in
the FA Cup final to Arsenal, City could only draw with West
Bromwich Albion and relegation was confirmed. The following
week, a 3–1 defeat at Everton brought down the curtain on a
disastrous season. Little did Joe know at the time but it was to be his
last appearance in the First Division.

A campaign that began with Joe being spoken about as a possible
England international ended with him sitting at home contemplating life back in English football's second tier. On reflection he
could at least take consolation from the fact that he was spared
the humiliation of England's cataclysmic World Cup defeat at the
hands of the United States in Belo Horizonte. As the domestic
season approached Joe shared the growing optimism swirling
around Maine Road that City could bounce straight back. The main
reason for this renewed belief was the arrival in June of Joe's former
team-mate Les McDowall as manager. McDowall had served his
managerial apprenticeship with Wrexham and jumped at the
opportunity to take over as Jock Thomson's successor. McDowall
possessed an infectious enthusiasm for the game and in time would
become widely regarded as an innovative manager who was not
afraid to experiment tactically.

Unfortunately for Joe, an injury sustained a week before the season started was to restrict his appearances. In the annual public trial match at Maine Road, played between the first team and reserves (light blues and maroons) on 12 August, 1950, Joe fractured a bone just above his left ankle. During the early stages of the first half he chased second-string forward Jones and went down awkwardly, his left leg taking his full weight, leaving him in a crumpled heap. Trainer Laurie Barnett dashed frantically across the pitch to treat him, but it was immediately clear that Joe could not continue. With the help of former City player-turned-coach Fred Tilson, Joe was carried to a waiting ambulance bound for Manchester Royal Infirmary where X-rays showed the full extent of the injury. He was immediately ruled out for the foreseeable future.

It was the first serious injury of Joe's career and, while not career-threatening, it was always difficult in those days to gauge how well a player would recover. Remarkably, within four months he was back playing and pushing for a first-team recall. To lose a player of his stature and ability had been a bitter blow to City's aspirations, but in his absence they raced out of the blocks. The summer signing from Swansea Town of Roy Paul as Britain's most expensive half-back, proved to be an inspirational acquisition. With Westcott and Smith banging the goals in, City were unbeaten in their first ten matches. By early December they were one point clear at the top of Division Two with a game in hand, and there was genuine concern on Joe's part that he would not be able to force his way back into the team.

Joe's standing as one of the club's longest-serving players, however, held much sway with the City selection committee. His loyalty was rewarded when, on 13 December, 1950, the *Manchester Evening News* reported: 'City have decided to disturb a winning team to bring back Joe Fagan.' The article went on to explain how he had played himself back into contention in the reserves and he duly took the place of the unfortunate Rigby for the visit of fellow promotion chasers Preston North End three days later. It was an ill-timed return: he found himself up against the diminutive but prolific Charlie Wayman, and City slumped to a 3–0 defeat. It was a sombre occasion all round with City donning black armbands out of respect for their former secretary-manager Wilf Wild, the man who handed Joe his first professional contract in 1938.

Despite this loss, Joe managed to hold down his place for the next five games. Results were mixed: two wins, two defeats and a draw, including a third successive exit at the first hurdle of the FA Cup, this time at Birmingham. A Boxing Day League defeat at St Andrew's removed City from their position at the top of the table. It was clear Joe was struggling to rediscover his form following the injury, and after figuring in the 1–1 draw at home to Leicester on 20 January, 1951, Rigby was recalled. Joe would never play a first-team game for the club again.

In his absence, City recovered to finish second and make an immediate return to the top division. Joe was delighted for the club and his team-mates, but the prospect of playing again in Division One was no longer on his agenda. His spell on the sidelines had provided him with ample time to mull over his future. In Rigby, City had a ready-made replacement and first-team opportunities would become even more limited. During the summer of 1951, Joe, now aged thirty, decided that it was in his best interests to cut his ties and move on.

He may not be remembered as one of City's legends, but he was highly thought of during his time there and has remained so ever since. Gary James, a lifelong City supporter and author of several books on the club, says: 'You have to remember it is goalkeepers and centre-forwards who have historically received the most adulation at City, so when fans talk about players from the past Joe Fagan is not a name that is generally mentioned. At the same time I've never come across any negative comments about him. They are always positive and I think he was always warmly welcomed when he came back.'

Though born and bred on Merseyside, there is no doubt that Joe's first footballing love was Manchester City, and they would always hold a special place in his heart. 'Maybe it was because Mum's family had been City supporters, or the fact they gave him his big break in football,' says his second youngest son Stephen. 'I suppose it's quite normal for an ex-player to have some sort of allegiance towards his former club, but I guess he must have really enjoyed his time there. In fact, he mentioned it quite a few times in later years that they were his second favourite club, and prior to joining Liverpool he'd have jumped at the chance to return there.'

Saying goodbye to City was a massive wrench. Having given the club thirteen years' unstinting loyalty, making one hundred and fifty-eight appearances and scoring two goals, it was not surprising that he left with a heavy heart. Ambitious to continue in the game, though, and with an eye on one day moving into coaching, Joe was keen to seek a challenge elsewhere and was prepared to step down a division or two to do so.

CHAPTER THREE

THE PROVING GROUNDS

DESPITE JOE'S INJURY problems there were plenty of offers on the table after he left Manchester City, including the chance to sign for Grimsby Town of Division Three North, managed at the time by a Scot named Bill Shankly. Having spent two years at Carlisle, Shankly was on his way to establishing himself as a manager of some promise. In his last year at Brunton Park he had taken Carlisle to third place in Division Three North, and before taking charge at Grimsby had been interviewed for the vacant Liverpool manager's job, only to be put off by the club's insistence that the directors picked the team. At Blundell Park he inherited an ailing team who had recently suffered two relegations, but he would soon have them challenging for promotion. Teaming up with Shankly was a move Joe considered seriously and years later he admitted: 'I'd have been delighted to join him.' But with his future boss unable to fix him up with a house in Grimsby, it was an offer that Joe had to turn down. Housing was often a key factor in attracting players to a club in the immediate post-War era.

Instead of prolonging his career as a player in the Football League, though, Joe chose to take his first tentative steps in the coaching world by accepting the part-time role of player-manager at non-League Nelson. A small Lancashire mill town just four miles from Burnley, Nelson had been a League club for a ten-year spell between 1921 and 1931. Within a season of becoming founder members of Division Three North, they celebrated the high point of their history by taking the title by four points in 1922–23. On the back of that success Nelson embarked on an overseas tour to Spain and recorded a remarkable 4–2 victory over Real Madrid. Another notable scalp soon followed during their one season in English football's second tier when Manchester United were beaten 1–0 away from home. Unfortunately, those good times were short-lived and they were relegated straight back to Division Three North, and a steady decline set in. They lost their Football League status in 1931 and disbanded in 1936. The club reformed after the War, rejoining the Lancashire Combination, and were on their way to establishing themselves as one of the top non-League clubs when Joe arrived.

Regaining Nelson's lost League status was a worthy goal, but it was financially a massive gamble for Joe to take. By now the Fagan family home was 4 Kintyre Avenue, a prefabricated house on Alexandra Park just west of Maine Road and still very much in the south of Manchester. Consequently, the £3-a-week wage he was paid was barely enough to cover Joe's bus fare for the long journeys north to Nelson. To help make ends meet, he established a painting and decorating business with a friend who owned a van. The supplementary income was welcome but, for Joe, football was always the priority.

Joe succeeded former Burnley centre-half Bob Johnson at Nelson and he inherited a team who in 1949–50 had clinched an historic double of Lancashire Combination League and Cup. The following season they were pipped to the title on goal difference and Joe's immediate brief was to reclaim the crown. It was not as easy a task as it first appeared. Nelson's recent success meant expectations were high and a lot of the players had already peaked. It was, however, a challenge Joe relished and, just as he would at Liverpool three decades later, he took over a successful team and not only maintained the high standards but also moved them up another notch.

*

In his first season at the helm he guided Nelson to the Lancashire Combination title in spectacular style. His team scored a remarkable one hundred and thirty-nine goals in forty-two matches, easily surpassing the previous season's tally of one hundred and twenty, while their thirty league wins equalled a club record. They won the title by eight points from Lancaster City and the trophy presentation took place amid ecstatic scenes on Saturday, 3 May, 1952, with a large crowd gathering in front of the Seedhill grandstand to see League secretary Mr C. Thornton hand over the silverware to Joe, who was also captain.

The mood of celebration continued in midweek when Nelson welcomed Scottish League club Stirling for a charity match. For a team with aspirations of regaining their Football League status it was viewed as a good test and one they passed with flying colours, fighting back from two goals down after twenty minutes to record a thrilling 5–2 victory. *Nelson Leader* correspondent 'Ledwin' supported the club's application for promotion to Division Three North and believed this was a performance 'which would have graced any turf and thrilled any crowd on either side of the border. It was the work of real champions: skilled, united, positive'. Victory over Stirling was a fitting way to bring down the curtain on Joe's first campaign in management. 'It's the best football we've played this season,' he said afterwards. Stirling manager George Patterson's post-match endorsement indicates that Joe's Nelson team were encouraged to adopt something similar to the 'pass and move' style of play that Liverpool would make famous in future years. 'The Nelson boys played excellent football,' Patterson said. 'They kept the ball low most of the time, they were keen yet clean, and they undoubtedly had the edge over my boys. I understand you are trying to get into the Third Division. I think you would do well.'

Unfortunately, Nelson's application to rejoin the Football League was unsuccessful, the sixth time in as many years they had been thwarted. Darlington and Workington were the two clubs forced to seek re-election after finishing at the bottom of Division Three North. Nelson were joined in challenging them by Wigan Athletic, New Brighton and North Shields. When it came to the voting process, Nelson received not a single vote. Wigan received nine, but Darlington and Workington, with forty-nine and forty votes respectively, retained their Football League status comfortably.

This latest failed election attempt was a bitter blow to everyone connected with the club, and especially to Joe who was ambitious to manage at a higher level. At just thirty-one years of age, though, he was well aware that time was on his side. In his first season at Seedhill he had successfully combined the role of manager with that of playing, appearing in forty-five of Nelson's forty-seven first-team fixtures and scoring four goals. As well as showcasing his managerial potential he had also proved that he could still play, albeit at a much lower standard.

His experience at the back was the rock on which Nelson's success was built, though he would have been first to admit that the quality of the players around him were exceptional for the level at which they were playing. Among the players at Joe's disposal was little Jimmy Ward, a former Manchester United reserve who had only been kept out of the first team by the presence of the likes of Charlie Mitten and Jimmy Delaney. A skilful inside-forward, Ward's versatility also allowed him to play wing-half; he is regarded by Nelson supporters of a certain vintage as the best player to grace the club. Then there was another front man, 42-goal top scorer Jack Webber, who had previously played in the First Division with Blackburn Rovers. Other players of note included Arthur Cowell, Harry Wolstenholme, Tommy McManus, Ted Wigglesworth and Jimmy Buchanan.

Another highlight of that 1951–52 campaign was an FA Cup first-round tie against Oldham Athletic which drew Nelson's biggest home crowd since 1929. Though Nelson were eventually well beaten by the high-flying Division Three side, it was such a memorable occasion that whenever he was reminded about it Joe would always say: 'How could I forget *that* match?' Recalling the tie in his column for the *Nelson Leader* thirty-four years later, local journalist Noel Wild wrote: 'For a Lancashire Combination club such as Nelson it was THE big occasion all right. It was an all-ticket match for a start – and there have not been many more of those at Seedhill, if any.'

More than twelve thousand packed into the rain-swept ground on 22 November, 1951. Wild said: 'When Joe Fagan, as player-manager, led his Nelson team out that day ... the old red blooded corpuscles fairly cavorted and somersaulted in a state of expectancy. The tiny Seedhill press box was packed up to overflowing for the first time in living memory. Even the BBC Sports Special reporter was there and afterwards Joe was interviewed by esteemed commentator Kenneth Wolstenholme. What mightier acknowledgment of the national media than that?' With Joe lining up in his usual position of centre-half, Nelson put up a brave fight but eventually succumbed 4–0. The result was slightly harsh on Joe and his team, but according to the local newspaper the player-manager led by example throughout and showed 'some of the same class' of their opponents.

Joe was certainly enjoying his time at Nelson and he had struck up a mutual bond of affection with the locals, as proved when addressing the visitors from Stirling at the end-of-season dinner. 'I am also a foreigner,' he said. 'I come from Liverpool, the capital of Ireland. But since I came to Nelson I have felt the warmth and friendliness of everybody in the town.' Unfortunately, a series of injuries to key players prevented a repeat the following season. Joe could only steer Nelson to fifth place in the Lancashire Combination, and towards the end of that campaign it was mooted around the club and the town that to cut costs Nelson should in future operate without the services of a permanent manager. Joe got wind of this and with a family to provide for, he could not afford to hang around to be made redundant. Shortly after the final whistle of the 1952–53 season he informed the club's directors that he would be relinquishing his position. Joe's departure signalled the end of Nelson's 'golden era'. Their fortunes gradually worsened in the years that followed, but their former player-manager has never been forgotten in the town. According to lifelong fan, and former club chairman, Malcolm Beckett, Joe remains 'the most well-known person to be connected with the club'. In the summer of 2008 Joe's memory was honoured when Nelson played Merseyside-based non-League club AFC Liverpool for the Joe Fagan Commemorative Trophy.

After leaving Seedhill, 32-year-old Joe Fagan found himself at another major crossroad in his career. His experiences at Nelson had only served to heighten his ambition to pursue a career in coaching, but with opportunities thin on the ground the prospect of having no involvement in the game when the 1953–54 football season got underway was looking more and more of a possibility. However, then came an offer from across the Pennines for him to prolong his playing career. It came from Third Division North side Bradford Park Avenue, via manager Norman Kirkman, a former full-back with Rochdale, Chesterfield, Leicester and Southampton. Kirkman was relatively new to the club, having joined five months before from Exeter City where he had cut his teeth as player-manager for a year.

Due to their present-day non-League status and the ascent of Bradford City, Park Avenue are now the lesser known of Bradford's two football clubs, but that was not always the case. A First Division club either side of the First World War, Park Avenue's heyday was undoubtedly in 1946 when, inspired by the phenomenal goalscoring record of England international Len Shackleton, they reached the quarter-final of the FA Cup. But they cashed in on their prize asset, selling him for a record £13,000 fee to Newcastle, which signalled the start of their demise. In 1949–50 they dropped into Division Three North and had failed to climb out again.

Joe's arrival was not viewed as a quick fix to rectify that situation. Instead, he was brought in by Kirkman to help with the second team, where it was hoped his experience would rub off on the youngsters hoping to push through the ranks. Having not played in the Football League for two years, and with plenty more youthful options available to the manager, Joe knew first-team opportunities at Park Avenue would be limited. He also had to account for the extra travelling that would be involved, especially as his ever expanding family had now moved further south to 34 Oakmore Road in Baguley, on the outskirts of Manchester.

It cannot have been an easy decision, but Joe's resolve to continue earning a wage from the game he loved was solid. He was happy to help Kirkman and saw the move to Bradford as an important step on what he hoped would be the pathway to a coaching career. His best playing days were well behind him, but Joe was still more than capable of holding his own on the pitch and became a regular in an otherwise fresh-faced reserve side in the Midland League. Just as Kirkman had hoped, he exerted a positive influence on all around him and the manager remarked: 'Should any of the lads – as we hope they will – make the grade, I am sure they will in later years ascribe much of the credit for that to the fact they have been able to play alongside Joe Fagan.'

One of those young players was Bradford-born Brian Jones. Jones had joined the club from local junior football, and would soon drift back into it without making a first-team breakthrough at Peel Park, but he clearly remembers Joe as 'a great student of the game'. On away trips Jones would always try to make sure he was on Joe's table at meal times, and he recalls: 'As captain of Bradford's reserve side he was always ready with a pre-match address. Such remarks as, "If you see a space get into it and then we can find you", were typical. Everyone had to pay attention and if anyone wasn't he would stop talking and look steadily at the culprit until the man started listening. He once did it to the club chairman who happened to be in the dressing room at the time.'

As well as mentoring the club's second string, Joe was also available to help out in the first team when emergencies arose. On 7 September, 1953, he made his senior Bradford Park Avenue debut in a 2–0 defeat at eventual champions Port Vale. Unfortunately he missed an emotional reunion with former club Manchester City in the third round of that season's FA Cup. Instead he was back on duty for the reserves that afternoon in a 5–4 defeat at Gainsborough Trinity.

Just two more first-team appearances followed, at home to Workington and Tranmere Rovers in late February, and at the end of a season in which Park Avenue finished ninth, Joe was, by mutual agreement, one of five players released on a free transfer. It was no surprise. His stint with Park Avenue was never going to be long-term, but he was keen to draw as much coaching experience as he possibly could from it. As much as players like Jones would have benefited from Joe's leadership, this opportunity to develop effective ways of nurturing young talent was invaluable for an aspiring coach. It was a marriage of convenience but it had run its course. The club accepted Joe's decision to move on and he left with the best wishes of Norman Kirkman, who was to remain at Park Avenue for only another eight months before being dismissed due to a 'deterioration in the club's financial position'.

During the summer of 1954, while England and Scotland competed for the World Cup in Switzerland, Joe once again took stock of his options before agreeing to join Altrincham for one last season in the Cheshire League. He scored on his debut in a 4–2 home win over Witton Albion on 16 October, 1954, and went on to make thirty appearances for the Moss Lane club before finally hanging up his boots at the end of the season. Joe was now forced to con-template a life beyond football. With potential earnings in the game very poor it was becoming increasingly difficult to justify financially his continued involvement in the sport he loved. The painting and decorating partnership had been wound up and, with a family to support, Joe was forced to seek employment checking British Gas meters manufactured in a local factory.

It was, however, impossible to exorcise the football bug. Whatever spare time Joe had would be spent watching football on the local park and helping out with coaching wherever he could. Fortunately his foreman at the factory was a football enthusiast and took a shine to the former City captain now under his charge. Whenever Joe needed to get away early to fulfil a football commitment a convenient blind eye was turned. Once again Joe's determination to forge a career in his chosen field came to the fore. To his close family and friends he made no secret of his desire to get back into football. He worked hard at maintaining his contacts, exhausting his network of friends and former colleagues in order to spread the word that he was available and willing to take on any legitimate coaching position. The longer he was out of the game the more he hankered for a return and the more effort he put into making it happen.

Eventually his perseverance paid off. In the summer of 1956, former Everton striker Harry Catterick came knocking with the offer of a coaching position at Rochdale. It was deemed an opportunity too good to refuse. Darlington-born Catterick was two years older than Joe. After his top-flight playing career was cut short by injury at the age of thirty-one he became player-manager at Crewe Alexandra before moving to Rochdale in 1953. Regarded by those who played under him as an authoritarian figure, Catterick was well respected by players and supporters alike at Spotland. However, after three years in charge he had experienced nothing but frustration in his quest to lift them from the Football League's lowest tier. He was well aware of what Joe had achieved in that first season at Nelson and believed him to be a coach of immense potential. So when Rochdale's long-serving trainer Joe Duff, who also doubled up as a coach driver in his spare time, was forced to relinquish his position following a road accident in July 1956, Joe Fagan was instantly earmarked as a potential replacement.

With a threadbare squad and dilapidated ground, life at Rochdale was certainly no bed of roses and Joe quickly discovered that there was a lot more to his role at Spotland than simply coaching. Among many other duties, he was responsible for cutting the grass, marking the pitches, painting the stands and washing the kit. During his first season at the club, he would also be in at eight o'clock each morning to start running the baths for when the players finished training, such was the length of time it took for them to be filled because of the poor state of the plumbing. After a year he took it upon himself to clean out all the water tanks so they worked more efficiently.

Joe could have been forgiven for thinking he had been employed as more odd-job man than coach. However, no task was too menial for him and, never one to complain, he quietly went about his business with the minimum of fuss, a trait that stayed with him throughout his career. Joe could still not afford a car and after work Catterick would drop him off not at his home but on Bury Road, and he would walk the remaining two and a half miles to the latest family home on Gainsborough Drive. If things were difficult work-wise for Joe at Rochdale, the time spent in the town was almost crippling for his family who had now grown to Lil, four sons, John, Roger, Kit, Stephen, and a daughter, Joanne. Rochdale seemed to be permanently windswept, cold and damp, but living just above the breadline the family had to do without anything but the very basics. Despite this, the family were considered 'posh' because of their Manchester accents and the unpleasant feeling of being outsiders was always present. To this day the children remember those bleak, hungry days of struggle with great bitterness. It is impossible to overstate how difficult it must have been for Joe to continue to pursue his career as a football coach when it would have been much easier to provide for his family through a more regular job. The already desperate situation was made worse by Lil suffering from ill health throughout this period.

Joe, though, remained positive that better times were ahead. Rather than wasting time worrying about where he and his young family were heading, he spent every spare minute at Spotland, throwing himself into his work and trying to improve every aspect of the club. Most Sunday mornings he would take his eldest sons to the ground and they would help patch up the players' boots and repair their studs. If the weight of Joe's workload was not enough, most of the training responsibilities also fell on his shoulders. This should come as no surprise given that the coaching staff comprised of just himself, the manager and assistant trainer Arthur Griffiths, later to be replaced (on Joe's recommendation) by former Manchester City defender Albert Emptage. With Catterick by now more of a suit-and-tie man, rather than a tracksuit manager, Joe found himself at the heart of much of the day-to-day work with the players.

A youngster coming through the ranks at Rochdale during this time was centre-forward Brian Green. He had joined the club as a 19-year-old shortly before Joe arrived and remembers his former coach fondly. 'He was one of the nicest blokes I ever met in football,' says Green, who went on to play fifty-four times for the club, scoring eight goals. 'Harry would leave the training to Joe. "Work them hard", he would tell him, but Joe was great and training was always enjoyable. We'd be put through our paces, starting off with several laps around the pitch, and Joe would always join in. Then it would generally be plenty of work with the ball and a game of head tennis to finish.' Green would later coach in Australia and Norway, as well as returning to Rochdale for a brief spell as manager in the mid-1970s, and rates Joe as one of the biggest influences on his career. He said: 'He wasn't one of these coaches who'd look down their noses at the young lads and bully them.'

Though never regarded as the most cultured of defenders, Joe was keen to get Rochdale playing football in what he considered to be the right way: on the ground, passing and moving. Though his old defensive instincts would scream 'safety first' when it came to playing from the back, he was never an advocate of the long-ball game, even if some of the players at his disposal were more suited to this tactic. According to Rochdale historian Steve Phillipps: 'The entertainment value varied quite a bit and Dale were rarely better than an average mid-table side.' But they did have their moments when everything clicked: twice during Joe's first season at the club they hit six goals in a game, the most notable being the 6–1 rout of Catterick's old club Crewe at Gresty Road. Consistency, however, was difficult to maintain and Rochdale finished 1956–57 in thirteenth position. The following season, though, was to be one of the most memorable the club had experienced since joining the

Football League in 1921. At one stage they threatened to make a strong challenge for the top, and with ten games remaining had risen to fourth. During a season in which a home draw with leaders Bury in October drew a record post-War crowd of 18,896 to Spotland, they hammered Hartlepool 7–0 and came back from 4– 1 down early in the second half to beat Darlington 5–4. They fell away to finish tenth, but that was enough to secure them a place in the newly-formed Division Three, as the Football League restructured the lower tiers by scrapping the two regional divisions.

While Rochdale were finally on the up, Joe was on his way out. Towards the end of the 1957–58 season Liverpool, then a team struggling to escape from Division Two, began the search for an assistant trainer and reserve-team coach to replace the outgoing Dickie Dorsett. The sterling work done by Joe had not gone unnoticed and after scouring the lower leagues Liverpool approached him, ironically after a chance conversation Catterick had with one of their representatives earlier in the season when he had sung the praises of his number two. In an interview with the *Liverpool Echo* many years later, Catterick recalled: '(Joe had) done a marvellous job. He did very well for me because he's always been a trustworthy type, who knows the game inside out and has no ballyhoo about him ... he isn't much of a talker but is incredibly knowledgeable.'

It planted a seed and when the time was right Liverpool acted upon it. The exact date when contact was first made is not certain, but on 17 April, 1958, the day after Rochdale had lost 2–0 at Chester, a letter with a Liverpool postmark arrived for Joe's attention. It was from the then Liverpool manager Phil Taylor and the content of it was to change immeasurably the course of Joe's life. It read: 'At our board meeting on Tuesday evening I was asked to invite you through to meet one or two of the Directors. In this way you can have an interview with a couple of our directors while they are here.' The letter continued: 'I have as yet not contacted Harry Catterick regarding a possible position here for you, but of course would do so if my directors are agreeable to take you on. I have no doubt that everything will be OK here for you, but I am quite happy that we shall be able to work together without any trouble.' The lure of a decent club house remained a big bargaining tool and Taylor added: 'We have as you know a house in Anfield and I would like you to see it before the game on Wednesday, so if you can get over here early we could get down and look it over. If you would like to bring your wife, all the better.'

An ambitious young coach like Joe did not need asking twice and he responded promptly. The following week, as arranged, he and Lil were among the crowd of 2,628 who witnessed Alan Banks scoring twice for Liverpool reserves in a 2–2 draw against Bury. Before the game they were shown around a neat semi-detached property in nearby Lynholme Road, just a few minutes' walk from the ground. Afterwards Joe met the directors in the boardroom. His mind was made up, and convinced that a better future lay ahead at Anfield both parties shook hands on a deal.

Twenty years after turning down Liverpool's offer to join their staff as a player, and leaving his home city in search of footballing fame, Joe Fagan was now heading back. Little did Harry Catterick know it at the time but his tentative recommendation would come back to haunt his future club across Stanley Park time and time again over the coming years.

CHAPTER FOUR

BIRTH OF THE BOOTROOM

T HE ANFIELD JOE Fagan walked into during the close season of 1958 was pretty bleak. Compared to the heights they would scale over the next twenty-five years, when they would become the pre-eminent club in England, Europe and, arguably, the world, Liverpool were scrabbling around in the foothills. The only mysticism that surrounded them at the end of the 1950s was how they had managed to get into such a mess in the first place. Since their last flirtation with the big time – the 1950 FA Cup final, in which they lost to Arsenal – hard times had fallen on Anfield. The stresses and strains of trying to revive the ailing giant had already seen off two managers, George Kay and Don Welsh, and a third would soon follow. A place in the First Division had been lost four years before, and three near-misses in the quest for promotion lent an air of resignation to the increasingly wide open spaces appearing on the Kop.

'Always the bridesmaid, never the bride, that is what they used to say about us and it was so frustrating,' recalled Alan A'Court, the outside-left who, as a youngster, had been part of the side who suffered the indignity of relegation in 1954. 'We would always be in the running until Easter and then somehow fall away. It was often commented at the time that the directors didn't want us to win promotion because they would have to spend more money if we went up. But this certainly wasn't true in the case of the players: we were crying out for promotion.'

Accusations that those running the club lacked ambition were commonplace among supporters of the time, and had been for a while, a point emphasised by author John Williams in his book *Red Men*. 'The club often trotted out the line about its responsibilities to shareholders as well as supporters, and the Liverpool board seemed quite unwilling to speculate to accumulate,' he wrote. The title-winning season of 1946–47 had been followed by the death of visionary chairman Bill McConnell, whose loss was undoubtedly a contributory factor in the club's demise as a major footballing force. Hailing from a large Liverpool-supporting family, McConnell had been following the club's fortunes since the turn of the century. He made his name in the catering trade, running a string of dockside cafés, and joined the Anfield board in 1929. He was elected chairman in 1944 and under his guidance, according to the local *Evening Express*, 'the club had never been in better hands'. His vision was for Liverpool to be the best team in the land. He played an instrumental role in the inaugural post-War title triumph, leading the players on an inspired pre-season tour of North America and having the foresight to splash out a club-record transfer fee to sign Albert Stubbins. Unfortunately, McConnell fell ill during the spring of 1947 and passed away shortly afterwards, living just long enough to see his dream fulfilled.

Without his inspirational guidance off the field, a catastrophic fall from grace ensued on it. Hindered by a reluctance to spend, great players were replaced by distinctly average ones, and a once mighty team withered away. In the dozen years since they paid £12,500 to Newcastle for the services of centre-forward Stubbins, there had been no improvement on the club's record fee; Liverpool would pay the ultimate price and relinquish their proud record of fifty years as a top-flight club. By the time of Joe's arrival, only two members of that legendary post-War side remained: the iconic Billy Liddell, who had almost single-handedly carried the team throughout this barren era, and whose influence was such that the club became widely known as 'Liddellpool'; and defensive lynchpin Laurie Hughes, a former England international who played in the

1950 World Cup finals. Both, however, were now past their best and edging closer to retirement. Other star names in the team were few and far between. A'Court, whose impressive form had attracted serious interest from Arsenal, was on his way to the World Cup with England, while goalkeeper Tommy Younger would captain Scotland in that summer's tournament in Sweden. Players of promise included full-back Ronnie Moran, winger Johnny Morrissey, playmaker Jimmy Melia and Jimmy Harrower, a recent signing from Hibernian. Then there was Johnny Wheeler, the man appointed club captain ahead of the 1958–59 campaign. Wheeler had also represented England and was on the losing side in the 'Matthews Cup Final' of 1953. But he had recently turned thirty and his best days were clearly behind him. The same could be said of honest journeymen like ball-playing wing-half Geoff Twentyman, Welshman Roy Saunders and strapping centre-forward Louis Bimpson. The remainder of the first-team squad was made up of bargain buys from the lower leagues such as Bishop Auckland-born Barry Wilkinson, the solid and dependable full-back John Molyneux and Dick White, a towering centre-half signed from Scunthorpe. All were capable of holding their own at this level but lacked the guile and class to perform any higher.

Mirroring the poor position of the club on the pitch, Liverpool's home ground was also falling into a decrepit state. Despite being on standby to host Manchester United and Bolton Wanderers if the 1958 FA Cup final required a replay, the old stadium was not in the best of health: grass was growing between the crumbling concrete steps on the terraces, dry rot eating into the wooden gates and paint flaking off the crush barriers. Since 1928, when a roof was put over the vast Spion Kop terrace, its appearance had hardly changed; the odd lick of paint here and there being the height of refurbishment until floodlights were installed in 1957. In addition, the toilets did not flush and there was no running water in the changing-rooms.

Over at Melwood, the club's recently-acquired training ground in a leafy suburb of the city known as West Derby, facilities were no better. In fact, they were probably worse. Once the site of a school playing field, Melwood consisted of nothing more than an old cricket pavilion, where the players changed, and an unkempt field on which they trained. For a club who had been champions of England five times, and who aspired to a return to that level, it was symptomatic of their fall from grace.

On the final Saturday of the 1957–58 League season, with all hope of promotion vanquished a week earlier in a 1–1 draw with champions-elect West Ham United, a crowd of just 26,440 gathered at Anfield to witness the end of another campaign that had failed to deliver on its promise. Until then Liverpool supporters had remained remarkably loyal. The average attendance for the season, despite the last-day low, was still 38,475, with six games attracting crowds of more than forty thousand and two topping fifty thousand. It was more than enough to keep the money men happy, but it would not be long before those who handed over their hard-earned cash at the turnstiles (admission prices ranged from two and four shillings, or ten and twenty pence in modern money, depending on whether you wanted to stand or sit) started to show signs of restlessness. Indeed, a week after Liverpool's fourth successive season of Second Division football had come to a close, J. Doyle of Wavertree, in a letter to the *Football Echo*, voiced his displeasure at the way supporters on the Kop had been treated. 'It would not have been out of place at Anfield last Saturday, if before the game a club official had publicly thanked the fans for their loyalty during the season. Such a gesture would have done much to show that the support each week is appreciated and not merely taken for granted.' The fans' loyalty was not blind. It was not yet at breaking point, but while the players continued to receive wholehearted backing from the terraces, supporters were slowly waking up to the fact their team was heading nowhere fast. The local press on Merseyside (*Liverpool Echo, Daily Post* and *Evening Express*) were generally perceived as being 'largely friendly and supportive' towards senior Anfield officials, but the ever-increasing mood of discontent aimed at those in the positions of power at the club could be gauged through the letters page, particularly in the Saturday 'Pink'. It reached a crescendo shortly before the arrival of Bill Shankly in 1959 when one fed-up fan wrote: 'Never in the history of the club have their local supporters' spirits and enthusiasm been at such a low ebb. We see no optimism or hope in the present team.' Another contributor, paraphrasing Prime Minister Harold Macmillan, warned: 'A drop down to the Third Division is a real possibility. We followers of Liverpool have never had it so bad.'

Into this melting pot of growing despair and questionable playing strength strode the 37-year-old Joe Fagan. His appointment, on Monday, 5 May, 1958, as assistant trainer was comparatively low-key and consequently was afforded little in the way of column inches. The *Liverpool Echo* and *Evening Express* both ran short pieces, but the *Daily Post* ignored it completely. 'Joe Fagan Gets Anfield Berth' read the *Echo* headline. But it was a story almost lost amid the inquests into the previous weekend's FA Cup final, in which Bolton had controversially defeated Manchester United. As an item of local news it was overshadowed by a rare visit to the city by the Queen Mother. The other club-related news centred on the signing of Mansfield Town's 27-year-old outside-right Fred Morris, who Liverpool had been monitoring for several weeks, and the departure of the man Morris had been bought to replace, Tony McNamara, a £4,000 capture from Everton just six months before. McNamara was the most notable of six players placed on Liverpool's end-of-season released list, which also included full-back Tom McNulty, half-back Don Campbell and forwards Joe Dickson, Brian Jackson and David Kerr.

Of greater importance to the club's newest employee were the names of those on the retained list: these were the men he would soon be working with, and, in particular, the youngsters in the squad whose talents he was expected to nurture in the reserves. When it came to second-string football, Liverpool did not have the best track record, but a greater emphasis was now being placed on achieving results at this level. In 1958, Liverpool were clearly concentrating on youth development and, eager to ensure that no promising young player escaped their clutches, they issued an open invitation to all boys aged between fifteen and eighteen in the Merseyside area to apply for a trial. No stone, it seemed, was being left unturned. Since the Central League had become the competition for the reserve teams of Midlands and Northern-based clubs in the 1920s, Liverpool's name had been conspicuous by its absence from the list of winners. That was until 1956–57 when, under the guidance of Bob Paisley, they were champions for the first time. Under Joe, the Liverpool reserve team would become a breeding ground for future internationals, and their unprecedented dominance of the competition comprised fourteen titles between 1968 and 1985. It was not lost on the Liverpool hierarchy that the Football League's most successful side of the 1950s – Wolverhampton Wanderers – also won five Central League titles in the same decade. During sixteen successful post-War years in charge at Molineux, Stan Cullis laid down a blueprint for developing home-grown talent that Liverpool would come to follow very closely. It was viewed as the way forward, especially by a board of directors reluctant to spend too much money.

Before getting to grips with his new challenge, Joe had the luxury of a few weeks off while Liverpool's 15-man squad embarked on a five-game, end-of-season tour to Spain. It gave him time to complete the formalities of his move from Rochdale and settle into life at 42 Lynholme Road, a house that would be the Fagan family home for the next four decades. Almost twenty years had passed since Joe upped sticks and left the city of his birth to join the playing staff at Maine Road. Yet while the promise of a neat and tidy semi in the then salubrious surrounds of L4 certainly played a part in enticing him back to Liverpool, it was more his burning ambition to coach at a higher level than sentiment that swayed him ultimately. According to his wife Lil: 'He was very ambitious to move to a bigger club, and the fact it was Liverpool didn't really matter. To him it was just another job.'

The Liverpool he was returning to was a much changed place to the one he had left in the late 1930s. His native Scotland Road was experiencing the start of a steady decline that would lead to large numbers of its inhabitants being moved out and re-housed on council estates in the overspill areas of nearby Kirkby, Huyton and Norris Green. The city may have recovered from the horrific damage inflicted by the blitz of 1941, but its pioneering overhead railway had since been pulled down, the last tram had run its course and the once bustling docks were no longer a hive of activity. The world was changing, but Liverpool would soon be back at the heart of it, both on the football pitch and in the pop charts. Like The Beatles and the Mersey Beat, Liverpool Football Club would also shake the Sixties.

While A'Court and Younger caught early planes home from the World Cup, Joe was eagerly counting down the days until his first day of work at his new club. Liverpool may have been languishing in Division Two for the past four years, but its stature and support meant it remained a big club, and from Joe's perspective it was a huge step up from his humble coaching beginnings at Spotland. In manager Phil Taylor, he would be working for a fine, upstanding club man who, while of a quiet and submissive nature, had earned the respect of everyone at Anfield. He had won a First Division Championship medal as a player in 1947 and was the first captain to lead Liverpool out at Wembley in an FA Cup final. After hanging up his boots at the end of the 1953–54 relegation season he accepted a position on the coaching staff and eventually succeeded Welsh as manager in May 1956. Initially, he took on the role in a caretaker capacity and was described by the board as merely a 'liaison man' in the dressing-room. This, of course, was the era when directors picked the team and they had the final say in all matters affecting the club. In Taylor's first season at the helm Liverpool missed promotion by one point from Nottingham Forest, though it was enough to earn him the job permanently. But, with another near-miss recently added to his *c.v.*, the pressure was building.

Also waiting to greet Joe in July 1958 was first-team trainer Bob Paisley. Like Taylor, Paisley was also a former playing adversary of Joe's. He, too, had won the title with Liverpool just after the War, but was also remembered for losing his place in the FA Cup final side three years later, despite scoring against Everton in the semi-final. A thigh injury forced him to miss the four League games before the final and, though fully recovered, Bill Jones was selected ahead of him. Paisley had joined Liverpool from noted amateur club Bishop Auckland in his native County Durham, shortly before the start of hostilities in 1939. During the War he served as a gunner in Montgomery's 'Desert Rats' and later established himself as a pivotal, if unsung, member of the successful post-War Liverpool team. When he retired in 1954 he followed Taylor on to the backroom staff as reserve-team trainer and added another string to his bow by studying a correspondence course in physiotherapy. With Taylor's elevation to manager, Paisley moved a rung up the ladder. He also began to take more control over the rehabilitation of the club's injured players, eventually replacing veteran sponge-man Albert Shelley. His methods were a far cry from the cold water bucket treatment favoured by Shelley and they helped drag Liverpool into the modern age. Honest and hardworking, quiet and unassuming, Joe had found a kindred spirit. More importantly, when it came to football they found themselves on a very similar wavelength. Neither could have foreseen then just how entwined their professional lives would become, but they struck up an instant rapport. 'Right from the outset they appeared to be very comfortable in each other's company and a very warm relationship developed,' remembers Bob's son Graham. 'They were never that close that they socialised together but, then again, none of the backroom staff ever did. They were essentially work colleagues and the conversation never seemed to stray from the topic of football.' Completing the Anfield backroom set-up was Reuben Bennett, a craggy Scot who joined as chief coach just a few months after Joe. Famed for working the players vigorously on the training pitch, the former Army physical training instructor was also an immensely popular figure among the squad who he regularly kept entertained with tall tales of his youthful heroic deeds. Following an undistinguished playing career as a goalkeeper at Hull City, Queen of the South, Dundee and Elgin City, Bennett excelled as a coach and was head-hunted for his role at Liverpool by chairman Tom Williams. Despite a failed attempt at management with Ayr United in the mid-1950s, where he resigned after two successive mid-table finishes in the Scottish Second Division, Bennett was regarded as one of the finest coaches in Scotland and his capture was viewed as a major coup.

Joe, Paisley and Bennett would play a crucial role in Liverpool's future and the significance of their coming together cannot be underplayed. It was with Paisley and Bennett, rather than the manager, that Joe spent the majority of his time. They shared a common bond: a deep-lying love for the game and a strong determination to put the club back on the map. Every spare minute would be spent discussing the finer arts of football. With such like-minded individuals around him, it did not take Joe long to settle in. 'It was like he'd been at the club all his life,' says Ronnie Moran. 'Normally there's a transitional period when someone new arrives, but Joe, and Reuben just after him, were like part of the furniture from day one.' But while the manager had his office and the players had their changing-room, the backroom staff had no real base where they could convene after training over a cup of tea or something stronger. Indirectly Joe was responsible for rectifying this and, in turn, creating the legendary Bootroom. Without him the room would probably have stayed what its name suggests, though there was no conscious decision to turn it into the equivalent of the school common room. The transformation, if that is not too strong a term, was down to Joe's association with an old school pal, Paul Orr, later to become Lord Mayor of Liverpool, and who was then manager of local amateur side Guinness Exports. As a favour to Orr, Joe would do a spot of coaching and arrange for injured Exports players to visit Anfield for treatment. As a thank-you, Orr would regularly despatch in the opposite direction supplies of the famous black stuff, and various other Guinness-brewed ales, marked for Joe's attention. Being rather partial to a drink or two it was a gesture that was much appreciated by Liverpool's assistant trainer, and he believed it only right that it was shared among his colleagues. The only problem was where to store it. Then he remembered the old cubby hole where the boots were kept.

In time that cubby hole, situated to the left of the main corridor as you walked towards the tunnel and dressing-rooms, would become furnished with luxuries like a rickety old table and a couple of plastic chairs, a tatty piece of carpet on the floor and a calendar on a wall which would later be adorned with photographs ripped from newspapers of topless models. Apart from an old Liverpool team photograph, and boots hanging on their pegs, there was little evidence to suggest that this room was even part of a football club. Seating arrangements were not ideal: upturned beer crates were among the best options, along with the baskets that carried the kit to away games. But the presence of a ready supply of ale, along with something to sit on, made it a natural place for the coaching staff to gather. 'We have a full and frank exchange of views in there in a leisurely atmosphere every Sunday morning,' recalled Paisley in later years. 'It's just like popping down to the local.'

Joe quickly set about his work at Anfield, assisting Paisley and Bennett with the day-to-day training, and flexing his managerial muscles with the reserve team he had inherited from the recently departed Dickie Dorsett. Those who came under his charge noted almost straight away a visible difference in their preparation for games. Among them was Alan Banks, a 19-year-old forward who lived within a minute's walk of Anfield and who was regarded as one of the better young prospects on the club's books. After scoring freely in the 'A' and 'B' teams as an amateur, Banks was just starting out as a professional. He had scored ten times for the second team towards the end of the previous season and would make his first-team debut in September 1958, scoring in a 5–0 win over Brighton. He admits his game improved greatly under the watchful eye of the new coach. 'It suddenly became a lot more organised under Joe,' he says. 'We began to practise set-pieces, which was almost unheard of before, and as a result our free-kick and corner routines became a lot more inventive. He was a lovely fella who made everyone around him so relaxed, but at the same time he also instilled in us all a will-to-win attitude. Every session was treated like a cup final and nine times out of ten we'd beat the first team in training.'

At Joe's disposal when it came to selecting his starting XI for the 'stiffs' was a mixture of promising youngsters, like Banks, and seasoned professionals, some of whom, in this era of the maximum wage, were simply content to play out their career in the reserves by doing just enough to earn another contract at the end of each season. 'He'd always stress that so long as a player gave one hundred per cent then everything would be fine,' says Banks, 'but he was well aware that not every player in the reserves was. It was difficult because some of these players obviously had no future at the club, but they couldn't be disposed of straight away.' It was a situation which a lesser coach may have found difficult to handle, but Joe looked upon this opportunity to work with these senior players as good preparation for the future.

In 1958, Roger Hunt signed amateur forms for Liverpool. However, because he was posted to an Army base in Wiltshire during his National Service, it meant he was only available to play once every three weeks, which restricted him to 'A'-team appearances. Having already been released by Bury, Hunt was starting to question whether professional football was the career for him. Towards the end of the 1958–59 season, he was called up by Joe for the reserves. On paper it appeared to be an inspirational selection. Hunt scored the first in a 3–0 win against Burnley at Anfield, and he admits it was an eye-opening experience. 'I was coming from the Army and the rest of the team were either full-time professionals or part-time professionals. It was like a trial game for me because I had done quite well in the 'A' team. I scored a goal early on, but the game was way too fast for me. I was not fit enough and I couldn't keep up. When I came in at half-time I was really blowing, I remember Joe stood over me and just said, "I want more from you".

I could barely breathe!' The rest of the game passed Hunt by in a blur, though within a few weeks he was handed a further chance to impress. It came against Preston on the final Saturday of the season, but after another bright opening Hunt's performance dropped off so markedly that midway through the second half Joe decided upon a tactical switch in which captain John Nicholson pushed up front and Hunt dropped back into his place in defence. 'It was obvious that I hadn't played too well and I was so down-hearted and depressed when I went into the dressing room,' Hunt remembers. 'Then Joe came up to me. He came and sat with me and explained exactly what I would have to do to make the grade. He said he wasn't trying to make a show of me but that that kind of thing was what professional football was all about. He said that if I wanted to be a professional I had to get used to it.' Despite what Hunt would go on to achieve in the game he never forgot that day. 'It had a big affect on me. I put a lot of my career down to that one game. That talk stuck in my mind. I still remember it vividly. I only had a few weeks left in the Army and I thought if I was going to make the grade I would have to do whatever Joe Fagan said. I decided to get much fitter, work harder, and if I didn't make it at least I had given it everything. I always remember that part of it because Joe was solely responsible. I was prepared to work hard but he explained to me exactly what I had to do. Obviously full-time training helped, but I needed someone to tell me what was required.'

The start of Joe's time as reserve-team coach was an encouraging one. An opening-day 1–1 draw at Blackburn was followed by six wins from the next nine, including a 4–2 victory at home against Everton, which attracted a crowd of more than nine thousand. Liverpool ran reigning champions Wolves close at the top of the Central League for most of the season before having to settle for second place. But while Joe's first season at the club could generally be considered a success, a fifth successive failure by the first team to gain promotion cast a dark shadow over Anfield during the summer of 1959. They had suffered seven defeats by the end of November, and while a mid-season run of eight successive wins raised expectations, the now ritual post-Easter dip put paid to top-flight aspirations. Horace Yates of the *Daily Post* lamented: 'Few club supporters can have had to endure the mental torments and tortures experienced by the Anfield crowd.' To compound this mounting sense of crisis it was also a season in which fans' favourite Billy Liddell was dropped for the first time in his Anfield career and non-League Worcester City dumped Liverpool out of the FA Cup in what is still regarded as the most humiliating result in the club's history. The already restless natives were on the brink of revolt and soon made their feelings known. However, their actions in the aftermath of a lacklustre draw at home to Portsmouth were quickly condemned in the local press. 'Nobody can pretend that the squandering of another home point was not disappointing, but this was no possible justification for the slow handclap to which the players left the field,' commented Yates. Taylor was on borrowed time as manager, but the situation only served to focus the resolve of everyone within the club to put things right, not least Joe. He had sensed that the pressure was building and was aware of the urgent need to bring through a player from the reserves who could come to the club's rescue. Fortunately, he had someone in mind, though it would prove too late to save the manager.

The close season of 1959 saw the now 21-year-old Roger Hunt demobbed and pitched into full-time training at Melwood. Thanks to Joe's influence, he had adopted a hardened realism about what he had to achieve. Early in his first season as a professional, and after scoring seven goals in five games for the reserves, Joe recommended him to Phil Taylor. Hunt made his first-team debut on 9 September and scored in a 2–0 home win over Scunthorpe. It was to be the start of a glorious goal-laden career, though had it not been for Joe's intervention it could have turned out differently. On the way home from that pivotal reserve-team game the previous season, Hunt's father had suggested to his son that he probably would not make it in the game and gently invited him to take his place in the family haulage business. However, Joe had judged his player correctly. By giving him a chance in the reserves, and then bluntly communicating to Hunt how far he still had to go, he had lit the competitive fire within the future World Cup winner. Knowing how to steer a young player in the right direction would become a hallmark of Joe's time in charge of Liverpool reserves.

Hunt was to become a permanent fixture in the first team after his debut, but not even his emergence could keep Taylor's position safe. Following a 4–2 defeat at Lincoln on 14 November, a game in which Hunt again scored, the stresses and strains of the job finally overcame the manager and he tendered his resignation. The team languished in eleventh position, ten points behind the leaders and eventual champions Aston Villa, with just six wins from their first eighteen games. Promotion already appeared out of the question for yet another year. Ever the gentleman, 42-year-old Taylor bowed out gracefully and wished the club well for the future.

It was a sad end to what had been an illustrious Anfield career and Joe was naturally disappointed to see Taylor leave. He was, after all, the man who brought him to the club and for that he would be forever grateful. Equally, though, he was well aware of the potential below the surface, and that all it needed was the right man to ignite the flames. At this stage of his still fledgling career this was neither the time nor the place for Joe to take on such responsibility. Nor was it for backroom colleague and fellow future Liverpool manager Bob Paisley. Tentative speculation that Reuben Bennett might step up to the managerial plate was quickly doused. He was, first and foremost, a coach and the memories of his time in charge at Ayr served as a stark reminder of that. Every member of the backroom staff had much to offer, but while the club remained without a manager their futures were in limbo. All they could do in the meantime was help steer the ship with steady hands. Nevertheless, it remained an anxious time for all concerned. Joe had only been at the club eighteen months and was keen to discover if he still had a role to play in its future. The arrival of a new manager at any club brings with it an air of uncertainty and Paisley later admitted that he went as far as putting 'a letter into the board to clarify my position'. His wife Jessie underlines the uncertainty.

'Bob and everyone else didn't know what was going to happen after Phil Taylor left. They thought they might be finished at the club because so many managers wanted to bring their own staff with them,' she says. Joe could have been forgiven for fearing his brief career might be over before it had really begun. Not only was he enjoying life at Liverpool, his family had settled and with a wife and five children to support – plus another on the way – Joe had no desire to up sticks again.

He need not have worried. On the evening of Monday, 30 November, 1959, a board meeting at Anfield rubber-stamped the appointment of Liverpool Football Club's fourth post-War manager. It was Huddersfield Town's Bill Shankly, the man who had once tried to sign Joe as a player for Grimsby. The appointment was officially announced in the following day's press and a caption beneath a picture of the new boss in the *Daily Post* read simply: 'Bill Shankly, newly-appointed Liverpool manager, has a solitary aim – to put Liverpool back in the First Division. If he succeeds he's the friend for life of all Liverpudlians.' Having spoken with Shankly, the reporter was clearly impressed and added: 'The new manager's confidence and firm resolve are infectious. Nobody can be in his company for more than a few minutes and not realise that here is a driving force who will spare himself no pains to get done the job he has in view.'

The supporters were, initially, sceptical and Shankly's arrival was met with a lukewarm reception. One fan even went so far as suggesting that Taylor should still be in charge. 'I see no reason why he should have been displaced,' wrote 'A Phil Taylor fan' in the *Liverpool Echo*. 'The power which, I understand, has been given to Mr Shankly should have been given to Mr Taylor. During his term in office he was not given any real power.' Though this view was an exception, the feeling among the majority of those who stood on the Kop was that Shankly had yet to achieve anything notable in management and until they saw concrete evidence that he was the man to lead the club out of the abyss, then they were reserving judgment.

In contrast, no one was happier than Liverpool's assistant trainer, especially when he was quickly assured that his job was safe. In a rousing, heartfelt opening address to the Liverpool coaching staff on the day after he first breezed into Anfield, the canny Scot announced: 'Now normally managers come into a new club and bring their trainers with them. I am not going to do that. You fellows have been here, some of you for a long time. I have my own training system and I will work in cooperation with you. I will lay down the plans and gradually we will all be on the same wavelength. I want one thing and that is loyalty. I don't want anybody to carry stories about anybody else ... If anyone tells me a story about anyone else, the man with the story will get the sack. I don't care if he has been here for fifty years. I want everyone to be loyal to each other. Everything we do will be for the good of Liverpool Football Club.'

Joe listened intently. Shankly's words were like music to his ears. The epitome of a clubman throughout his playing and coaching career, Joe was now in the presence of someone who was preaching the principles he had been quietly following for so long. In his eyes the club could not have made a better appointment. 'When I heard Bill was coming to Liverpool I was delighted,' Joe recalled in later years. 'Not only would it be a pleasure to work with this man whose concept of the game I respected so much, I also knew that with his enthusiasm, Anfield would soon be buzzing.' Just as there had been with Bob Paisley, there was instant chemistry between the pair and a mutual respect that would last a lifetime. '"Hullo, Joe, remember when we hammered you at Maine Road?" That was how Bill Shankly greeted me on the day he arrived at Anfield. He had a great memory – but hammered us? Rubbish. Preston North End had only won by a single goal. But that was Bill Shankly. A fantastic memory, an interest in every person he ever met, and the ability to turn a lucky victory into a magnificent success or a heavy defeat into a day when everything went wrong – the referee, the ball, the weather, anything. I must be one of the very few people to achieve a remarkable double: not only did I refuse to join Liverpool as a youngster, but I said "No" when Bill Shankly wanted to sign me for one of his teams. And he remembered it that day he arrived at Anfield because the second thing he said was, "You should have come to Grimsby, Joe. We'd have gone up if you'd come".'

Bill Shankly had the vision and the personality to transform a soundly sleeping giant into Britain's most successful football club. Born in the Ayrshire mining village of Glenbuck, Shankly first found fame as a half-back for Preston. He helped them win the FA Cup in 1938 and later played as a Wartime guest for Liverpool. He cut his managerial teeth at Carlisle United, the club where he had begun his playing career south of the border. After two years at Brunton Park, he moved to Grimsby Town in 1951, and it was around this time that he first appeared on Liverpool's radar, when he was interviewed for the managerial position vacated by George Kay. He scuppered his chances on that occasion by insisting he would only accept the job on the proviso that he had full control over team selection. This did not go down well with the directors of the time and the job was given to Don Welsh. Shankly's burning passion for the game had made a lasting impression, though, and his managerial progress was monitored closely, next at Workington and later at Huddersfield. At each club money had been tight and his reputation for making players, rather than buying them, was particularly attractive to the Liverpool board.

Though he had yet to manage at the top level, Shankly was fiercely ambitious. Within hours of accepting the job he was telling the *Echo* that Liverpool were 'among the top grade teams in the football land', adding: 'When the challenge was made to me I simply could not refuse to accept it. There is a job to be done, perhaps a big job, but with the cooperation of Mr Williams, the directors and staff, I feel certain we shall see the task through together.' Two days before officially taking charge, Shankly had sat incognito at the back of Liverpool's Main Stand, along with 2,533 spectators, and watched Stan Woodall score a hat-trick for Joe's reserve team in an emphatic 5–0 victory over Manchester City. Without knowing it, Joe had made a good first impression. But

upon further investigation into the general state of the club Shankly
was horrified to discover quite how far Liverpool had fallen. When
addressing the players on his first day, he said simply: 'There are
going to be a lot of changes here. If you want to play for Liverpool
you'll have to earn it. If you don't want to, you'll be gone.' It would
take Shankly just one game to come to the conclusion that 'the team
as a whole was not good enough'. Within a few weeks he had drawn
up a list that contained twenty-four players he deemed surplus
to requirements. 'We were overburdened with players,' he later
explained. 'The maximum pay then was twenty pounds and the staff
was too big.' Twelve months later every one of the twenty-four had
been moved on, including the hat-trick hero Woodall. 'It was not
that I had anything against those boys, but it had to be done –
transferring them, letting them go for free, helping them to get
other clubs.' The Anfield revolution was underway and as Alan
A'Court remembered: 'In no time at all, Anfield and Melwood were
buzzing with an electric atmosphere. It was rather as if you were
on board a powerful new racing car and he had just switched on the
engine.'

Bill Shankly had come to Liverpool to build a great club and he had
the inspiration and drive needed to achieve it. Like many great
leaders he also enjoyed his fair share of luck, not least in the
lieutenants he inherited. Brought up in comparable working-class
backgrounds, they were made from similar stuff to himself and he
knew that he could rely on every one of them. 'He looked at what
was good and he kept it,' remembers captain of the time Ronnie
Moran. 'Reuben, Bob and Joe were loyal men and they backed the
manager to the hilt in every situation.'
    Despite an inauspicious start on the pitch – a 4–0 defeat at home
to Cardiff followed by a 3–0 reverse at Charlton – Shankly's arrival
gave the entire club a much-needed lift. Suddenly, Roger Hunt
remembers, 'everyone seemed to be walking about with a new sense
of purpose'. Joe hit it off immediately with the new boss. According
to Lil Fagan: 'They got on like a house on fire.' Crucially, so too did

the rest of the backroom staff. 'That's why they went on to be so successful,' said Lil, 'because it was such a close-knit group. They'd have these meetings and everyone was allowed to have their say. They wouldn't agree on everything all of the time, but they'd each chip in with ideas, then debate together what would work and what wouldn't.'

Slowly but surely progress was made. From twelfth place on Boxing Day, Liverpool rallied to finish third, narrowly missing promotion again but restoring some lost pride and dignity along the way. Contrary to popular belief, though, Shankly did not change everything straight away and Joe's day-to-day tasks altered very little. 'He made so few changes initially,' said A'Court, 'that it was at least a year before anyone outside Anfield began to realise that things really had changed.' Among Shankly's first priorities was establishing a Liverpool way of playing and this required a complete overhaul of how the players trained. Not long after taking charge the local press were proudly informed that he and his backroom staff had 'reorganised the whole training system'. It would be a long-term project, and though instigated by the manager, Joe was central to its implementation. The traditional training at most clubs, including Liverpool, was based on physical fitness, and the players did not see much of the ball during the week. Shankly changed that: he tried to make training like a match. Everything was quick, sharp and with a ball. Apart from the pre-season training when a lot of running was needed to get the squad to a basic level of fitness, everything was geared to game situations. A simple style of football was drilled into the team. 'Pass it to the nearest red shirt' became one mantra, 'pass and move' another. Training became more enjoyable for the players. They did not have full-sized practice matches, but would play small-sided games. Joe, Bob Paisley and Shankly would play against the youngsters, while the professionals played their own games elsewhere.

Joe fully embraced these changes. 'On his first afternoon the call came. "Get a ball out, three a side, lads". The pattern was set and the three-, four- and five-a-side matches were established as part of the Anfield training routine. Bill knew that not only was it a training exercise, it also taught ball control, accuracy in passing, running off the ball; in a word, simplicity. The message was, "Give it, help your mates". And this was his theme throughout his time at Anfield. Pre-season road running was abolished at the start of the following season because Bill said, "You don't play on tarmac, you play on grass". The famous sweat box was also soon in operation. Four boards, placed on each side of a 20-yard rectangle against which a player would play the ball, play it and play it. A minute in there was enough for anyone, particularly with Bill's strident Scottish voice demanding maximum effort. It taught concentration under pressure and that paid its way many times in crucial moments of big games.'

Though Shankly was the inspiration behind Liverpool's style of play and their training methods, he was never really a training-ground coach; he was purely a manager, or an overseer. And though Paisley was officially a coach, he was more of a quiet observer day to day, as well as carrying out an important role as chief physiotherapist. Joe spent a good deal of time helping Paisley give injured players treatment, but his main job was to continue planning the individual training sessions, and lead them alongside Bennett. This suited him down to the ground. Combining his day-to-day coaching responsibilities with reserve-team management duties allowed Joe to operate predominantly in the background, away from the larger-than-life manager of the club. Never one to seek the limelight, in this respect he was the exact opposite to Shankly. But there was regular contact between the two, and he was trusted to report back with anything that would be of note to the first-team manager.

With Roger Hunt now an established first-team regular, Joe set to work on nurturing the next graduate from the reserves. His second Central League season began with an 8–1 thrashing of Barnsley, included a remarkable 7–5 home defeat by eventual champions Manchester United, and ended with a second successive runners-up spot. Of greater importance, however, was the breakthrough into the senior side of outside-right Ian Callaghan, who had recently turned eighteen. Callaghan, from the Toxteth district of Liverpool, had signed professional forms with the club just six weeks earlier and had played only four times for the reserves. Joe had been well aware of his progress in the 'A' team and he did not hesitate to push his claims for a senior call-up. 'Joe would always be on hand with words of encouragement for the young lads who were coming through the ranks, and he was no different with me,' says Callaghan. 'Although I'd played only a few games for him he obviously believed in my ability and I'll always be grateful to him for putting my name forward to Mr Shankly.'

Replacing the legendary Billy Liddell was no easy task. However, Callaghan experienced an afternoon he would never forget when Liverpool welcomed Bristol Rovers to Anfield for what was essentially a meaningless end-of-season fixture. With the number seven shirt hanging off his slight frame, Callaghan belied his tender years and completely stole the show with a display of youthful zest that few in the 27,317 crowd that day would forget. Describing how he set up three of Liverpool's four goals in a comfortable win before being applauded off at the end by everyone including both sets of players and the referee, Jack Rowe of the *Daily Post* questioned whether 'any other young player has made such an impact on Liverpool supporters'. The following day Callaghan woke up to headlines such as the *Sunday People*'s 'Baby-face Ian dazzles 'em', while Graham Fisher in the *Daily Express* described Callaghan's debut as the most accomplished he had had the pleasure to witness. Ronnie Moran, a team-mate of Callaghan's that day and the man who would ultimately follow in Joe's footsteps as reserve-team manager, concedes that: 'A player with the talent of Cally is always going to force his way through the ranks no matter what club he is at.' But he adds: 'The role of the coach, who is there to guide him, cannot be underestimated. Fortunately for Ian that man was Joe. He'd have had a big say in him being selected that day.'

Callaghan may have been the man of the moment, and indeed

played in three of the four remaining games that season, but he still had plenty to learn before a senior shirt would be his on a permanent basis. He was one for the future and Shankly wanted him to continue his football education in the best place possible: back in the reserves with Joe. 'I enjoyed my time with the first team,' said Callaghan, 'but dropping back into Joe's reserve side wasn't a problem. In fact, it was a pleasure to continue my football education under him. There were no airs or graces about Joe and just because I'd played in the first team and created a few headlines didn't matter one iota as far as he was concerned. I was treated the same as everyone else in his team, and that's the way it should be. I would never have got above my station anyway, but even if I had there's no doubt Joe would have been on hand to quickly put me back in my place. It was a great grounding and I'm sure I became a better player for it.'

It would be another season and a half before Callaghan firmly established himself in the first team, but he would go on to make more appearances for Liverpool than any other player. During this time another reserve-team regular made a successful step-up to the senior side. Gerry Byrne was an uncompromising, hard-as-nails full-back who had grown up around the same Scotland Road streets as Joe. He had made his debut as far back as September 1957, but it coincided with a crushing 5–1 defeat at Charlton, in which he had the misfortune to score an own goal, and he had rather harshly been dumped on the transfer list. With no offers coming in, Byrne became almost ever present in the second string during Joe's first two years at the club, and in that time his obvious talent came to the fore. Byrne finally secured a regular first-team place towards the end of Shankly's first season, but he has never forgotten the part Joe played in helping resurrect his career. 'I was playing for him in the reserves while on the transfer list and it would have been easy for me to let my head drop in such circumstances. But he made sure I didn't with constant words of encouragement. Only when Shanks took over did things really take off for me, but I'll always be grateful to Joe for how he helped me when I was at a really low ebb.'

Not every reserve player Joe recommended for the senior side turned out to be a success, especially during the transitional 1959–60 season. Reg Blore, John Nicholson, and Willie Carlin, for example, were all handed first-team debuts after impressing under Joe, but failed to seize their opportunities. Each of them made a solitary senior appearance before moving on to earn a living in the lower leagues – Blore with Wrexham and Oldham, Carlin most notably at Derby County, where he played under Brian Clough and won a Second Division Championship medal, and Nicholson with Port Vale and Doncaster before he was killed in a road accident the day after his thirtieth birthday.

Shankly, though, never doubted the extensive football knowledge of Joe or the other backroom boys. He was well aware that they were, almost literally, ready and willing to help build a football club with him. Bob Paisley was a bricklayer by trade and he would be busy building the dugouts while Shankly was arranging for the installation of new toilets or similar much-needed improvements. Meanwhile, Joe, fresh from his jack-of-all-trades role at Rochdale, marshalled the club's groundstaff boys who would be responsible for anything from painting the crush barriers on the terraces to sweeping the stadium on a Sunday after a home game. It was a system based on the principle that no one was too big or important to help with the most menial of tasks. That kind of manual labour inevitably establishes a trust between co-workers and a grounded atmosphere around the club. One of Joe's early charges was Tommy Smith, later to become captain of Liverpool, a European Cup winner and an England international. Smith's father had died in 1959 and when he joined the groundstaff a year later, aged fifteen, he was happy to claim the £7 a week to take home to his mother. In later years he would be quick to remind new players that no airs and graces would be accepted at Liverpool. It was a lesson Joe taught him at a young age. 'I remember one day when I was eighteen, I had been on the groundstaff for two or three years and was just about to turn professional. Joe's advice was to just keep going, keep working and not to get excited. But it was difficult not to get excited. I was playing with the reserves with maybe eight or nine other blokes all pushing for the first team, and now I was turning pro. The groundstaff lads said to me, "Hey, Tommy, can you give us a hand sweeping the home dressing room so we can get away quickly?" "I am not going to be doing anything like that," I said. "I'm going to be signing in five or ten minutes. No more sweeping up for me, no more cleaning boots." In my mind I was a professional now. There was a brush on the floor and they picked it up and gave it to me saying, "Come on, Tommy, just once more, as a going-away present." I told them to sod off. As far as I was concerned I didn't have to do anything like that anymore. Only then did I catch in the corner of my eye the sight of Joe standing behind me. I was horrified to think he had heard me on my ego trip. "Tommy", he said, shaking his head. "Pick up the brush, son". He didn't shout or rant but he didn't need to, I picked up the brush and got on with it.'

The work off the pitch, establishing new attitudes as much as new facilities, would only be worthwhile if the playing side could be put right. A key factor in this was persuading the board to invest in the team. With gates continuing to fall – the 1959–60 season produced a post-War all-time average low of 30,268 and the following season it was to drop below thirty thousand for the first time since 1938 – a return to the top flight, with its added gate revenue, was becoming a necessity. Shankly's arrival had raised the morale of players and staff, but the fans were yet to witness much change. The football they were watching may have been a little more pleasing on the eye, but results were showing no sign of improving. It was becoming evident that Liverpool were never going to escape the murky waters of Division Two without an influx of new players. Other clubs were spending large sums and Liverpool were in danger of being left behind for good. Increasingly desperate Liverpudlians would cast envious glances across Stanley Park and see Everton, the so-called 'Mersey Millionaires', spending freely and flaunting the wealth of their chief benefactor John Moores, the founder of the Littlewoods Pools empire. In a letter to the *Liverpool Echo* Mr E. McDermott, one of many disgruntled supporters, wrote: 'When I hear that Liverpool have signed one centre-forward, one winger, one full-back and some good reserves I will be back with twenty thousand who just want to see a team who can make Liverpool proud.' While Liverpool's biggest transfer outlay remained the £12,500 it took to prise Albert Stubbins from Everton's clutches in 1946, their Merseyside rivals had surpassed that figure many times, and in February 1960 they forked out £30,000 for teenage defender Jimmy Gabriel from Dundee. In November the same year they had returned to Scotland with a cheque for £40,000 to secure the services of Hearts forward Alex Young.

The red half of the city could only dream. But, crucially, Moores, though a true-blue Evertonian, also had a financial interest in Liverpool. His family had shares in the club and he was kept abreast of happenings at Anfield through his bridge-playing friendship with Liverpool chairman Tom Williams. It was thanks to Moores that accountant Eric Sawyer was elected to the Liverpool board and the purse strings were gradually loosened. Targets such as Jack Charlton and Brian Clough were still deemed out of Liverpool's league financially, but during the summer of 1960 the club's long-standing transfer record was broken and then surpassed again on Sheffield United winger Kevin Lewis (£13,000) and Preston half-back Gordon Milne (£16,000). In both cases it proved to be money well spent. However, though Lewis's goals return in the season that followed was impressive – nineteen in thirty-two League games – the old saying that you only get what you pay for had never rang truer, and £13,000 was not enough to buy Liverpool a place back in Division One on this occasion. Yet another third-place finish had Liverpudlians tearing their hair out and the local press sympathised. 'Failure to gain promotion tends to make one come to the conclusion that a little more enterprise on the part of the management might have done the trick, not only this time but several seasons previously,' commented veteran observer Leslie Edwards in the

Liverpool Echo. 'There has been too marked a tendency for the club to believe that players elsewhere are no better than those already on the books. Promises that big signings would be made and that the size of transfer fees would not frighten or deter is in sharp contrast with history.'

It had been an equally frustrating campaign for Joe's reserve team who, for the third season in a row, failed to win the Central League title, this time by two points from Sheffield Wednesday. Had top scorer Alan Banks not been drafted into the first team as cover for the injured Dave Hickson at a crucial point, it might have turned out differently. In Banks's absence, the reserves lost three and won just one, the only consolation being that during his brief time with the seniors he made a considerable impact, scoring four times in as many games. Together with the twenty-one goals he registered in the Central League, Banks topped the club goalscoring charts in 1960–61, but when his contract expired that summer he was released as part of the rebuilding process. He was not alone: Younger, Wheeler, Arnell, Wilkinson, Campbell, Slater, Rudham and Harrower were all moved on. Out, too, went centre-forward Hickson, so a new strike partner was needed for Hunt. That man was Motherwell and Scotland's Ian St John.

To land him Liverpool would have to pay more than double their previous record outlay. Once Shankly had identified St John as his number one target he then had to persuade the board to release the funds. The directors initially baulked at the asking price of £37,500, but the manager argued that Liverpool could not afford *not* to sign him. With the backing of Sawyer the deal was eventually pushed through. It was a momentous couple of months in the transfer market for Liverpool and the capture of St John was quickly followed by the arrival of towering centre-back Ron Yeats from Dundee United for £30,000. 'Six feet four and strong as an ox,' proclaimed a proud Shankly. Yeats was the 'colossus' needed to help shore up the defence.

Both signings were pitched straight into the first team, but they would still come into contact with Joe on a daily basis, and he made an indelible impression on them during their opening weeks on Merseyside. 'He'd just turned forty but what struck me was the great a shape he was in,' says St John. 'You could tell he'd been a player and obviously he kept himself in good nick. More importantly, he just oozed enthusiasm and had this manner about him that got the best out of everyone. It was great to see and only served to heighten my belief that I'd joined the right club.' Yeats concurs: 'From the first moment I walked into the club I found Joe to be one of the most unassuming and down-to-earth men I was to come across in football. It was a great time to join Liverpool and people like Joe helped us settle.'

With Yeats at the back and St John up front Liverpool, it seemed, were finally ready to escape from the Division Two wilderness. A run of ten wins and a draw from their opening eleven games consolidated top spot and there was never any danger of them being knocked off their perch. On the day their top-flight return was confirmed, Joe was at the Baseball Ground overseeing a drab goalless draw against Derby's reserves in front of just a few hundred spectators. But in the side who defeated Southampton 2–0 on a rain-sodden afternoon at Anfield to end an eight-year exile were three players who had been touched by Joe's influence: 41-goal marksman Roger Hunt, ever-present full-back Gerry Byrne and the first team's new number seven, Ian Callaghan. On an occasion to rank alongside some of the most memorable in the club's history, the celebrations went on long into the night. 'A constant downpour could do nothing to dampen the emotional scene, or the excitement of the crowd on the memorable day they had been waiting for,' wrote Michael Charters in the *Liverpool Echo*. Captain Ron Yeats still rates it 'the biggest thing in Liverpool's history because without it, the success that followed would never have happened'. Long-time fan Mike Glover remembers it purely for the overwhelming sense of relief: 'After eight years of suffering abuse from Bluenoses, we never thought it would happen, so when it did it was just unbelievable.'

As the news sank in that Liverpool were finally back in the

Promised Land, congratulatory telegrams poured in from all corners of the country, some from the most unlikely of sources. Matt Busby, a popular Liverpool captain of the pre-War era and now manager of Liverpool's soon-to-be intense rivals Manchester United, said: 'A club like Liverpool deserve to be playing in the highest class.' Even those in the blue half of Merseyside seemed to welcome their return: larger-than-life local MP, and staunch Evertonian, Bessie Braddock, admitted it would be good for the city to have two clubs competing against each other in the top flight again. Speaking at the time, Bill Shankly described leading Liverpool to promotion as his proudest moment in football and was quick to acknowledge the contribution of his backroom staff. 'Without their help we could have achieved nothing,' he said. 'No praise can be too high for these men who have worked so hard and who normally receive no public recognition.'

So, 21 April, 1962, became a red-letter day in the club's history. Though not there in person, Joe had certainly played his part. Everything was clicking into place and the ethos laid down in the Bootroom was at last beginning to reap its rewards.

CHAPTER FIVE

THE SHANKLY YEARS

I N AN ERA when football coaches were rarely seen and, most definitely never heard, to the supporters who turned up at Anfield every other week Joe Fagan was simply another name on the backroom staff rota. His role in the Shankly-inspired Liverpool revival in the early 1960s was deemed, from the outside, at best a bit part. Only the real die-hards, those who religiously followed the second XI when the first team played away, would have been remotely aware of the job he was doing. His true worth was known only to those who worked closely with him on a daily basis. Though he may have been one of the lowest earners on the Anfield payroll, taking home a weekly wage less than the national average, to them his value was already considered priceless.

In the four years since joining the club from Rochdale Joe had gone about his business in a quiet but supremely efficient manner. As the recently crowned champions of Division Two prepared for their return to the top flight, Joe's sterling work in the background suddenly began to attract admiring glances from other clubs. Word spreads quickly in football circles and during the summer of 1962, as England went out in the quarter-finals of the World Cup in Chile, the grapevine was buzzing with whispers that Liverpool had a bright young coach of immense potential.

Among those who showed an interest were neighbours Everton, still widely regarded as the pre-eminent club on Merseyside.

Everton were now managed by Harry Catterick, Joe's former boss at Rochdale and the man who had initially recommended him to Liverpool. After a successful stint in charge of Sheffield Wednesday, Catterick took over at Goodison Park in May 1961. His arrival followed the highly-publicised sacking of Johnny Carey, who was told of his fate by John Moores in the back of a taxi as the pair left a League Management meeting in London. As Catterick set about assembling his backroom team he did not hesitate in making Joe his number one target and the audacious attempt to prise him away from Anfield threatened to throw a spanner Liverpool's resurgence. Not long before she passed away in October 2010, Lil Fagan confirmed that an approach was made to tempt her husband across Stanley Park. Fortunately for Liverpool, it was one Joe never considered seriously. 'He was more than happy at Anfield,' she explained. 'He had made good friends there and the club was progressing as he would have hoped. He felt part of something and saw no reason to go elsewhere.'

As acknowledged by Peter Robinson, Liverpool's club secretary from 1965, and later a close confidant of Joe during his time as manager, there would be further temptations put in Joe's way in future years. Though the identity of those other clubs who would try to poach him have never been disclosed, the reasons for him staying did not change. 'He was a man of such high principles,' says Robinson, 'and the reason he didn't mention any of this to us at the time was because he thought it would look as though he was just trying to get extra money out of us. Of course, he'd never do such a thing and I do know that he turned down several offers of a lot more money even before I joined.'

How the course of football history might have changed had Joe accepted Everton's offer is anyone's guess, but hindsight tells us that the mere thought of it would be enough to make every Liverpool supporter break out in a cold sweat. No individual is bigger than a club, not even the manager. Yet so crucial was the role each member of the Bootroom performed that to take one of them out of the equation could have had dire consequences. According to Ian St John: 'No football men have devoted themselves to a cause so thoroughly and self-effacingly.'

Due to his involvement with the reserves, Joe was slightly detached from the first-team squad, but he was very much part of the club's 'think-tank'. Consequently, he often offered a different perspective to those put forward by Paisley, Bennett and Shankly. Ron Yeats remembers him being 'just as important to us as Bob and Reuben were'. He confirms: 'There was no coaching hierarchy in our eyes.' Because Joe was so heavily involved in the day-to-day training of the players, he also enjoyed a good relationship with them. He was content to take a ribbing for his viciously short haircuts and happy to give back banter in kind. This placed him ideally for dealing with requests for help from players. He was always unflinchingly loyal to Paisley and Shankly, but at the same time a different type of character to them. 'Joe would come and have a chat, offer advice where he could and generally say whatever he thought,' explains Roger Hunt. 'I would go to Joe to talk about my form or to see if he could see anything that he thought I could improve on in my game.'

While responsibility for training was shared between all three coaches, one of Joe's duties was to carefully plan and meticulously log each day's schedule. It was a system put in place to ensure that in times of trouble the coaching staff could refer to these 'manuals' to see if any comparisons could be drawn and a solution found to the problem. The compilation of such notebooks was hardly revolutionary: in his autobiography Bill Shankly admits accumulating many over the years, filling them with all manner of information, picked up from anything or anyone so long as he deemed it valuable. Joe's 'little black books' were different. They focused more on Liverpool's training routines and are now often referred to as 'the Anfield bibles'. In reality they are nothing more than a collection of tatty-looking, A4-sized notebooks. The passage of time has discoloured and loosened some of the pages, but it was what was written inside that mattered. As Ronnie Moran testifies, they were the encyclopaedias that would define Liverpool's approach for the best part of three decades. 'Every day after lunch Joe would get his book out and write in what we had done that morning, what treatment had been applied if any of the players was injured, what training routines we'd done and so on,' says Moran. 'They became such an integral part of life at the club. Joe later taught me all about them and it was a tradition that carried on. They were a priceless source of reference.' According to legend, hidden inside these revered tomes was the magic formula that gave Liverpool the longevity to stay at the top. In truth, there was not one. The principles on which Liverpool's success was built were based on good footballers and a common sense attitude to training them.

For Liverpool's players there was no running up and down sand dunes in the summer, as a lot of teams would do, nor plodding along the road like generations of their predecessors had done. The training was tough but never too tough. It was a question of finding the right balance. Overtraining intensified the risk of injury. But fitness levels had to be maintained and the manager took immense pride in the fact that his team was widely regarded as the fittest around. The number one priority during pre-season was to reach peak fitness at just the right time, as opposed to going flat out through the summer and running the risk of being exhausted for the opening game. After clinching promotion in April 1962, Shankly remarked: 'We won the championship in the first month when we were fitter competitively than our rivals.' Jimmy Melia, a veteran of the side who had languished in Division Two for so long, later recalled: 'That was the first time I'd played in the first match of the season and felt I could play again afterwards.'

Contrary to popular belief there was much more to Liverpool's training than the legendary five-a-sides. A typical session would begin with a series of short warm-up exercises that consisted of light jogging and stretches. The squad would be split into groups for sprints, shuttle runs, endurance running and circuit training. Sessions were never over-complicated. Set-pieces were rarely worked on. When the balls came out it was basic drills: running round cones, head tennis and shooting practice. Those in the first-team squad were already good footballers, so it was just a case of honing their skills and ability. 'Above all, the main aim is that everyone can control a ball and do the basic things in football,' said Shankly. As Joe remembered: 'It was simplicity itself.' Invariably training would end with small-sided games.

On the pitch Bill Shankly had given the fans something to shout about once more. A sense of pride returned to Anfield and the fans came flocking back for the start of the 1962–63 season. With Liverpool bucking a national attendance trend by attracting their highest average gate for thirteen years, the extra revenue generated meant there would soon be more investment in the team, long overdue improvements on the ground and better training facilities at Melwood. The club were, at last, moving with the times. It was an upturn that went hand in hand with a resurgence in the city's standing. With the 'Mersey beat' movement led by The Beatles soon to rock the world, Liverpool was suddenly the place to be. According to author and journalist Paul Du Noyer, Liverpool was 'the pride of great Britain and – increasingly – a source of wonder to the world. The media was infatuated. Everyone was talking about this damp, grubby town that nobody had thought twice about for fifty years ... Liverpool, so often out of step with the national mood was now it's very model: cheeky and young, un-posh, un-stuffy, democratic to the boot heels'. The city was on the crest of a wave and so was the club who proudly carried its name. For Joe Fagan professional life had never been better.

The club's new-found ability to go out and spend large sums in the transfer market meant Joe's role in bringing youngsters through from the reserves was to become even more challenging. So long as it was done with the best interests of the club at heart, though, that was fine by him. This is what he had been striving for: to be coaching at the top level, at a club where everyone was pulling in the same direction. Now that the early excitement of working under Bill Shankly had been translated into genuine progress, the future seemed bright indeed. Only the surprising and controversial sale of winger Johnny Morrissey to Everton for £10,000 in August 1962, threatened to shatter the equilibrium. It was a deal that had been conducted behind Shankly's back and it left him incandescent with rage, and revitalised memories of his earlier battles with the board. He threatened to resign on the spot and had he done so maybe his loyal lieutenants, including Joe, would have gone with him. Fortunately, he was persuaded to bite his lip and stay put. A compromise with the board was reached whereby no future deals, outgoing or incoming, would be done without the manager's say-so. It was a significant turning point in the club's history. Having gained control of the purse strings, Shankly was able to turn Liverpool into the big club he always believed it to be. Over the next few years, Shankly recruited left-half Willie Stevenson from Glasgow Rangers for £20,000, Preston's flying winger Peter Thompson for a club record £40,000, followed by a similar fee to Arsenal for utility man Geoff Strong.

Liverpool's first season back in the top flight was all about consolidation before they could think about re-establishing themselves as one of England's foremost clubs. Three early graduates of the Joe Fagan finishing school – Byrne, Hunt and Callaghan – were mainstays of the side who finished eighth. Only an agonising defeat against Leicester City at Hillsborough denied them a place in the FA Cup final. The club were clearly on the up.

With the last of the dead wood from the pre-Shankly era finally shifted, Joe now had the opportunity to stamp his authority on the club's reserve set-up. Whereas in the past the second-string squad had too often been cluttered with unambitious, ageing professionals, the class of 1962–63 had a youthful zest about it. Bobby Graham, a young inside-forward brought down from Motherwell as an apprentice in 1960, rated it 'formidable'. Helping to lower the average age was an influx of youngsters from the team who reached the final of the FA Youth Cup for the first time that season. Half of the side who eventually lost on aggregate to West Ham figured in Joe's reserve side, with more to follow.

As far as results were concerned, 1962–63 was not a vintage season for Liverpool's second XI. However, in terms of bringing through aspiring young footballers it was one of the most fruitful. Several players made their first-team debuts, and while not all of them would establish themselves as regulars, three in particular would soon become household names. Goalkeeper Tommy Lawrence was the first to cement his place in the senior side, ousting Jim Furnell after just thirteen games of the season. A Scotsman brought up in Warrington from an early age, Lawrence would hold down the number one position for the remainder of the decade. Also making his breakthrough was a baby-faced Chris Lawler. A former England Schoolboy and youth international, Lawler was widely regarded as one of the most promising young defenders in the country. Raised just a few miles from Anfield in Norris Green, he had joined the club as an apprentice in 1960 and was quickly taken under Joe's wing. Lawler's debut came as replacement for the injured Ron Yeats in a 2–2 home draw with West Bromwich Albion and, such was the faith of the club's coaching staff, there were no qualms about pitching him into a match as important as the FA Cup semi-final against Leicester just five weeks later. Though it would be another two years before Lawler fully established himself in the team, his potential was recognised beyond the confines of Anfield. Manchester United manager Matt Busby was a known admirer, even attempting to sign him, along with another of Joe's reserve-team members, Tommy Smith. Fortunately for Liverpool's future it was an audacious double swoop that was wisely rebuffed by Shankly.

Smith was eighteen months younger than Lawler, but seeing his close friend called up to the senior side only served to heighten his burning desire to follow suit. He would constantly pester the reserve-team coach about when his time would come. Smith remembers: 'Joe was always very approachable and looking back I must have got on his nerves the amount of times I chatted to him about why I wasn't in the first team. "You're not good enough", he'd say, and when somebody answers you as honestly as that there's not a lot more you can add. "Erm, OK, but when am I going to be good enough?" I'd reply, and he'd simply add, "I'll tell you when you're good enough, son". It was as simple as that and, although I didn't always agree with him, I admired the bluntness of his response.'

On Easter Monday 1963 Smith was given further reason to feel aggrieved at being deemed 'not yet good enough for the first team' when Liverpool's defence leaked seven goals in a First Division game at White Hart Lane. It prompted him to confront the manager about his future. 'I'd just turned eighteen and was thinking, "If I can't get into this team now, after such a heavy defeat, then when will I?" On reflection, questioning the manager at such a young age was probably not the wisest thing to do, but I was so frustrated at what I perceived to be a lack of progress.'

Of all the players Joe worked with during his time at Liverpool Smith was perhaps the one to whom he was closest. They hailed from the same part of the city, their childhood homes being just a few streets apart, and their backgrounds were remarkably similar. 'Joe sensed my frustration and was much more sympathetic to my cause. "You'll get there eventually, Smithy", I remember him saying, and I really appreciated his arm-around-the-shoulder approach. It was just what I needed at the time.' Unknown to Smith, Joe was constantly championing his cause to Bill Shankly. 'So many players came through the system that he recommended,' says Roger Hunt. 'If you were good enough you got a chance. Shankly trusted what Joe told him about players.' The manager was well aware of Smith's ability, having promised Mrs Smith that he would take good care of her son when signing him as a 15-year-old apprentice. He had taken a keen interest in the boy's development and was impressed by how he had progressed. But while Shankly was interested in his players' footballing ability and nothing else, Smith remembers that Joe took a more paternal approach to his young charges. 'He really did take care of us and that was very good for me,' says Smith. 'I was never a tearaway, but with my dad dying when I was only fifteen, it was important to have a father figure like Joe in my life at this time. There was a big England-Scotland rivalry among the lads at Liverpool back then and training could often get quite heated. The Scots all thought they were prize-fighters, but I knocked hell out of a couple of them with nobody's permission. Joe would just pull me to one side and tell me to relax, be careful, not get myself into any trouble.' With a physique that belied his tender years there was no doubt about Smith's capacity to handle himself in the hustle and bustle of the First Division. However, whether he had the character and temperament to handle the pressure that comes with making the step up was a decision only Joe could make. It was not long, though, before Smith made his Liverpool first-team debut, lining up in defence alongside Ron Yeats in a comfortable 5–1 home win over Birmingham. 'Joe didn't quite tell me, but I know he had a word with the boss,' Smith recalls, 'and for that I'll be forever grateful.'

As with Lawler, Smith still had to bide his time before he was able to call himself a first-team regular. He continued his education under Joe in the reserves as Liverpool completed their transformation from also-rans to top dogs by pipping Manchester United and Everton to the First Division Championship the following season. Liverpool's first League success for seventeen years was confirmed amid ecstatic scenes at the final home game of the season against Arsenal. On an occasion to savour, the BBC cameras were present to investigate the 'new phenomenon' of singing at football matches and an exultant Kop did not disappoint. The atmosphere was helped by an emphatic 5–0 victory, and as Shankly basked in the glory he was quick to insist: 'Liverpool's triumph is no one-man affair. My training and coaching staff have done a wonderful job. Every man in our organisation has been taught the importance of looking after the small things. From the boardroom to the groundsman, every cog in the machine has functioned perfectly. Everyone has given one hundred per cent effort.' The manager's grand master-plan for world domination was taking shape. The likes of Smith and Lawler would soon have an integral part to play in the next stage of that development as a first taste of European football and a much-coveted first triumph in the FA Cup beckoned.

Victory over Leeds United at Wembley in the FA Cup final of 1965 is regarded as the pinnacle of all that Shankly achieved at Liverpool and is still remembered as the greatest day in the club's history. It had taken seventy-three years for Liverpool's name to be inscribed on the trophy and during that time their followers had to put up with merciless ribbing from Everton supporters whose team had won the competition twice. Local mythology even went as far as suggesting that the city's iconic Liver Birds on top of the Liver Building in the city would fly from their perch should a team from Anfield lift the coveted trophy. 'To think a club like Liverpool had never won the FA Cup was unbelievable,' said Shankly. 'So many had prayed for it to happen over all the years but it had never come to pass. So when we beat Leeds, the emotion was unforgettable. Grown men were crying and it was the greatest feeling any human could have to see what we had done.' Though Joe was not directly involved on the bench at Wembley, it was a collective effort, involving all the players and backroom staff. Indeed, Joe was famously photographed drinking from the Cup in the changing-room afterwards. The *Football Echo* hailed this momentous achievement with a front page headline that roared: 'Ee-Aye-Addio The Reds Have Won The Cup.' More than a quarter of a million people packed into Liverpool city centre the following day to welcome home the Wembley heroes. It was a win that meant so much and Ron Yeats recalls: 'As captain, I received a tremendous amount of mail after the final, congratulating me on our victory. Some letters were from older supporters who actually wrote that they could now die in peace after Liverpool had won the FA Cup.' It may be difficult for modern football supporters to appreciate but before the advent of the Premier League and Champions League this was *the* trophy to win. The importance of capturing it for the first time can not be underestimated. In Shankly's eyes, until this so-called jinx had been broken, Liverpool could never truly be considered a big club. It was, he believed, a millstone around their neck which was preventing them moving on to future success.

In addition to that elusive FA Cup triumph, the 1964–65 season is also fondly remembered for the progress made in the club's first season of European football. Competing against the cream of the Continent provided a new challenge for the Liverpool coaching staff. In the second round against Anderlecht they proved they were not afraid to experiment tactically if they believed it could outwit the opposition. Until then, Shankly's Liverpool had generally adopted the old W-M formation that had been favoured by most British clubs since it was introduced by Huddersfield Town and Arsenal manager Herbert Chapman in the mid-1920s. In modern-speak it would be best described as 3–2–5, a formation that consisted of three full-backs, two half-backs, two wingers, two inside-forwards and a centre-forward. Having been impressed by how the Belgium national team had held England to a 2–2 draw at Wembley, Shankly returned to Melwood and consulted his coaches about the best way to handle Anderlecht, who he expected would play in a similar style. The four great minds got together and the outcome was what Tommy Smith firmly believes to be 'the start of a flat back four in this country'. Though Smith had come through the ranks as an inside-forward, the coaching staff had noted how he also had the potential to play in defence. On the night Anderlecht came to Anfield, despite running out with a number ten on his back in the days when a player's number was an indication of what position he would be playing, Smith dropped back and 'acted as Ron Yeats's right leg'. It was a switch that left the Belgians bemused, and on a night when Liverpool wore their now famous all-red strip for the first time, they ran out comfortable 3–0 winners. The champions of West Germany, F.C. Koln, were despatched in the next round on the toss of a disc after a play-off in neutral Rotterdam. A controversial defeat at the hands of reigning world club champions Internazionale ended Liverpool's run in the semi-finals, though not before an exhilarating first leg at Anfield that Joe later described as one of the club's greatest European nights. He recalled in an interview almost twenty years later: 'The atmosphere was tremendous. They say you could hear the singing in the city centre, and we played brilliantly. I'm quite glad I missed the return leg because all anyone could talk about afterwards was the refereeing.'

The 3–0 second-leg defeat in Milan, following the 3-1 Anfield lead, was tough to accept, but the disappointment of missing a place in the final was softened slightly by the knowledge that this Liverpool team had taken yet more giant strides. Internazionale coach Helenio Herrera certainly thought so and was quoted afterwards as saying: 'Liverpool are progressive. They are really thinking about football. The way to win the European Cup is to pass man to man fairly short and then make the fast burst. Liverpool have developed this and have the fitness to carry it out.' These early years in Europe acted as a valuable learning curve for everyone at the club. But tactically Liverpool still had a long way to go before they could master the art of conquering the Continentals. Further progress was made the following season when they reached their first European final. They beat Juventus, Honved and Celtic along the way in the European Cup-Winners' Cup. But on a filthy night in Glasgow, the occasion proved to be a huge anti-climax: Borussia Dortmund took the trophy thanks to a bizarre own goal by Ron Yeats in extra-time. Nevertheless it was a great time to be associated with the club: just four days before suffering that 2–1 defeat at Hampden Park, Liverpool's victory by the same scoreline at home to Chelsea was enough for them to be crowned champions for a record-equalling seventh time. That put them level with Arsenal as the most successful League team in English football. It was the club's third major honour in as many seasons and supporters brought up in the doldrums of the 1950s had never had it so good.

Other players who learned their trade in Joe's reserve team, and made notable first-team contributions during this time, included centre-forward Alf Arrowsmith, a 15-goal marksman in the title-winning campaign of 1963–64; defender Phil Ferns, who figured eighteen times that season; outside-right Gordon Wallace, the

scorer of Liverpool's first goal in European competition; and Bobby
Graham, who scored a hat-trick on his League debut in September
1964 against Aston Villa.

While success at first-team level was what everyone at the club
ultimately worked towards, the sheer consistency shown by those
in the senior side in the mid-1960s made Joe's job increasingly
difficult. Between 1964 and 1967 the Liverpool team was so settled
that when asked what the team would be for the weekend, legend
has it that Shankly would quip: 'Same as last year.' Exceptional
circumstances aside – such as the last League game before the 1965
FA Cup final when Shankly was reprimanded by the authorities for
making seven alterations to the side who lost at Wolves – changes
in personnel were few and far between.

Graham, Arrowsmith, Ferns and Wallace would probably have
walked straight into most other First Division sides at this time. So
would others like George Scott, the prolific reserve-team forward
in the first half of the 1960s. In those days before substitutes he did
not progress further than 'twelfth man carrying the skip'.
Aberdeen-born Scott joined Liverpool as a 15-year-old in January
1960. He remembers how Joe met him from the train at Lime Street
and during the taxi ride to his digs on Anfield Road warned him to
stay out of the many pubs they passed along Scotland Road. For
three years between 1962 and 1965 Scott was almost ever present in
Joe's reserve team and regularly topped the Central League scoring
lists. Being able to keep players motivated in such circumstances
remains one of the key strengths of any successful reserve-team
manager and, according to Scott, Joe had this in abundance.
'Towards the end of my time at Liverpool I did start to get a bit
frustrated, but Joe always used to urge me to keep giving one
hundred per cent,' Scott remembers. 'He had no time for sulking or
moaning and used to tell me to never give up and keep giving
myself targets. "Be the top scorer this season in the reserve team,
that's all you can do", he'd say.' It was in the aftermath of the FA
Cup win that Scott was informed by Bill Shankly that his contract
at the club would not be renewed. However, he looks back with no

regrets, especially when he considers that during the following season, when Liverpool regained the First Division title, only fourteen players were used and one of them, Bobby Graham, made just one appearance. Scott says: 'I will always remember my last meeting with Joe after Bill told me he was letting me go. He told me that I would be successful not only in my future football career but in whatever I chose to do. I could see it in his face that he seemed genuinely upset. He said that I should never think of myself as not having succeeded in my ambitions during my time playing for him at Anfield. I never saw Joe again after I left Anfield, but like Bill and Bob he had a tremendous influence on my early life.'

The summer of 1966 was dominated by the World Cup finals, staged in England. The hosts' squad included three Liverpool players, Roger Hunt, Ian Callaghan and Gerry Byrne, all of whom had in some way been influenced by Joe in their formative years at Anfield. With all England's matches taking place at Wembley, excitement on Merseyside centred on Goodison Park, the chosen venue for three group games involving reigning champions Brazil, plus a quarter-final and semi-final. Like every football fan Joe became fully engrossed in the spectacle. Along with Shankly and Paisley, he attended all five games at Goodison. Son Stephen remembers being taken to one of them and being told by his dad 'to keep an eye on this lad Pele'. Stephen, then eight, admits to having no real interest in football before this and was taken aback at how many people seemed know his dad on the short walk from Lynholme Road to the ground. 'I think it was Reuben who couldn't make the game that day,' he recalls, 'and with me being the first home from school Dad asked if I wanted to go along. We made our way through Stanley Park and it took ages because everyone we passed kept stopping Dad for a chat.'

Despite Joe's declaration to his son that 'Pele was the best player in the world', Brazil's number ten endured a tournament to forget as the holders were eliminated at the group phase. Down in London, Roger Hunt was ever present as England swept to a momentous victory over West Germany in the final. With three goals in the tournament, Hunt had sealed his reputation as one of the great goalscorers of his generation. Not that Joe, or anyone at Liverpool, needed convincing of his qualities. Nor did they get carried away by the hype surrounding Ramsey's so-called 'wingless wonders'. Adopting a 4–3–3 formation that involved operating with no out-and-out wide men ultimately carried England to World Cup glory, and in its aftermath brought about a sea-change in tactical thinking at clubs up and down the country. Almost everywhere, that is, apart from Liverpool where it never caught on. That is not to say those in the Bootroom were stuck in their ways and unwilling to embrace change; far from it, especially where Joe was concerned. Not long after England's success, a delegation from Liverpool, led by Shankly and including Joe, attended an FA-organised coaching course at the Lilleshall training centre in Shropshire. Unimpressed by having to spend so much time in a classroom, Shankly cut short his stay, famously remarking to Paisley: 'Come on, Bob, we've heard enough.' An open-minded Joe took it more seriously and proceeded to make detailed notes; his view was that anything that could possibly make the team better was worth considering. According to Ian St John: 'Joe, too, wouldn't have been a big fan of what went on down there, but he always seemed open to new ideas.' Joe eventually came to the conclusion that the course contained too much theory work which 'was easier to explain in person than on paper', and admitted: 'I don't think it's anything new.' Not that it stopped him encouraging other people to try it themselves. 'Towards the end of my career I attended the Lilleshall training centre to start studying for my coaching badges,' says St John. 'This was something that was frowned upon by Shanks and Bob, but Joe never seemed to have a problem with it.'

With Liverpool firmly established at the summit of English football, Shankly's side were expected to go on and dominate English football for the foreseeable future. However, over the next few seasons it became apparent that the team who had risen from the Second Division were losing some of their lustre. Admittedly, between 1966–67 and 1971–72 Liverpool did not finish outside the top five in the First Division and gates regularly topped fifty thousand. More importantly, though, during that period Liverpool did not win a single trophy. Given the club's recent run of success it was a worryingly barren spell. In today's climate of fans' forums, radio phone-ins and almost blanket television coverage, the comparative drought would have been built up into a crisis. Though the press often suggested that Shankly's first great team had 'peaked', the Anfield crowd stood by their side. Despite having enjoyed a modicum of success in the mid-1960s, those who stood on the Kop were yet to be spoilt by a conveyor-belt of trophies like their sons would be in future years. With the pre-Shankly era still a vivid and painful memory, the majority of Liverpool supporters were a lot more tolerant and appreciative of the situation. Despite a 6–1 drubbing of Nottingham Forest in their final home game of the 1967–68 season, results elsewhere meant Liverpool's title ambitions were thwarted for another year. But Chris James, writing in the *Liverpool Echo,* said: 'The fans showed what they thought when they applauded both teams off and the Kop refused to budge for ten minutes as they chanted for Bill Shankly to appear.' Deep down, though, the manager knew changes had to be made. 'We had a mediocre time for a while in the late 1960s as we prepared for the 1970s,' Shankly later admitted in his autobiography. 'A lot of our players were about the same age and I had given them a set time as to how long I thought they would last. I thought some of them would maybe have gone on longer than they did, because of their experience. Maybe the success they had shortened their careers. They had won the League, the FA Cup and League again, and they had been in Europe so often. Perhaps they were no longer hungry enough.' In contrast, Liverpool's second string really began to prosper.

As always, the main task of the reserve-team coach was to produce players for the first team. So that transition was as seamless as possible the philosophy was consistent between the two sides.

Joe trained and educated his players in much the same way as Shankly and Paisley ran the first team. This meant every player knew exactly what was expected of them. Now, that included winning trophies. Under Joe's guidance Liverpool reserves won three successive Central League titles between 1969 and 1971. The winning mentality that Joe instilled in his team was the template which would be passed down through the Bootroom ranks, and strictly adhered to by his successors, Ronnie Moran, Roy Evans and later Chris Lawler. Throughout the 1970s, and into the 1980s, the club dominated the competition, topping the table a further eleven times. This success bred a level of confidence that was important for the whole club. Reserve-team players graduating to the first team were already used to winning games. Indeed, the success of the second team famously prompted Shankly to quip: 'The city of Liverpool has two great teams: Liverpool and Liverpool reserves.' It was a tongue-in-cheek barb aimed in the direction of his great rivals across Stanley Park, but deep down Shankly was extremely proud of the important work Joe was doing. According to Dave Bowler, author of Shankly's official biography: 'Knowing that his great side were coming to their end, Bill stepped up his observations of the reserve strength … working on them in training and letting Joe Fagan and Ronnie Moran mould the side on Saturdays'.

Successive fourth-place finishes in the Central League in 1966–67 and 1967–68 were the prelude to Liverpool's dominance for the next twenty years. Just as Shankly is remembered for assembling two successful sides during his tenure as Liverpool manager, Joe can be credited with a similar job at reserve level. While his side of the early 1960s provided the first team with players such as Lawrence, Lawler and Smith, the team who swept to a hat-trick of Central League titles at the turn of the decade, provided the breeding ground for an equally exciting crop of youngsters. Bowler says: 'Behind the scenes, Liverpool were working feverishly to create a new side. On the face of things, though, Liverpool were hanging on for their lives and the going was getting harder.' As with most reserve teams, Joe worked with an eclectic mix: the squad were mainly made up of home-grown talent, like Doug Livermore, Phil Boersma, John McLaughlin, Kevin Marsh, John Webb, Steve Peplow and Roy Evans. Some of these boys, like Tommy Smith before them, came to regard Joe as their 'father in football'. Evans remembers: 'We all joined the club around the same time and Joe was the one who taught us how to play. His personality made him perfect for that role. He was a very caring man. I remember Dougie (Livermore) losing his dad and Joe really helped him through what was a tough time. He wanted to see everyone do well and would go that extra mile for his players.' Alongside the local lads were promising youngsters who had been brought in from the lower leagues. These included Peter Wall, a cultured full-back from Wrexham, Bury wing-half Alec Lindsay, dominant Bristolian centre-back Larry Lloyd and goalkeeper Ray Clemence, an £18,000 signing from Scunthorpe United. 'Joe was a very, very good man-manager,' remembers Clemence. 'Perhaps in the reserves that is even more important than the first team because you are dealing with three types of players. You have the young players coming out of youth-team football: they need to learn everything but will try as hard as they possibly can. Then you get first-team players coming back to the reserves who don't really want to be there, so trying to get them to commit one hundred per cent can be a problem. Then there is the middle lot who are stuck in the reserves. They are either striving to get into the first team and can't make it, or they are never going to get into the first team and it is everybody's fault but their own. You have to deal with all those; Joe handled it all so well.'

Captain of the side was Glaswegian Ian Ross, a former apprentice who had signed professional forms as a 17-year old in August 1965. 'Shanks had joked that we were the second best team on Merseyside and Joe instilled in us a belief that we were,' Ross recalls. 'It really was all about winning matches with Joe; draws were never any good. He sent us out to win every game and for a spell we almost did that.' Between August 1968 and May 1971 Liverpool reserves lost just fourteen of their 126 Central League fixtures.

The first of those three early titles was clinched with plenty to spare on Easter Monday 1969, with both goals in a 2–0 home win against Derby County from Steve Peplow, a slightly-built but skilful forward who ended the season top scorer with nineteen goals. With an average home crowd of more than three and a half thousand, Liverpool reserves were one of the best-supported teams in the Central League. Consequently there was no shortage of fans with an opinion. The letters page of Saturday's *Football Echo* became a regular platform for calls for some of Joe's second-team players to be promoted to a first team who had just experienced a third season without a trophy. A typical example was submitted by M.T. Mills, of Liverpool 14, who wrote: 'I would like to thank Liverpool reserves for some of the most entertaining football I have ever seen. The games against Everton and Bury exemplified what football, as a game, is all about.' *Liverpool Echo* reporter Chris James was in no doubt that there was great potential in Joe's team. 'The reserves' record speaks for the ability in the team and, introduced gradually, they could form the basis of the first team in the future,' he suggested.

One of the first players to be blooded towards the tail-end of the 1968–69 season was Brian Hall, a diminutive midfielder who had taken an unorthodox route into professional football. Having graduated from university with a degree in mathematics, Hall joined the club on a full-time basis at the comparatively late age of twenty-two. He was a world away from the archetypal footballer of the time. At any other club he might have struggled to be accepted in predominantly working-class dressing-rooms, and sensing this Joe made it his business to look after him. 'Joe never differentiated between players because of their backgrounds,' recalls Hall, 'and he helped introduce me into the family that is Liverpool Football Club. His thinking was always football-orientated, but above that he was a real people's person. He understood my situation and was a constant source of encouragement from my first days at the club as an amateur.' As Hall adapted to life as a full-time footballer one aspect he struggled with was the boredom in the afternoon once training had finished. Having been used to having his mind occupied constantly during his university days, the concept of being ordered to do nothing but rest when away from Melwood was an alien one. After several months of feeling lethargic, Hall consulted the club doctor who suggested he should try and keep his brain active. Joe had a solution and set him up with a part-time teaching job at a local school.

Hall had been at the club as a professional for less than nine months when he was handed his first-team debut. He went on as a substitute for the injured Roger Hunt in a 1–1 draw at Stoke, coincidentally on the day his regular team-mates were clinching the Central League title at Anfield. He soon found himself back with them as he continued his development, but the good impression he made opened the door for others. Liverpool's second string retained the title the following season in spectacular style, losing only twice and scoring eighty-nine goals in the process, conceding just twenty. They were the first team to win back-to-back titles at that level for more than a decade. But more importantly Joe had produced another six first-team debutants – McLaughlin, Evans, Peplow, Boersma, Lindsay and Lloyd. With the first team suffering another disappointing season, Joe's protégés were emerging at just the right time.

The FA Cup quarter-final defeat by Watford in February 1970 is generally accepted as marking the watershed between Bill Shankly's two great Liverpool teams. 'After Watford I knew I had to do my job and change my team,' he admitted later. 'It had to be done and if I didn't do it I was shirking my responsibilities.' Only a select few – Callaghan, Lawler and new captain Smith – survived the cull that followed. Peter Thompson was given a brief stay of execution, but veterans such as Lawrence, Yeats, Hunt and St John were soon moved on and a new guard brought through.

Joe now had another role to play and that involved using all his man-management skills when left to pick up the pieces from the fall-out between Shankly and an unhappy first-teamer. The transition from first-team stalwart to cast-off was uncomfortable for all parties and it was not a process the manager dealt with particularly well. Though Shankly did care deeply about his players, he could often give the opposite impression and even the most loyal servants could be treated to his infamous cold shoulder. Joe tried where possible to make these awkward situations easier for all concerned. His tact and sensitivity helped to ensure that players left with the dignity their years of service had earned. 'Towards the end of my ten years at Liverpool I ended up playing a few games under Joe for the reserves,' remembers St John. 'I had the hump with Shanks and had fallen out with him because he'd left me out of the team. Joe immediately embraced me into the team and treated me like the senior pro I was. In team-talks he'd always ask my opinion in front of the lads and gave me the captaincy. It was a sign of respect and it certainly made what was a difficult time for me that bit smoother. Other coaches may have thought I was a "big head" who needed putting into place, but that was never Joe's style. He gave me back my credibility and I really appreciated what he did for me back then. This only lasted for a matter of weeks before I eventually left the club but it gave me the lift I needed.'

While St John and his former team-mates were on their way out, several more members of Joe's Central League champions were waiting patiently in the wings. Shankly knew this moment would one day come and had been preparing for it. 'Gradually we were bringing players into the team,' he wrote in his autobiography. 'Some of them already had a couple of Central League championship medals before they got their chance in the big time. I could afford to buy players in their teens from the lower divisions and prepare them for a couple of years in the reserves.' Big-money signings such as Emlyn Hughes (£67,000 from Blackpool in March 1967), striker Tony Hateley (£96,000 from Chelsea in June 1967) and Britain's then most expensive teenager Alun Evans (£110,000 from Wolves in September 1968) aside, it was common practice for new arrivals to 'serve their time' in the reserves. Ray Clemence was advised that he would learn his trade in the second team for about six months before being considered for the seniors. Others were given similar assurances of a swifter passage to the first XI, but these promises proved to be somewhat wide of the mark on many occasions. Shankly obviously had to attract players to the club and telling them that they would have to wait patiently in the reserves would probably not have been an effective sales pitch. However, the presence of several new team members with great expectations and varying degrees of patience did not make Joe's job easy.

Clemence recalls: 'Even though there were a few of us who had been told we would soon be in the first team there was a great spirit. That's why we won the Central League every season. An awful lot of that was down to Joe, though he would never admit it. He somehow kept everybody happy, or as happy as a reserve team can be.' As a goalkeeper Clemence had to be more patient than most. He had only one position to aim for and Tommy Lawrence had filled it admirably since 1962. Clemence's two full seasons in the reserves both yielded Central League championship medals, but he had joined Liverpool to win first-team silverware. During the last half-season before Lawrence finally stepped aside, Joe made a point of reassuring Clemence that his chance would come. 'It was so important to me because if he hadn't put his arm round me I would have lost all motivation and probably left the club,' Clemence admits. 'He knew that I had improved as much as I could and I needed that next challenge, whether that was going to be at Liverpool or somewhere else. Joe kept me focused and really hammered home that when the opportunity arrived I had to be ready to take it. Thankfully I did, but a lot of that was down to Joe.'

As he had done with numerous would-be first-teamers in the past, Joe carefully weighed up the ability and character they showed in reserve-team fixtures. He would always report back to the other staff if someone was doing particularly well. Or particularly poorly. Players would be taken to one side and told simply what they needed to do to make the next step. Sometimes this was little more than 'keep it going', but often there were specific improvements that needed to be made. For Clemence, this involved a number of technical changes. Unusually for an English team at that time, Liverpool's back four would push up very high to support the midfield, leaving a large gap between defence and goalkeeper. Lawrence was well known for rushing off his line and clearing long balls played over the top of the defence. At a time when most goalkeepers were loath to leave their penalty areas, Lawrence was the original 'sweeper-keeper'; Clemence had to be ready to do the same job. 'I hadn't been asked to do anything like that at Scunthorpe, so I had to learn new starting positions and how to deal with certain situations,' he remembers. 'Joe helped me with all that. Obviously he had never been a 'keeper, but basically Joe did everything. His knowledge of goalkeeping was good enough.' Clemence was very hard on himself and tended to believe that every goal he conceded was his fault. Joe took the time to talk through performances with him, explaining how there were usually several mistakes from several different players before a goal was conceded. Joe also took the time to develop Clemence's kicking, which had been a significant weakness. They would spend hours kicking footballs to each other until the goalkeeper's kicking was up to standard.

By the start of the 1970–71 season Clemence had established himself as the first team's undisputed number one. He was joined in the senior ranks by fellow Central League title winners Lloyd, Hall, McLaughlin and Lindsay. Another young reserve who briefly broke through to the first team that season was Joe's then 20-year-old son Chris – or Kit as he was more commonly known. Like his dad, Kit was a defender, but 'an attacking right-back who could score goals', according to his younger brother Stephen. He made his debut as an extra-time substitute for Steve Heighway in a League Cup tie against Mansfield Town in September 1970. Kit had joined Liverpool as an apprentice after playing junior football for Shorefields in the local amateur leagues. He rose through the club's youth ranks and featured in the reserve team's success the season before. Keen to avoid accusations of nepotism, Joe treated Kit like any other player; on occasions he was perhaps even more demanding of him. Even when he received his well-deserved senior call-up, it was typical of the Fagans' laidback demeanour that this milestone moment in his life was kept very low-key within the family. 'I don't remember there being any big fuss made about it which, when I think back on it now, is a bit sad really,' says youngest brother Michael. 'He was making his first-team debut as a professional footballer and that is a massive achievement, but it was hardly mentioned.'

Liverpool had just regained the lead through Alun Evans when Kit entered the action in the one hundred and second minute. He was introduced to shore up a defence who had already conceded twice against the Fourth Division minnows. However, it was at the opposite end that he almost made an impact. 'He had a chance near the end but put it past the post,' recalls Stephen. 'I remember there being talk afterwards that if that had gone in Kit would have played again the following week, and who knows how far he would have gone then?' After appearing as an unused substitute in a Fairs Cup tie at home to Hibernian three months later, Kit's second outing came at Manchester City near the end of the season. It was a match played two days before Liverpool's Fairs Cup semi-final second leg at Leeds and a makeshift Liverpool XI came away with a creditable point in a 2–2 draw. Sadly for Kit that was his last first-team appearance in a red shirt. When his contract expired that summer he was released and he moved across the Mersey to Tranmere where he enjoyed a lengthy run in the first team before emigrating to New Zealand.

Despite reaching the last four of the Fairs Cup, and losing narrowly to Arsenal in an energy-sapping FA Cup final, it was clear throughout the 1970–71 season that Liverpool still lacked the spark to reignite their search for honours. By this stage the club had joined the big spenders in the British game: they splashed out around £100,000 on three occasions between 1967 and 1970 to sign strikers Hateley, Evans and then John Toshack. However, it was a buy from the lower divisions who proved to be the missing piece in the puzzle. In November 1970, the same month Toshack was signed from Cardiff City, Joe accompanied Shankly and Paisley on a scouting trip to Goodison Park for the second replay of an FA Cup tie between Scunthorpe United and Tranmere Rovers. Andy Beattie, a scout for Preston, had tipped off his friend Shankly about a young player called Kevin Keegan. The evidence of that one game was enough for Liverpool to buy the 20-year-old prodigy for £35,000 at the end of the season.

Keegan signed for Liverpool just before their Cup final defeat by Arsenal. With several members of the first-team squad on international duty, the club had to take a weakened team on their post-season tour of Scandinavia. This gave Keegan his chance to impress. Shankly and Paisley also skipped the trip, leaving Joe and Ronnie Moran in charge. After making his debut in a 3–2 friendly defeat against Aarhus of Denmark, Keegan scored his first Liverpool goal two days later in a 5–0 win over Swedish team I.F.K. Lulea. He was also voted man of the match and followed that up with another goal in a 4–0 win against Gif Sundsvall. 'That tour was important for me,' Keegan recalls. 'I was treated like you would expect to be treated at a top football club having come from where I had come. I was a reserve-team player, just twenty years of age and nobody knew me. That trip to Sweden meant Joe Fagan saw me play very soon after I had joined. That must have put something in his mind. I think Joe was very influential in my eventual selection for the first team. I know he liked my type of player because I worked hard, and I am sure he would have pushed me forward after Sweden. When we came back for pre-season I was probably fitter than any of the lads there because I used to do a lot of long running over the summer months. I think that won over people like Joe because they saw the determination in me.'

Joe had been so impressed by Keegan that his sons remember their father returning from training full of praise for this relatively unknown new signing. Keegan clearly had a burning desire to be successful that complemented his ability. Along with Moran, Joe strongly advised Shankly to waste no time getting this lad into the first team. Keegan played just three reserve-team games and impressed Shankly in the traditional firsts versus reserves match the week before the season. He was thrown straight into the first team at home to Nottingham Forest on the opening day of the 1971–72 season, scoring in a 3–1 win. Keegan's arrival was the catalyst for Liverpool's next golden period. Shankly's second great team had been assembled.

Throughout the transitional years Joe's quiet psychological approach was crucial to the Bootroom dynamic. Though he was fulfilling an important job for the reserve team, at the end of the 1970–71 season his contribution was officially recognised with promotion to the position of first-team trainer. He left his post as head of the second string after guiding them to a third successive Central League championship, the first time the feat had been achieved since Wolves had done so in the early 1950s. Of Joe's three title wins at that level this was perhaps the most challenging. It may not have been won in as impressive a style as the previous two, but in terms of having to overcome adversity it was the one of which he could be most justifiably proud. Having lost a significant number of his reserve-team 'stalwarts' to the senior ranks, it was a much-changed team who made it three in a row. Because of first-team call-ups, and an abnormal number of injuries, Joe fielded thirty-two players that season. Among them were a quartet who would serve on the club's coaching staff in future years: Roy Evans, Steve Heighway, Hughie McAuley and a spindly-legged teenager from Kirkby named Phil Thompson. Thompson has never forgotten the first time he played for Joe in the reserves. 'It was a goalless draw away at Sheffield Wednesday and what sticks in my mind is his reaction to my performance,' recalls Thompson. 'He actually gave me a bollocking. He said, "I know it's your first game, son, but can't you play the ball forward? Every ball was sideways or backwards. Use this as an experience and have the confidence to play the ball forwards". Being my debut Joe knew I would remember his words. Of course, it was sound advice, even if it did shake a 16-year-old who thought he had done fairly well.'

Joe's promotion prompted a backroom reshuffle in which Bob Paisley became assistant manager and junior Bootroom member Moran was put in charge of the reserves. Moran had only recently hung up his boots after winding down his playing career in Joe's reserve side. He had already taken great heart from Joe's encouragement during his time as a player and he knew that the elder man would be an invaluable mentor as his coaching career began. 'The one man I learned the most from was Joe Fagan,' says Moran. 'When I was playing for the reserves at Newcastle, he threw me the number eleven jersey. I told him, "I'm not quick enough to play outside left", and he just said, "Go out and play". He knew I was a worrier so he didn't fill my brain with ideas of what I should or shouldn't do. It turned out he had Roy Evans playing behind me at left-back, so it didn't matter that I wasn't the quickest of movers – I didn't have to go haring back after the winger. Playing for Joe in the reserves, at the end of my career, were some of the best times I had playing for Liverpool.'

As first-team coach Joe continued to take the training sessions as he had done, but now had even more hands-on contact with the senior players by doubling up as 'sponge-man' on matchdays. 'He used it as a way to have a few indirect words with the referee who would always be in earshot,' remembered Emlyn Hughes. 'The conversation would go something like this, "What was that goal disallowed for, Emlyn? It looked a good goal to me, but we have to accept these decisions, don't we, Emlyn?" It put that little bit of doubt in the referee's mind – but in the nicest possible way. Who knows the next decision might have gone Liverpool's way because of it.' Joe also continued to assist Paisley with physiotherapist and masseur duties. He may have had no qualifications or formal training in this field, but he often donned a white coat to administer treatment to an injured player. While some clubs had clearly defined roles for each coach, Liverpool did not. Everyone mucked in. It sometimes meant managing the manager. As much as Shankly was a great visionary, a peerless motivator and possessed a superb football mind, he was also very abrasive. The others, including Joe, would often have to smooth over the effects of the manager's habit of upsetting people. Shankly's Liverpool could be a volatile place and occasionally even Joe was known to lose his temper. 'He was definitely no soft touch and if you needed a telling off you got a telling off,' remembers Roy Evans. 'He very rarely went ballistic, but if he did you knew it was serious.' Generally, though, Joe was the peacekeeper. On one occasion during the 1970s, Tommy Smith was left seething after Shankly snubbed him on an away trip to Arsenal. Smith was certain that he was going to be dropped from the squad and had asked to remain in Liverpool to train, rather than travelling down to London to sit in the stands at Highbury. Shankly insisted that he had not decided on his team and demanded that Smith travel with the squad. Smith remembers: 'I stormed out of the room and Joe stopped me on my way out. He asked me what the hell I was doing and I explained that I thought Shanks was taking the mick out of me. In the end Joe persuaded me to go down to London. Shanks read out the team and of course I wasn't in it. I picked up my bag and walked straight out. For the second time in two days Joe confronted me. I explained that I was going home and he said, "OK, well, I will see you tomorrow morning and you just make sure you come in to the club".' Smith duly turned up at Anfield the following day and Joe put him through his paces, running the player up and down the terraces before sending him inside to shower. As Smith was about to leave, Shankly popped his head around the dressing-room door: 'Hello, Tommy son, I just thought I would let you know that I would have done exactly the same thing as you did yesterday.' It was as close as Shankly would come to calling for a truce. Knowing that Shankly and Smith were both hot-blooded characters, Joe had typically taken the edge off a potentially explosive situation. By making sure that Smith acted in a professional way, and by knowing that Shankly would be impressed to see the dissatisfied player working away on the terraces at Anfield, Joe ensured that the Liverpool machine kept running smoothly.

Joe was a perfect counterbalance to Shankly. As Kevin Keegan acknowledges, he was sensitive to the different personalities who combined to make a squad. 'Joe was good to talk to. He was one of those crucial people at a football club who would come over and spend time with you. The manager has so much on his plate, he has to look after so many things. But Joe, in particular, would spend a bit of time to come over to you individually and say, "Come on, lad, what's up?" He would notice the little things and that's what made him so great. He knew when you needed a little boost. Or if you were getting carried away with yourself he would put you back on the straight and narrow. A lot of his work was not done in team meetings or even in front of anybody. It was definitely not done on camera to impress people. It was done quietly, privately, to get the best of you for Liverpool FC.'

After the disappointment of losing the 1971 FA Cup final and narrowly missing the First Division title the following year, all the work put into Shankly's rebuilt Liverpool came to fruition in 1973. The championship was clinched in a goalless home draw against Leicester on the final Saturday of the League season. With one trophy in the bag Liverpool travelled to Germany to defend a 3–0 first-leg lead in the UEFA Cup final against Borussia Monchengladbach. The club's first European trophy should have been a formality. But as captain Tommy Smith remembers it did not quite go according to plan. 'In Germany we were 2–0 down after about twenty minutes. We hung in until half-time and got a real bollocking off Shanks. The way they were playing it would have been about 10–0. The second half started and I just started growling and snarling, getting stuck into a few tackles. We could have won the second half as it happens but we held on to lose 2–0, which meant we won 3–2 on aggregate. Anyway, they gave me the cup, which weighed half a ton, the bottom end of it was a brick! While the lads were running around celebrating, Joe came up to me quietly and said, "Smithy, that was the best game you have had for a long time". He didn't shout or go over the top and I liked that.

I thought, "Fucking hell, Joe has never said anything like that to me before. That will do for me".' The effect that such a simple endorsement could have on an experienced player like Smith shows the kind of respect that existed between Joe and the Liverpool team.

However, even though they may have won two trophies, as the mid-1970s approached football was evolving and in terms of tactics it would soon be time for a another change. This hit home after Liverpool lost both legs of the following season's European Cup second-round tie against Red Star Belgrade. The Yugoslavs' slick passing, and the way they patiently built from the back, made a lasting impression on Joe and the Anfield backroom team. 'Joe had a great understanding of how players should play football and, without a shadow of doubt, he'd have been incredibly influential in how our style of football changed,' claims Brian Hall. The next morning the coaching staff convened as normal in the Bootroom. This time, though, the manager joined them. Everyone had their say and between them the Liverpool brains trust decided that a less hectic style of play was required to conquer the Continent. 'The top Europeans showed us how to break out of defence efficiently,' recalled Bob Paisley in later years. 'The pace of their movement was dictated by their first pass. We had to learn how to be patient like that and think about the next two or three moves when we had the ball.' The fall-out of those defeats marked the end of the old-style 'stopper' in the shape of Larry Lloyd to be replaced by a more comfortable ball-playing centre-half in young Phil Thompson. He recalled in his autobiography: 'It was a clever decision by the boss and his staff. They were ahead of the time. All of a sudden we were looking to play from the back. If it took fifty passes to score we didn't care. The coming together of Emlyn (Hughes) and myself in that partnership was the start of the Total Football that would be made famous by the Dutch that same year.'

Liverpool's new style of play was never better illustrated than on that memorable afternoon at Wembley in May 1974 when, as commentator David Coleman so eloquently put it, 'Newcastle were undressed'. Keegan scored twice as Liverpool recorded a 3–0 win in one of the most one-sided FA Cup finals of all time. Joe, resplendent in an all-red club-issue Umbro tracksuit, sat three seats away from Shankly on the Liverpool bench. However, it was the last time Shankly would lead Liverpool. Like everyone else, Joe had no idea of the bombshell that was to drop on 12 July, 1974. 'It is with great regret, as chairman of the board, I have to inform you that Mr Shankly has intimated to us that he wishes to retire from League football,' said a sombre-looking John Smith at a packed Anfield press conference. To the assembled gathering of journalists who had turned up in expectation of a new signing, it was a moment of such jaw-dropping significance that even the most hardened of the hacks struggled to comprehend what they had just heard. 'I was present in the club's trophy room and can still hear the gasps of astonishment,' says former *Daily Express* reporter John Keith. 'At first people simply refused to believe Shankly had gone.' As the news slowly sunk in, cameras flashed frantically while Shankly shuffled anxiously in his seat. 'This was not a decision that was taken quickly,' he said. 'It had been in my mind over the last twelve months. I feel it is time I had a rest from the game. It was the most difficult thing in the world to make a decision like this and when I went to see the chairman to say I was retiring it was like walking to the electric chair.'

The shock announcement that Liverpool's modern-day founding father was to step down as manager after fifteen years shook the Kop to its core. When word filtered down to the streets, everyday life seemed to stop momentarily in its tracks. No sooner had the *Liverpool Echo*, with the headline 'Soccer Bombshell – Shankly Retires' emblazoned across the front page, rolled off the presses than copies were being snapped up by a public seeking confirmation. Some distraught fans had to leave work early as they struggled to come to terms with the prospect of life at Liverpool without him. In his book, *Talking Shankly*, Tom Darby wrote: 'The pubs of Liverpool were strangely silent that evening. It is said that the later demise of John Lennon was met with nowhere near the sense of loss Liverpool felt at Shankly going.' Many, including

Tommy Smith, were in denial. 'The close season's always too long for Shanks, never mind retirement,' was his immediate and dismissive response to the news. 'I had to hear it from two or three people and then on the radio before I believed it,' recalls Ray Clemence. It had been such a guarded secret that not even those closest to Shankly at the club had been warned. 'Every year, virtually, he'd say he was going to pack in,' said his assistant Bob Paisley. 'You didn't take him seriously. When he finally did I was lost for words, shocked. It was the day I got back from holiday and it was like a bomb being dropped.' As for Joe, his reaction remains something of a grey area. With it being the close-season there was no entry in his diary, but with pre-season training due to begin the following Monday he was at Anfield that day getting everything ready for the players' return. Yet his views on the matter were not sought and he has subsequently never been quoted about it. Two of his sons, however, have contrasting views on how he took the news. 'Nothing much shocked Dad,' insists Michael, 'especially where Shankly was concerned.' But Stephen remembers him 'being as shocked as everyone else'. The truth probably lies somewhere in between. Horace Yates in the *Daily Post* immediately raised the question: 'It's not so much who will follow him, as how can anybody follow him?'

Fortunately Liverpool had a safety net in place. It was called the Bootroom. Like the Royal Family, within it was a hierarchy that meant that when the King had gone there was another waiting to take his place. Club secretary Peter Robinson was a key figure in the decision to look within for Shankly's successor. But Robinson admits it was not so straightforward. 'When Bill resigned we had two options,' he says. 'One was to look outside the club, and Jack Charlton was one of the names Bill actually recommended to us. The other was to promote from within which, of course, was what we eventually opted for. We discussed both possibilities and I must say that opinion was divided on what course we should follow.'

One name never mentioned publicly in connection with the vacancy was Joe's. However, Michael Fagan maintains a belief that his dad was recommended to the board by Shankly. 'Mum told me years later,' Michael reveals. 'Apparently, he found out through Bob as they passed on the stairs at Anfield one day around this time. "I hear Shanks has put your name forward as his replacement", Bob told him, but Dad was like, "No, no, no, you take it and we'll just carry on as we are".' Peter Robinson admits to having no knowledge of such a recommendation and with no one else now available to validate Michael's claim it is one that can never be proved. Robinson does insist, though, that Shankly had always held Joe in high esteem. 'Bill once said to me that the one man he knew he could always rely on to express an opinion was Joe and I think that says an awful lot. He rated him very, very highly.' Even if Michael's version of events is true, it is unlikely the board would have seriously considered promoting Joe to the position of manager when there was already an assistant in place above him. Eventually the view was taken that Bob Paisley was more than capable of continuing the good work Shankly had started. But Robinson is quick to add: 'The fact that Bob would have such a strong staff behind him, headed, of course, by Joe, was a contributory factor in the high level of confidence we placed in Bob.'

It was an appointment made with the former manager's blessing and one Joe wholeheartedly supported. Bringing in an outsider could have undermined all that he had helped build during the previous sixteen years. Shankly's dream had been to see Liverpool 'conquer the bloody world', and even though the great man had gone, none of his disciples was going to rest easy until the target had been achieved. Joe's time would come, of course, but until then there was plenty more important work behind the scenes to be getting on with.

CHAPTER SIX

THE PAISLEY YEARS

FOR THE MAJORITY of Liverpool fans the summer of 1974 felt like the end of the world. Their King had abdicated and there was a genuine sense of trepidation about what the future held. The void left by Bill Shankly was huge. For a brief spell the club seemed rudderless and the danger was that the players would lose direction. Even those within the club were concerned whether Bob Paisley could possibly follow Shankly. 'Most of the players at that time, if they are honest, would admit they were not sure that Bob could do the job,' recalls Kevin Keegan. 'Bob was a good number two, but he wasn't very good communication-wise.' Ray Clemence says: 'I think when he first succeeded Shanks he was a bit overawed. I'll never forget him standing in the dressing-room in the summer of 1974 on the first day of pre-season training and telling us, "Shanks has gone and they're giving me the job, even though I didn't really want it. But we must try to carry on what he's started".'

Paisley, with his awkward habit of muddling his words, and a penchant for forgetting names, was the complete opposite to Shankly in terms of personality. He admitted as much when he said: 'I knew, taking over from him, there would be difficulties to combat because of the type of extrovert personality Bill was and the fantastic record he had. I knew comparisons would be made.' However, Paisley was equipped with a keen football brain, an eye for a good player, a good deal of common sense and a thorough understanding of Liverpool Football Club. After all, he had been there, along with Joe Fagan, on Shankly's first day. They had both been instrumental in implementing Shankly's ideas, and it was now down to them to ensure the Anfield machine continued to run smoothly. Many football managers are eager to stamp their authority immediately upon arrival: training routines change, new tactical ideas are implemented and personnel overhauled. Sometimes the changes are necessary and for the better, but Liverpool in 1974 were a successful team, fresh from a dominant display in English football's showpiece game. Also, Bob Paisley did not have a large ego to satisfy: he was happy to keep things almost exactly as they were.

Joe's official position was now chief coach, though job titles were never important at Liverpool. In practice he continued his previous duties and took on some extra ones. Where in the past Paisley would have been the one to point out tactfully to a player that he needed a rest, or that he was not quite ready to return to the team, this would now be Joe's domain. As second in command, he was now responsible for relaying the manager's decisions to the unfortunate player. Joe did not relish this side of his job, but neither would he hesitate to give his own frank appraisal of where a player was going wrong. 'He knew when people needed a kick up the backside, when they needed time to themselves and when they needed a quiet word or a boost,' says Ray Clemence. 'He could do it all and he did it quietly and without a fuss.'

In addition to Joe's promotion, the Bootroom reshuffle moved Ronnie Moran to first-team coach and 25-year-old Roy Evans, a key member of the reserve side for nearly a decade, was made manager of the second team. Evans became the youngest coach to work in the Football League. Born in the Liverpool district of Bootle, his star had dimmed somewhat after representing England as a schoolboy. His playing career at Liverpool had stalled after a handful of first-team appearances and he was facing a transfer away from the club he loved. On announcing the appointment, chairman John Smith said: 'We wanted to keep the promotions and changes within the club to maintain our family atmosphere. We have not made an appointment for today but for the future. One day, Roy Evans will be our manager.' It was a prescient comment by Smith: Evans would indeed go on to manage the club twenty years later, but back in 1974 he was struggling to weigh up the pros and cons of giving up his playing career at such a young age. 'I initially refused the coaching job, but Joe played a big part in persuading me to give it a try,' says Evans. 'Joe spoke to me, Ronnie too; even Tommy Smith had a word. All of them influenced me to do it, but when you get someone like Joe saying, "Just give it a try", you listen.'

Joe had noticed Evans's enthusiasm in training and the way he was always looking to help his team-mates. As Paisley put it: 'Roy knows the game well and has the right approach to control and guide players.' Early in Paisley's first season Joe pulled Evans to one side and told the rookie coach: 'Look, when you come with the first team, when you sit on the bench, if you have something to say, then bloody well say it. Because sometimes when you are slightly on the outside, not travelling with the team every week, you will see something different to us. You might be wrong, you might be right, but if you just say that one little thing that helps us, that is what we are looking for.' Not only did Joe's prompting give Evans the confidence to speak up, it also made him feel a relevant and valued member of the coaching team early in his career. This kind of intervention was the hallmark of Joe's work during Paisley's reign. His attention to detail was amazing. He simply would not let the club drop below the standards that had been established. He would chastise the players after a below-par performance with his trademark lament: 'You buggers, you've done me today, you bloody berks.'

With Paisley now moved into the manager's office, the Bootroom was manned on a daily basis by Joe, Ronnie Moran and Roy Evans. But while Shankly had been slightly removed from the Bootroom, Paisley still found time for the all-important marathon conversations with his staff. As ever, all opinions were considered and even if a particular point was later discarded, it would have had equal consideration, no matter who put it forward.

With Shankly's departure, the club had suffered a significant loss in the field of man-management. For years the great man had inspired players to greater heights through praise or intimidation. Shankly could persuade even an average player that he was the greatest talent in Europe. For some players, notably Kevin Keegan, it was a real struggle to raise themselves to the same levels without Shankly there to inspire them. Joe was not one for hyperbole or inspirational speeches. In the dressing-room before games he would go about his business in a quiet manner, but from time to time casually reminding certain players of a weakness in the opposition ranks or of a special instruction they had been asked to carry out. He was no replacement for Shankly, but his personnel skills became more and more important as Paisley's tenure progressed. If players had a problem or needed something explained they would normally speak to Joe. He kept an appropriate distance from them but always remained approachable. While Shankly had told fantastic stories, and excited his players by telling them how good they were, Joe calmed their fears and cajoled them into form by being the voice of reason and common sense. Discipline was another area Joe took over. Always quick to pull people back into line with a glare or a grumpy call of 'Hey you buggers, behave yourselves', Joe would make sure he stamped out promptly any disquiet in the ranks. A cup of tea would be offered after training and a disgruntled player would be gently coaxed back into toeing the company line. Football teams always contain fiery personalities who will inevitably clash from time to time, but Joe would step in with: 'Hey, we can't win football matches when you are arguing with each other. You are already fighting eleven of the opposition, you can't fight one on our team as well.' Solutions were always simple and reasonable. Above all, Joe was down to earth and he had no time for egos, self-indulgence or posturing.

Keegan remembers that Joe would come to the fore when the team had under-performed; he knew instinctively when to confront players with a few home truths, and when to say nothing. Joe would not hesitate to ruffle a few feathers even after a victory or a draw if he thought the team were showing even an ounce of complacency. Everything was carefully aimed at keeping things on an even keel: not too uptight and not too laidback. 'Joe was a man of relatively few words, so when he did speak, people listened,' Keegan recalls. 'If someone is talking all the time, shouting and ranting, people start to take it with a pinch of salt; they switch off. With Joe, I would think maybe we had played quite well, perhaps been a bit unlucky, and he would come in and say, "You buggers, that was a game you should have won. You have let yourselves down, you have let the club down, you have let the staff down and you have let the fans down". It always hit home. You knew what the standards were.' Off-field discipline was equally important. As Keegan flourished to become one of football's first superstars, he was offered all kinds of endorsement deals from newspapers, boot manufacturers and other sponsors. 'You've just got to keep doing what you are doing,' Joe told him. 'Don't change anything and don't take too much on. Don't lose your focus. There is only one contract that matters and that is with Liverpool Football Club, because if you are playing well they will always come and ask you to write columns, to wear boots and to put your name on footballs.'

Liverpool remained a happy ship, but as the first post-Shankly season loomed the burning question was, would it sail smoothly onwards? That 1974–75 season, Paisley's first in charge, was only partially reassuring for Liverpool fans. The team's performance did not drop off noticeably. Yet apart from the Fair Play trophy, Liverpool finished it with no silverware. They were runners-up to Dave Mackay's Derby County in the League and went out in the cup competitions early on. It was a solid if not glorious start. The highlight was a club-record 11–0 victory against Stromsgodset Drammen in the European Cup-Winners' Cup. A couple of key moves made midway through the season, however, hinted at what was to follow. Paisley showed his eye for a bargain by snapping up for £60,000 future Liverpool captain Phil Neal, a 23-year-old full-back from Northampton Town, and strengthening his squad with the shrewd acquisition of Newcastle United's Liverpool-born midfielder Terry McDermott, a future Footballer of the Year. The manager also underlined his footballing nous by shifting Shankly's final signing, Ray Kennedy, from the forward line into midfield where he would be a dominant force for years to come.

Topping the Fair Play League may have been seen by some as a softening in attitudes at Anfield and a sign that, post-Shankly, Liverpool had lost their ruthlessness. As was proved on an end-of-season break to Benidorm, however, that could not have been further from the truth. Trips like those were chiefly about relaxation, but the club had to justify taking the entire playing staff on holiday by including some friendly matches in the itinerary. Faced with a meaningless game against a local amateur team, Liverpool's players decided not to over-exert themselves. To Joe, this thinking was alien. With a glint in his eye he beckoned Tommy Smith to the touchline. 'Start a fight, Smithy,' he said. Thinking he had misheard Smith asked Joe to repeat his instruction. He got the message loud and clear a second time. Never one to duck out of anything, Smith duly obliged. A trademark no-nonsense challenge provoked a skirmish. The crowd started to get into the game and, suddenly, so did Liverpool's players. A few strong challenges were delivered, the blood started to boil and Liverpool won at a canter. Joe had reminded the players of their obligations: every time they put on the red shirt they were expected to give their all, even in a friendly match against a bunch of part-timers.

This level of steel and commitment was carried into the next season when the doubters were won over. With Ray Kennedy's conversion from occasional goalscoring striker to lethal left-sided midfielder, and exciting local youngsters Jimmy Case and David Fairclough emerging from the reserves, Paisley's team surged to the 1975–76 League title in thrilling fashion. The season was decided in a dramatic final fixture away at Wolverhampton Wanderers. With their nearest challengers, Queens Park Rangers, having completed their season, Liverpool were left knowing a win or low scoring draw would be enough to clinch a record-breaking ninth title. Wolves were in equally desperate need of the points to stave off the threat of relegation, so the stage was set for a night of drama. There were an estimated twenty thousand Liverpudlians inside Molineux, and they created memorable post-match scenes after Liverpool's 3–1 win.

To complete a successful season, and show they could succeed without Shankly, they also won a tense, two-legged UEFA Cup final against Belgian side F.C. Bruges to clinch a memorable Double. After coming back from two goals down to win 3–2 at Anfield, a single Keegan goal was enough to claim a draw in Belgium. 'The lads proved their character, guts and know-how in this game,' Joe jotted down in his diary after the second leg. 'Well done the lot of you … you buggers!' Everyone at Anfield breathed a sigh of relief and no one begrudged Liverpool their triumph. Derek Wallis in the *Daily Mirror* wrote: 'Seldom has a team been more deserving of the honours that have poured on them this season.' But Joe's standards were so high that he was not totally satisfied. 'I am happy, of course, but can I still say we failed this season? The League Cup and FA Cup are still in somebody else's hands!'

This second UEFA Cup success in three years proved that Liverpool were at last coming of age in Europe. Brian Glanville of *The Times* later reflected: 'Working diligently on their tactics, Liverpool emerged as a new, more sophisticated team, refusing to give the ball away to European teams who would not give it back.' A star-studded Barcelona team, including the Dutch legend Johan Cruyff, had been beaten before a record Anfield crowd for a European tie in the semi-final and many, including Wallis, believed the performance in Bruges intimated that they were now ready to launch a serious assault on the ultimate prize. He wrote: 'The European Cup may not be beyond them next season.' Tommy Smith agrees that it acted as the perfect springboard for future success. 'The UEFA Cup was always regarded as the lesser of the three European competitions, but it was the hardest of them all to win,' he says. 'There was an extra round for starters, and the two-legged final didn't make it any easier. You'd also come up against emerging clubs who were on the verge of great things, like Monchengladbach and Bruges, for example. So in that respect it was the perfect breeding ground for teams going into the European Cup.'

With Liverpool-born forward David Johnson, a summer signing from Ipswich, the only addition to the squad, Liverpool's early progress in the European Cup the following season was more steady than spectacular. Crusaders of Northern Ireland and Turkey's Trabzonspor were defeated with relative ease to secure a place in the quarter-final. A successful first defence of their League title since the 1920s was also looking probable as Liverpool led the table for much of the campaign. The only black spot on the horizon concerned the future of Keegan. News had broken on the eve of the season that this would be his last in Liverpool colours. The reigning Footballer of the Year had made no secret of his desire to try his luck abroad, but the announcement was met with a lukewarm reception by the fans who had once idolised him. At some clubs this situation might have led to awkwardness between player and staff. Not at Liverpool. The coaches were all hugely pragmatic about players leaving and none more than Joe. Whenever a player decided to move on, he would thank them for their efforts, wish them well and then move on. Whenever a good player was lost, another was found. It was not personal; former players were always made welcome if they returned to Anfield or Melwood. It was simply the belief that the only players who were important to Liverpool were those who could be selected to pull on a red shirt that coming Saturday. 'They never treated me any differently that season, never preferentially, never badly,' Keegan recalls. 'The club was the only thing that ever mattered to them. Yes, the players were important, but no player was ever too important.'

Had Liverpool's form dipped Keegan might have found life more difficult. But his final year at the club was shaping up to be the greatest yet in Liverpool's history. As well as the League and European Cup, an exciting run in the FA Cup gave rise to talk of Liverpool completing an unprecedented Treble. A surprise goalless draw at home to Third Division Crystal Palace in the third round was the only scare until the last few minutes of the semi-final against Everton at Maine Road. With the score level at 2–2, Bryan Hamilton looked to have booked Everton a place at Wembley until referee Clive Thomas ruled his 'goal' out for handball.

Everyone at Liverpool knew they had been let off the hook and were determined not to make the same mistake in the replay at the same venue four nights later. After the first meeting Joe pulled Tommy Smith aside. Smith recalls: '"What is it Joe?" I asked. "The winger …" "Yes, what about him?" "He nutmegged you, didn't he?" I just looked blankly at him. "Won't happen again, will it?" he frowned. And it didn't. A nice early tackle in the replay saw to that!'

With Duncan McKenzie not so effective, Liverpool cantered to a 3–0 win to reach the final and maintain their increasing hopes of a three-pronged trophy assault. Just over a fortnight later, on 14 May, 1977, Paisley's side clinched the League with a home draw against West Ham. 'Shit game, but we won the championship, so well done everybody,' was Joe's frank assessment that day. Given the title-clinching drama of twelve months before, it seemed like a comedown. But with the season gearing up to a climax of epic proportions it could be forgiven.

The route to the European Cup final in Rome had become more eventful. The 3–1 quarter-final win over St Etienne at Anfield is still widely acknowledged as one of the greatest evenings of drama the old stadium has hosted. It was summed up by Horace Yates in the following morning's *Daily Post* as 'a night of tension, drama, elation, frustration, and sheer jubilation'. Liverpool had lost 1–0 in France, but Keegan had them back on level terms with an early goal at the Anfield Road End. When St Etienne snatched an equaliser just after half-time, though, the away-goals rule left Liverpool needing to score twice. Ray Kennedy halved the requirement with a trademark strike and then, with just six minutes remaining and the Kop doing its best to suck a goal in, substitute David Fairclough latched on to a long forward pass. He controlled the ball on his chest, steadied himself and coolly slotted it under goalkeeper Yvan Curkovic. Anfield erupted in ecstasy; those present that night swear the ground shook. 'I have never known anything like it,' admitted captain Emlyn Hughes afterwards. 'I have played in front of one hundred and thirty thousand for England, but the noise and enthusiasm didn't compare with this.' Liverpool were into the semi-final for the first time since 1965. The fans belted out a rousing chorus of 'We shall not be moved', and Joe was left to reflect on what he described as 'one hell of a game'.

Fairclough's match-winning entrance remains one of the most iconic moments in Liverpool history. It is a night he has never been allowed to forget, and one that pigeon-holed him as 'Supersub', the nickname by which he is universally known. His uncanny knack of coming off the bench late and rescuing lost causes made him a secret weapon in Liverpool's armoury. He enjoyed many other magical moments in a red shirt during the course of his nine years as a professional at Anfield, yet when he looks back on his career the memories are tinged by a case of 'what if'. No player warmed the bench more during Paisley's reign than Fairclough. In total, he pulled on the number twelve shirt one hundred and thirty-six times between 1975 and 1983. While his relationship with Paisley suffered as a result, Joe also played a part in this. Often the manager would watch the game from the stands where he had a better view of the action. If Paisley wanted to make a substitution he would come down to the bench and tell Joe what he was thinking. 'Bob would then go back upstairs and leave the final decision to Joe,' Fairclough remembers. 'Sometimes, if Joe then noticed a slight change in the pattern of the game he would leave things as they were and I never went on. So, as you can imagine, on occasions when this happened he was not my favourite person.'

From his vantage point in the dug-out, though, Fairclough gained an insight into how Joe reacted to certain situations during the course of a game. 'Just like in training he wasn't as vocal as Ronnie on the bench, but he did a lot of talking. He was a man who kept his emotions in check. I can never remember him becoming embroiled in angry exchanges with the opposition bench, but there were times when he had to calm Ronnie down if things were getting heated on the touchline,' says Fairclough. 'He'd always be watching the game intensely and would be pulling players into position. He could also be a bit of a pessimist when watching from the sidelines and one of his favourite sayings would be, "Oh, they've shit it", meaning the team were going to collapse and be beaten. He was a big worrier in that respect and always seemed to fear the worst.' Against St Etienne there was no need to worry. 'When he went through you just knew David would score,' Joe later admitted. 'He could always be a match-winner.'

A comfortable 6–1 aggregate victory against FC Zurich in the semi-final enabled Liverpool to qualify for their first European Cup final against the newly-crowned Bundesliga champions Borussia Monchengladbach, a side peppered with internationals. But first there was the small matter of the FA Cup final at Wembley, where Manchester United stood between Liverpool and the second leg of a potential Treble. The prospect of two finals in the space of four days whipped the red half of Merseyside into a state of unbridled frenzy. The clamour for tickets and drawing up of dual invasion plans for London and Rome meant the football briefly took a back seat. The job of maintaining the players' focus amid all the off-field distractions was left to Joe. On the Monday of Wembley week he admitted it was a struggle. 'Training was bloody awful. The lads had two meetings about arrangements for Wembley then came out expecting an easy-osey time. They didn't get it. I bollocked them and told them it is the football that counts, not bloody tickets.'

Perhaps the players did lose some concentration in the build-up, but nonetheless they were unlucky to lose on the big day. Despite Jimmy Case scoring one of the greatest FA Cup final goals of all time, Jimmy Greenhoff's freakish winner capped a 2–1 win for

United. The beaten finalists looked physically and psychologically drained as they trooped off the sun-drenched pitch. Having looked like they were cruising to the Treble, the shock of the defeat was going to be a hard one from which to bounce back. 'It was as I feared,' Joe conceded in his diary. 'The adrenalin didn't seem to be flowing as it should have been. Too many players did not play well enough on the day. They did try, though, so hard luck.'

There was barely time for the players to pick themselves up from the crushing disappointment before they were due to play in Rome. The morale of the team was inevitably a worry, but Liverpool were desperate for a chance to wash away the misery of Wembley. They did just that on a night Paisley was to rate as the greatest in the club's history. 'It was one of those rare occasions that had everything,' Joe said later. 'Two fine sides capable of scoring goals, some great individual players and a wonderful atmosphere. I'll never forget our fans on that day. They were enthusiastic and wonderfully behaved, and the support they gave us was unbelievable. We scored three fine goals and Kevin Keegan gave just about the best performance he ever gave for Liverpool. We could easily have lost, because one of their fellows hit a post – but what a match it was.' Goals from Terry McDermott, Tommy Smith and a Phil Neal penalty secured a 3–1 triumph. It was a glorious dream-come-true for the thirty thousand travelling Liverpool supporters, and also for Joe, who admitted in his diary that the Liverpool players had been 'out of this world'.

Bob Paisley famously did not touch a drop of alcohol at the celebration banquet in Rome, preferring to stay sober and savour the moment. The same could not be said for Joe or his two youngest sons, Stephen and Michael. 'We went to Rome for four days with a few mates,' says Stephen. 'Dad had told us where he was staying and after the game we made our way over to the hotel to meet him. He took us into the room where this big banquet was taking place. All the players were there and everyone was celebrating. Dad gave us a bottle of Champagne each.' Joe sat at a table with three fellow members of the Anfield old guard: Ronnie Moran, Tommy Smith and Ian Callaghan and their respective partners. As the celebration dinner wore on, more and more Liverpool fans started sneaking in through the fire escape. Never one for fanfare, Joe could see how the evening was going to unfold and told Smith to commandeer 'one bottle of everything' from the bar. This standby supply was left in a corner until the festivities started to get too rowdy. Joe and company then took their booze and retired to a hotel room where they would later be joined by the defeated Monchengladbach captain Berti Vogts – who had been given a torrid game by an inspired Keegan – and some of his team-mates. It was typical Joe: even after the club's greatest victory to date, he opted for the more reserved celebration over the raucous party.

The press were fulsome in their praise of Liverpool's achievement. 'Kop Kings of Europe' screamed the front-page headline of the following morning's *Daily Mirror*. The *Guardian* explained that it was 'their ultimate reward for thirteen years of dogged perseverance in Continental competitions', and that 'no one could by any stretch of the imagination deny the English champions their full credit'. Closer to home, Michael Charters in the *Liverpool Echo* wrote: 'Liverpool are the masters of Europe – and the masters of how to play European football with style and efficiency, class combined with effort, individual brilliance with superb teamwork.' He hailed it as 'a night that will live forever as the highlight of a thousand sporting memories', and declared: 'You can get no higher than this in football.' For Joe, there was time for just one more diary entry: 'Thoughts on the season … fantastic.'

Kevin Keegan left for Hamburg that summer and Liverpool reinvested the majority of the £500,000 fee in Kenny Dalglish of Celtic. Taking over Keegan's number seven jersey could have been a poisoned chalice, but not for Dalglish, then twenty-six years old and already an established Scottish international. He turned out, whether by luck or design, to be a perfect fit for the team he had joined. The Liverpool management team were not going to complicate things with welcome speeches or instructions that would add to the pressure on Dalglish. They just let him get on with his job. The player recalls: 'The great thing about when I arrived is that there were a lot of people at Liverpool who were well set in their ways, and Joe had been instrumental in that. When I got there it wasn't difficult to get into the Liverpool way of doing things because if I hadn't I would have been out of tune. Everything was set up for me to just slot in. But it wasn't like a machine because a machine doesn't have any feeling.' Dalglish was quickly into his stride, scoring on the opening day of the 1977–78 season at Middlesbrough, and again on his first appearance in front of the Kop three nights later. By the end of the season he was way out in front as the club's leading goalscorer, with the last of his thirty-one being enough to win a second European Cup at the expense of FC Bruges. 'Only one goal scored, but worth many more,' noted Joe after the final. 'The main thing was winning.'

Dalglish's goal at Wembley lit up an otherwise dour game. But his stunning first season south of the border did not earn him any special treatment. 'Joe and I had the same kind of relationship that he had with everyone else,' Dalglish recalls. 'We all enjoyed each other's company but there was always a distance kept.' Once, Dalglish was apologising for arriving late for treatment at Anfield, only to have his explanation cut short. 'I'm not interested in excuses,' Joe told him. 'You were told to be here at six o'clock, you fucking get here at six.' As others would discover, Joe did not take kindly to lapses in punctuality. Alan Hansen, who arrived at Anfield from Partick Thistle just a few months before Dalglish, remembers: 'If you were late once a month Joe and Ronnie just laughed, but if it happened more than that, especially during a period when the team were struggling, they would go ballistic. And that's how it would be until we got back on track. Then it was free, easy and flexible again.' Generally, though, the atmosphere was relaxed most of the time. Players were given a long leash and trusted not to abuse the privilege. The message was clear: 'Win games and we will look after you; lose and we will be hard on you.'

Completing the trio of Scottish signings who would help carry

Liverpool into the next decade was Graeme Souness, a British record buy from Middlesbrough in January 1978. The tough-tackling, ball-playing midfielder made his debut at West Bromwich Albion shortly after joining and he admits the pre-match preparations came as a culture shock. 'I had trained all week with the lads at Melwood but was given no specific instruction by the coaching staff,' Souness remembers. 'On the day of the game I'm sitting in the dressing-room at The Hawthorns and the clock is ticking round to about a quarter to three. Still none of the coaches or Bob had said anything specific to me about how they wanted me to play, which I thought was a bit strange seeing as they'd just spent so much money to buy me. So with this in mind I approached Joe and whispered in his ear, "Joe, how do you want me to play?" Now Joe wasn't one to raise his voice, but suddenly in this big, booming voice he just looked at me and said, "Fuck off! We've taken a lot of time and effort and spent an awful lot of money to sign you and you're now turning around and asking me how to play football? Do us a favour, son …" I felt about two feet tall and what made it worse was everyone in the dressing-room heard him. The place fell silent and the lads just got their heads down and tried not to laugh.'

With one of his first touches of the ball at The Hawthorns Souness hit a sublime pass which had Liverpool fans drooling. Four months later, it was from his visionary pass that Dalglish scored the goal to win the European Cup. His natural ability, which was what initially earmarked him as a potential Liverpool player, was unquestionable, but his temperament remained suspect. As a headstrong youngster Souness walked out on his first club, Tottenham, believing he was good enough to be in the first team; while at Middlesbrough he upset some Liverpool fans by getting involved in a scuffle with Jimmy Case during a feisty League game at Anfield. Never one to back out of a challenge, Souness found his name was being taken by referees on an increasingly frequent basis. Three bookings he picked up at Middlesbrough during the first half of the 1977–78 season were carried over with his transfer to Liverpool. After he collected another two, taking him to twenty penalty points for the season, he received an immediate three-match ban. He became the first Liverpool player to fall foul of the system of totting up disciplinary points introduced by the Football Association three years before. As he recalled in his autobiography *No Half Measures*, it took a timely intervention by Joe to help curb his tendency to make reckless challenges. He wrote: 'It was Joe Fagan who gave me some good advice around this time when he told me that if I stayed on my feet and did not go lunging into the fray I wouldn't get booked so often.' It was simple but effective advice. Though Souness would be no stranger to a yellow card throughout the remainder of his Anfield career, the fact he was never sent off while wearing a Liverpool shirt is remarkable. Joe also played an influential role in helping Souness slot seamlessly into the Liverpool set-up. Having arrived from the North-East with a reputation as a 'jack the lad', negative headlines about his off-field activities were never too far away. 'I was still only a young lad and like everyone at that age I was full of myself and thought I knew all the answers,' Souness admits. 'But Joe soon hammered this attitude out of me. It might have taken a good six months to a year until I knew the boundaries, but thanks to Joe I then matured as a player.'

Excellent man-management skills and a clear philosophy were high on the list of Joe Fagan's main strengths as a coach. He was equally comfortable talking to individuals as he was a group and he always made it obvious what he was trying to achieve with a particular training session. 'He knew exactly what he wanted, which is the art of a great coach,' Roy Evans remembers. 'Then he knew how to get it across to the players. Joe kept it very, very simple, but he would never stop a player from expressing his own talent. He would say, "There is a time and a place for using your skills. There is a team pattern of play, but within that team pattern you are an individual and we want you to express what you can do".' Men like Dalglish, Souness and Hansen did not need to be taught how to play football. Training and coaching was more about making sure the players were fit, sharp and geared up mentally. 'Joe was tremendously influential on the mental side of things,' remembers Hansen. 'He was not a guru who could solve everything, but he could always point you in the right direction. If you were having a bad time, he would look at you and he might say, "Well, you are living your life wrong, you are eating too much or drinking too much, you need to look after yourself". But equally he might tell you to go and have a good night out. He never had any strict rules or regulations on what should be done, he just looked at individual situations with a common sense approach. He was unbelievably flexible and seemed to have a great knowledge about everything.'

The passing of time and the change of manager had done little to alter Joe's daily routine at Liverpool. However, as the years went by he took on more of a watching brief during training as Moran became the vocal presence on the training pitch and in the dressing-room. Joe would still take part in the five-a-sides, and Souness described him as a 'formidable player who no one could get past'. As an observer, Joe missed nothing and reported back to Paisley each day. Earlier in his career Paisley had been an enthusiastic participant in training, keeping goal in staff matches, but in later years he would stay in his small office at Melwood, venturing out only to deliver news, such as which team Liverpool had drawn in the European Cup. Even so, Paisley and Joe worked closely together and would regularly share their views on a team or player.

Once the tough physical work of pre-season was done, with Joe often still leading from the front, training was agreeable for most players. 'Training under Joe was always exactly the same, but it was never boring,' Hansen recalls. 'Apart from pre-season, the only time it ever got hard was when you were struggling, when you had maybe had a run of no wins in four. Then they would run you.' Having hugely talented players at his disposal makes a coach's job easier. However, top-level football players are often the kind of characters who speak out forcefully and without delay if they do not agree with what they are being asked to do. Players are quick to confront or lose faith in coaches or managers who cannot gauge when to work players hard, when to ease off, when to allow a bit of light-heartedness and when to keep things deadly serious. The minute a manager or coach loses the respect of the players, he is almost useless. During his time as manager, Paisley could trust Joe to get these decisions correct each time. Liverpool's players knew they were being led by men who were unrivalled in football knowledge and whose devotion to success was as strong as theirs. 'As a coach, you will be judged by the players on what they perceive you to know about football and, of course, Joe knew loads,' Hansen recalls.

Everything remained geared towards the 'pass and move' style of play that Shankly had brought to the club. Standing and admiring a pass was an unacceptable sin. Having given a pass, the player had to move immediately into a position to receive the ball again, thereby giving the man in possession a number of options. Joe was fond of saying: 'Football is a simple game, made complicated by fools.' Another favourite catchphrase was: 'Just pass it to the nearest red shirt.' Liverpool's basic tactics were really simple. 'There was no such thing as "dropping into the hole" or "blind-side runs",' says Souness. 'Joe would just laugh whenever he heard anything like this. Whoever came up with these phrases may as well have been speaking another language as far as he was concerned.' The team routinely turned out in a 4–4–2 formation, players tucked inside when they did not have possession and opened out when they did. Players knew their roles. This doctrine was drummed into players at all levels and the reserves and youth teams were all set up in the same way. It even extended to Joe's youngest son Michael, who was following in the footsteps of elder brother Kit and battling hard to make a name for himself in the reserve team at this time. A promising schoolboy player who represented the city, Michael had given up the game for two years in his early teens until Joe persuaded him to start playing again. Before long he was training twice a week at Melwood alongside the rest of the city's most talented schoolboy players and under the watchful gaze of not only Tom Saunders, Roy Evans and Ronnie Moran but also his dad. 'I never got any special treatment,' he recalls. 'Dad would usually just remain in the background and say nothing. But that was hard, just having him there watching. The only advice I really remember him giving me with regards to football was one day out on the training pitch, he said to me, "Always go and meet the ball, never wait for it to meet to you".'

As with Kit, Joe took a back seat in Michael's development as a footballer, preferring to let nature take its course and determine whether he was good enough to make the grade. It was a philosophy that had done Joe no harm as a young player in the 1930s and one he firmly believed in. Of course, Joe would have liked nothing more than to see one of his sons go all the way to the very top of the game, but he was well aware of just how competitive it could be and the pitfalls that lay ahead. Michael impressed head of youth development Tom Saunders sufficiently to be offered terms as an apprentice professional on leaving school. 'But Dad wanted me to get a trade so I took a job and I've regretted it ever since,' Michael admits. 'It was then that I really needed him to put an encouraging arm around my shoulder and say, "No, go on, son, follow your dream, you're good enough", or even, "Well, you might be good enough, just give it a go". I suppose there was time to go and look for a job afterwards if things didn't work out, but his was the old-fashioned way.'

Joe was also a realist. His second youngest son Stephen had shown similar promise, but deep down they both knew he did not have what it took to become a professional. It was a conclusion they reached after Stephen had spent a week training at Melwood one summer. The fact that no such conversation took place between Joe and Michael suggests he did have more faith in his youngest son. Despite his amateur status, Michael continued to make good progress, holding his own in the 'A' and 'B' teams alongside players who were training full-time. He helped them to Lancashire League titles in 1977 and 1978, and captained the side who competed in the FA Youth Cup. He broke into the reserve team in the 1978–79 season and made ten appearances, scoring one goal, as another

Central League title was claimed. However, in his third year at the club, when the promise of a full-time contract failed to materialise, Michael reacted angrily and walked out. 'They wanted me to continue as an amateur for one more year but I'd had enough,' he explains. 'I had missed out on an awful lot during those first two years, like going on overseas tours, and in the end it probably hampered my progress. It was so frustrating. A switch just flicked in my head and I was off. I couldn't believe what they'd done, but it was at this point that I needed to be yanked back by the scruff of my neck and told, "You're going nowhere". My dad said nothing, though, and for a long time I resented that.'

Michael's bitter experience at Liverpool had a damaging effect on his career and following a brief spell at Blackpool he drifted into non-League football representing, among others, one of Joe's former clubs, Altrincham. He played one more time at Anfield, though, in April 1987, for local amateur side Kirkby Town against Liverpool Reserves in the final of the Liverpool Senior Cup. A now retired Joe watched from the stands with mixed emotions as Michael and his team-mates pulled off a shock 3–2 victory. 'I didn't speak to Dad afterwards because we were all straight out on the town to celebrate and I didn't come in until the following morning. Anyway, I asked Mum where he was and she said, "Oh, he's not feeling too well, he drank a bottle of whisky last night". He never expressed what he really thought, but it later transpired that on that night it hit home that maybe if he had helped me a bit more I could have gone a lot further in the game. And I assume it would have been the same with our Kit. It is sad that we never got the chance to sit down and talk properly about it. Just before he died I got a message that he wanted to see me in the hospital and he mentioned that game I had played for Kirkby, but it was too late then.'

Liverpool may have won back-to-back European titles, but in 1978 a fresh threat to their dominance had emerged. It was to start an intense rivalry that supporters on the Kop still sing about today. In 1975, Brian Clough had taken over as manager of Nottingham

Forest, then an unfashionable club languishing mid-table in Division Two. Within two seasons he had transformed their fortunes and they had won promotion to the top flight. To everyone's surprise, Forest took the First Division by storm, taking the title from under Liverpool's noses and also defeating them, albeit controversially, after a replay in the League Cup final. Clough's admiration for Liverpool and what they had achieved was such that he adopted the same principles and reaped similar rewards. 'We at Forest learned from Liverpool,' he later admitted. 'For a while we had the Indian sign on them. They knew it, we knew it and it bothered them.' On Saturday, 17 December, 1977, as Liverpool laboured to a 1–0 home win over Queens Park Rangers, Forest displayed their title credentials with an impressive 4–0 drubbing of Manchester United at Old Trafford. It was a result that maintained their lead at the top of the table, leaving third-placed Liverpool trailing in their wake by six points. After watching highlights of the game on *Match of the Day* Joe was overcome by a feeling of *déjà-vu* and mused: 'Watched Notts (sic) Forest on the telly. They have no "stars" – but all good players. Their motto is (like ours used to be, and which I have believed in for years, and practised in the first and second teams): The back four pass it quickly and crisply to the midfield men – who need the time – the midfield men then pass it quickly to the front men, who also need the time. It is so simple that players can't see it. Most players think that if a colleague is open and no one near him they are not doing anything constructive by giving the ball to him.'

Over a four-year period the two clubs fought for the game's top honours. But despite the rivalry that developed there was a mutual respect between Clough and those on the Anfield backroom staff. 'Some of the best ideas came from the Bootroom,' said Clough. 'There was no mystique about it, though; it was the fellas who used it. I've been in there after matches and all I got was a drink, an occasional "well done" or "bad luck" and away.' Ronnie Moran remembers Clough visiting the Bootroom after games and says: 'He'd come in but never say much, just sit there like a schoolboy taking it all in.'

In 1978–79 Liverpool and Forest were drawn together in the first round of the European Cup. It was a tie that aroused enormous interest, but uncharacteristically Liverpool were lulled into the trap of playing in the style of a League match rather than a two-legged European tie. Trailing 1–0 away from home in the first meeting they pushed for an equaliser when their normal mindset in Europe would have been to settle for a slender defeat before completing the job at Anfield. As a consequence they were caught by a late sucker punch, conceded a second goal, and faced an uphill task in the return that ultimately proved insurmountable. It was a bitter blow, but it enabled Liverpool to concentrate domestically and take football in England to what many observers believed were previously unscaled heights. Just before the European Cup tie with Forest, Paisley's team sent out an ominous warning that they were ready to reclaim their domestic crown. Newly-promoted Tottenham Hotspur, with their recently-acquired Argentines Osvaldo Ardiles and Ricardo Villa, were the team who suffered, sent packing from Anfield after a 7–0 annihilation. The final goal that afternoon, scored by Terry McDermott, is regarded as one of the finest seen at Anfield. It was a prime example of the free-flowing football played by Liverpool at this time. 'Have you ever heard fifty thousand people purr with pleasure?' pondered Michael Charters in the following Monday's *Liverpool Echo*. 'Well, the Anfield spectators were doing that constantly as Liverpool stroked the ball around with one-touch moves of staggering accuracy. This display confirmed for me that the current Liverpool team is playing better, more exciting, attacking football than any side I've seen since the War.'

It was the highlight of a memorable League campaign in which Liverpool took the title by eight points from Forest. But Joe and the Bootroom would not allow themselves to wallow in praise, even after a win as good as that against Tottenham. 'We used to have a weekly joke,' remembers Ronnie Moran. 'If we won we'd say, "That's us OK for another week", but if we lost it was, "Could be out of a job now!" There's no way you could afford to sit back.'

Even so, the coaching staff took great pride in Liverpool's near-perfect season, one in which numerous records were shattered along the way, including the least number of goals conceded (sixteen), and the highest points haul under the two-points-for-a-win system (sixty-eight). Indeed, a reminder of that season, in the shape of a fixture list with the scores scribbled on it, hung proudly on a wall in the Bootroom for years afterwards.

Joe's increasing influence behind the scenes earned him another promotion during the summer of 1979 when he was given the official title of 'assistant manager'. It was, in effect, the job he had been doing since Shankly retired, and there was no visible change in his day-to-day routine. But it was at least recognition of the valuable role he was playing in the club's ongoing success. The fascination within football for finding out Liverpool's 'secret' was such that David Johnson, the club's top scorer the following season, remembers his England team-mates quizzing him for the inside track on the club's methods. 'We'd go away on international duty and the coaches would always be like, "Come on, what's the secret? Something is going on there behind closed doors at Anfield and Melwood". The Liverpool lads would just look at each other and say among ourselves, "What are these guys on about?" All we used to do was the simple things. It was just common sense to us.' Liverpool contributed a steady supply of players to the England squad during this time, with a record six lining up against Switzerland in 1977. If the international manager Ron Greenwood had his way there may even have been a coaching call-up for Joe. 'He liked our approach,' said Paisley after a meeting with Greenwood. 'It was also suggested by Ron that I, or Joe Fagan or Ronnie Moran, should go to England training sessions, not to run the place but as observers and perhaps to offer constructive criticism.'

As the 1980s dawned, Liverpool's success kept coming. The sheer consistency was astonishing. Between 1978 and 1981 Liverpool went eighty-five home games unbeaten in all competitions. They won the League again in 1980. The League Cup followed for the first time a year later, when they beat West Ham in the final after a replay at Villa Park. Another European Cup was won following a 1–0 victory over Real Madrid at the Parc des Princes. Alan Kennedy's winning goal confirmed Liverpool's return to the European summit after a two-year hiatus. Having thought they had mastered the art of Continental competition, successive first-round exits at the hands of Nottingham Forest and Dinamo Tbilisi had given Liverpool a harsh dose of reality.

By May 1981 the lessons had been learned. Joe's final words to the players before they left the dressing-room in Paris were: 'They will take quick free-kicks, so be ready. Don't forget that running off the ball will help your team-mates who are man-to-man marked. Remember to close up when we lose the ball. This is a one-off game, you must put everything you have into it!' Joe recognised that the game was changing as players became fitter, faster and more tactical. 'People will say it was a poor game,' he reflected after the final. 'In this modern day players have no time to indulge in solo performances, there is too much closing up and denying space to opponents.'

With stalwarts such as Callaghan, Smith, Toshack and Hughes having all now left the club, once again the Liverpool squad had been steadily remodelled. Among the new faces to establish themselves were latest reserve-team prodigy Sammy Lee, a chunky pocket-dynamo-style midfielder, and Alan Kennedy, the hero of Paris, an attacking left-back who arrived from Newcastle in 1978. Kennedy, nicknamed Barney Rubble after the popular television cartoon character of the time, admits that he struggled during his early days at Anfield and is another who benefited greatly from Joe's coaching techniques. 'Coming from Newcastle I was more used to the long-ball game and it took me time to settle into the Liverpool way of playing,' Kennedy recalls. 'Ray Kennedy would often come short, and so too would Graeme Souness, but the next minute I'd launch the ball and no one would be there. It was a difficult time, but Joe was sympathetic and always there to encourage me. "Come on, son, you know you can do a little bit better than that", he'd say. He knew how to get the best out of me and he had two other favourite sayings that I remember: "You're a good player so go out there and express yourself", and "When not in possession be in position".'

With Ray Clemence and Steve Heighway next to depart, soon to be followed by Case, Ray Kennedy and McDermott, Liverpool found themselves in the biggest transition of playing personnel since the one prompted by defeat to Watford in 1970. New blood was needed and it arrived in the shape of youngsters Ronnie Whelan, a midfielder signed from Home Farm in Ireland, and Ian Rush, a striker from Chester City. Both had spent time learning their trade in the reserves and were now ready to be pitched into regular first-team action. Higher-profile arrivals were Middlesbrough's livewire attacking midfielder Craig Johnston for £650,000 and Mark Lawrenson, an elegant, long-striding central defender from Brighton, who cost a club record £900,000. Straight away Joe joined Paisley in explaining to Lawrenson that, despite the size of his fee, he might have to wait before getting a chance in his favoured position of centre-half as Hansen and Phil Thompson had built up a solid partnership. They assured Lawrenson that they considered him good enough to play in a few different positions and that he would be playing while he waited for a central-defensive position to become available. Immediately a player joining the club was told what to expect and thus any potential confusion or annoyance was averted. Lawrenson's Liverpool career panned out exactly as he had been told it would. He made many appearances as a left-back, and even in midfield, before finally settling into central defence when Thompson's career began to wind down. 'Joe and Bob were great for me as soon as I arrived,' Lawrenson recalls. 'And although it sounds a bit egotistical, I think they knew that I had realised how to give them what they wanted.'

With the squad being gradually overhauled, a new-look Liverpool set out in the autumn of 1981 to re-assert their domestic supremacy.

They had suffered an alarming lapse the previous season and had finished an uncharacteristic fifth in Division One, the club's poorest League position for ten years. If Liverpool's consistency was seen as a reflection of the club's good management, comparative slumps such as this were viewed as a severe slight on it and would not be tolerated. The management were clearly not happy at seeing Aston Villa, Ipswich Town, Arsenal and West Bromwich Albion accumulate more points than they did in 1980–81. Even though the European Cup had been reclaimed, it was success in the 'bread and butter' of the First Division that Liverpool set out to achieve at the start of every season. Joe's grumpiness was assured if the team had not performed well. Ranting and raving, though, was generally not his style. He was not a man quick to lose his cool, but he also understood that it was necessary to hold something back to provoke a reaction when the team really needed one. 'There's two ways a manager can get his message across to his players,' says Souness. 'You can be noisy, argumentative and demanding of people. Or you can do it Joe's way, where just a few quiet words, or even a single look, can say it all. He could be hard and I remember on a number of occasions that he would say something really harsh to one of the lads, but he'd do it oh-so-quietly and that was his way of trying to emphasis the point.' Ronnie Moran would generally be the one to dish out the 'bollockings'. But on the rare occasions Joe let rip, Mark Lawrenson admits: 'It felt like the end of the world had arrived.' One afternoon at Melwood Alan Kennedy was the recipient of a rare Joe Fagan tongue-lashing. Souness explains: 'Joe got us all together and was talking about what we weren't doing right. The whole speech was intended for Alan but not aimed at him individually. Of all the lads in the group, though, Alan was the one not paying attention and I remember Joe just blowing his top. "Hold on a minute, son, this is all for your benefit, work it out!" Everyone was taken aback because it was unusual for Joe to lose his cool like that.'

His fury was perhaps most famously employed after an embarrassing 3–1 home loss against Manchester City on Boxing Day

1981. Liverpool had endured a dismal first half of the season. Defeat against City was their fifth in the League and John Bond's side were the third to have taken all three points from Anfield. Considering Liverpool had lost at home only eleven times in the League during the entire 1970s, this statistic added further fuel to the fire of those who felt the club had sunk to their lowest point since the pre-Shankly era. Liverpool were now languishing in twelfth place, nine points adrift of leaders Swansea. As the majority of the 37,929 crowd trooped dejectedly home that wintry afternoon, the doom and gloom merchants were predicting an imminent end to the all-conquering Liverpool dynasty. The chorus of boos that greeted the final whistle was evidence of the growing disenchantment among the fans. Much of the flak was aimed in the direction of rookie goalkeeper Bruce Grobbelaar, a former Rhodesian Army soldier who had been signed the previous season from Vancouver Whitecaps. Spotted while playing on loan for Crewe Alexandra, it was anticipated that he would serve his time in the reserves before being thrust into the first team. However, Ray Clemence's surprise departure to Tottenham hastened his senior baptism, and it had not been an entirely happy one. Grobbelaar handed City two of their goals, but in his diary Joe recorded his disgust with all the players and judged that only two of the eleven were playing to the standard he expected. The season was threatening to fall apart and he had had enough. 'It was on the following Monday as we were getting ready for training,' remembers Lawrenson. 'Joe sat us all down at Anfield before we went on the bus to train at Melwood. Bob, Ronnie and Evo would all have been there in the dressing-room, but they all walked out after Joe spoke that day. He really went berserk. There was nothing they could have added, he said it all.' Joe let rip at the players about their attitude and their approach to the season so far. He told them the current performances were unacceptable. 'There are people in this team who aren't pulling their weight – they know who they are,' he roared. Phil Neal was equally taken aback by the venom of Joe's outburst. He says: 'He had a go at every single player. He said, "We've had more meetings in the last month at this club then I've had in seventeen years. Hansen, start heading the ball; Souness, you haven't won a tackle; Dalglish, you should have twice as many goals by now ..." We all got it.'

It was rare for individual names to be mentioned, but Lawrenson admits: 'It had an unbelievable effect. It had a far bigger effect than anyone else at the club doing it – even Bob Paisley or Kenny Dalglish afterwards.' The next game was a potentially hazardous FA Cup third-round tie at Swansea, now led by John Toshack. Journalists were standing by to report that Liverpool's long-awaited demise had arrived. Not so. With their minds re-focused, Liverpool, with Souness captaining for the first time, blew Swansea away in a comprehensive 4–0 win. 'We were by far the better team,' Joe wrote in his diary. 'This was due to attitude and commitment to the job in hand. The question now is, "Can they keep it up?"' The answer was an emphatic 'yes'. Paisley's side went on an amazing run that included eleven consecutive League wins to sweep to yet another First Division title as well as a second successive League Cup. It is too simple to attribute the eventual success of the season to Joe's post-Boxing Day rant, but all those present would acknowledge that it was certainly a turning point. Joe even took temporary charge of the team for two games in April when Bob Paisley was consigned to his sick bed with a bout of pleurisy. Joe took the extra responsibility in his stride and emerged with a one hundred per cent record following a 1–0 home win against West Bromwich and a 3–2 victory at Southampton.

Liverpool ended up winning the League with a game to spare. A 3–1 home victory over Tottenham secured the trophy once more, so the following Tuesday night's outstanding fixture at Middlesbrough had nothing on it. As usual, the team coach drove up on the morning of the game, the players had lunch at a hotel and were then due to go to their rooms and have a sleep to prepare for the evening game. Mark Lawrenson takes up the story: 'All of the players went for a walk and we stumbled over a pub. You can imagine what it was like, we decided to go in and quite a few of us were feeling pretty worse for wear. We rushed back for half four because Roy Evans would be knocking on all the hotel room doors turning the lights on and getting everyone up to go to the game. We all made it back at 4.29 and jumped into bed pretending we were asleep.' Needless to say, the game was contested with a slightly reduced intensity. Unbeknown to the players, the coaching staff had also been enjoying a bottle of whisky and could not have cared less what the players had been up to. As far as they were concerned the League had been won and the staff and players had earned the right to start their summer holiday a little early. Joe's diary entry after a game would normally be at least a few lines long. On this occasion, tellingly, it simply read: 'Forget about this game.'

The story is not untypical of the Paisley reign. While the club was run extremely professionally, the players were treated as adults and trusted not to take things too far. There was always a great rapport within the squad and they were encouraged to build a strong team spirit. Quite often a European away trip would mean a hotel stay and a night out for the players. The coaching staff knew what was going on and would tolerate a slight drop off in training performance the day afterwards. Similarly the players were allowed to relax and enjoy a Christmas party together. The management understood that this kind of thing would happen anyway so did not try to control it. Indeed, Joe recognised that in moderation, a night out could act as a release and prevent players becoming worn down by the pressure on them. The trust given to the players also strengthened the bond between them and the staff. Dalglish points out: 'There was a huge amount of respect between everybody. The likes of Joe showed respect for the players, so they got it back automatically.'

Another reason Joe held the respect of the Liverpool players was that very little got past him. He was a quick judge of character and equally quick to work out what was going on in a given situation. Hansen remembers him being very astute in cottoning on to the kind of in-jokes and banter that go on between players in any dressing-room. He would let the players have their fun, but would also make it clear that he knew what they were up to. 'This kind of thing would be going on for up to twenty minutes before we went on to the pitch to play,' says Hansen. 'A lot of coaches might have told us to concentrate on the game, but the kind of players we had all knew what they were doing and Joe recognised that.' At other times it might be a quiet word in a player's ear. 'He wouldn't embarrass you in front of anybody else,' Lawrenson recalls. 'He always asked you the question so that you asked yourself the question. It was just his way of letting you know that he had spotted what was going on and hinting that you might want to change your behaviour slightly.' Very rarely would these one-on-one chats be negative, it just was not the Liverpool way. Paisley would only go over and see a player to let them know that they got away with a few mistakes the previous Saturday, and Joe was the same. At most, he might approach a player who was playing really well and say, 'Keep it going, lad.' 'That was tantamount to five pages in the back of the newspapers saying you were absolutely brilliant,' says Lawrenson

Joe genuinely cared for the fortunes of the players. His wife Lil used to joke that aside from the six children he had at home, Joe had countless more at Liverpool Football Club. 'He was very straightforward and honest,' says Dalglish. 'If something wasn't going right for an individual then Joe was as disappointed as that individual. You knew that he cared, you knew he got no pleasure out of anybody not doing well.'

Throughout Liverpool's glory years, Joe and his colleagues in the Bootroom remained remarkably level-headed. There were never any airs and graces about them. In December 1982, Watford chairman Elton John visited Anfield with his recently promoted club for the first time. With both sides challenging near the top of the table it was an important match. But as a clash of cultures there could not have been a bigger mismatch than the diva-esque pop star and those grounded inhabitants of the Bootroom. After an impressive 3–1 home win, the ever hospitable Joe welcomed Elton into the hallowed cubby hole. 'Hey, lad, would you like a drink?' he asked. 'I'll have a pink gin please,' replied the Watford chairman. With a shake of his head and look of horror on his face, Joe said: 'Pink gin, lad? You can have a brown ale, a Guinness or scotch, lad, and that's yer lot!' The story was related to the authors by journalist John Keith, who added: 'Elton thought it was brilliant and when he came out later he told us, "You know what, I've just played in front of thousands at Central Park in New York, but I was far more nervous going in that Bootroom. There's a mystique about the place". We said, "Well, you're very privileged because not everyone gets invited in".'

Joe's hospitality towards opposition managers and coaches was renowned throughout football. Visiting teams would usually return home with nothing in the way of points, but a post-match drink and friendly chat could always be guaranteed. Unlike dominant champions in other sports Liverpool remained a universally popular club. They did things the right way and these subtle touches helped. After one game around this time, Tottenham coach Peter Shreeves was telling reporters: 'Joe and the others are the friendliest people before the game, and afterwards they invite you in for a drink and maybe compliment you on how you played. They are good companions. But during the ninety minutes the way they behave is, well, the ultimate in professionalism.' To which, Joe, as he passed in the corridor, with a nod of the head and knowing smile, replied: 'Yes, during a game we're bastards.'

At the start of 1982–83 Bob Paisley announced his decision to retire at the end of the season. After forty-four years of loyal service a true giant of the game was set to depart. With the striking partnership of Rush and Dalglish now well established, Hansen and Lawrenson showing signs that they were a classic central-defensive pair in the making and Souness captaining the team from central midfield, it was a safe bet that Paisley would go out on a high. After three months it certainly looked that way. On the last Saturday of October a 3–1 win against Brighton took them back to the top of the table and they were never displaced. The run to a fourteenth First

Division title became such a procession that the campaign ended with a string of defeats which, while not enough to alter the outcome, disgusted Joe. On the day the title was won, Liverpool lost 2–0 at Tottenham, but their closest rivals Manchester United also lost. Joe remarked: 'It is pitiful, needing a point to win the title we didn't even look like getting it. We are struggling along with eight players and three also-rans. Not good enough.' It was a subtle hint that all may not have been well at the club. With the champions crowned amid such little fanfare, it was clear for all to see that expectations had risen remarkably since Paisley took control.

But if the climax to Paisley's last season in charge was something of a damp squib and easily forgotten, the memories of him climbing the thirty-nine steps at Wembley two months earlier to lift the Milk Cup were a more fitting finale. It came after Liverpool had come from behind to beat Manchester United and claim the trophy for a third successive season. Souness stood aside and invited Paisley to take the plaudits on what was his last appearance at the stadium. It was a moment Paisley later reflected on with great pride. It was a proud moment for Joe Fagan, too, because it meant his great colleague, boss, confidant and ally was bowing out where he had spent most of his managerial career: at the very top with silverware in his hands.

The Paisley era spanned nine seasons, yielding an incredible six League titles, three European Cups, a UEFA Cup and three League Cups. In two of the non-championship years, Liverpool finished runners-up. Six times Paisley was manager of the year. However, it is not doing him a disservice in any way to recognise that this success was a team effort. The Liverpool that Shankly built had been fine-tuned until English and European football had been conquered. The partnership of Paisley, Fagan, Moran and Evans was close to football perfection. Between them, they had all the bases covered: talent evaluation, ruthlessness, discipline, tactics, coaching talent, football knowledge, communication skills and man-management. Each one of them was crucial to the success of the club. They were all boyishly enthusiastic about their jobs and would very rarely take a day off. Though they spent a lot of time together, none of them really socialised with each other apart from official club functions, of which there were very few. Their camaraderie was clear for all to see, and never more so than during a testimonial or end-of-season friendly when there would often be a bottle of whisky passed along the bench.

The high regard in which Paisley is held is richly deserved. His genius in signing players has arguably never been matched in English football. (Joe readily admitted that he could not pick an emerging talent nearly as accurately as Paisley could.) He was an astute selector of teams and knew instinctively when to move a player on. But it is far from certain that Liverpool would have enjoyed such a sustained streak of dominance without Joe Fagan's every-day input. 'If you speak to most of the people who were there at the time, they will say Joe was right up there with Paisley,' says Alan Hansen. 'I don't think there was anybody during my time at Liverpool who was more influential. Bob was incredible at spotting strengths and weaknesses, at being ruthless with his team selections. But Joe played as big a part as anybody. He was an amazing man. Bob never said a lot, Joe would say it. If you were going great it would be Joe to caution you about getting carried away. If you were going badly he would go the other way. Joe was the man who ran everything. He was the main man.'

As the most successful English manager of all time, Bob Paisley left behind a glorious legacy. Following in his footsteps was an unenviable task. Only one man had the credentials to take it on.

CHAPTER SEVEN

BECOMING BOSS

FOUR MONTHS BEFORE Bob Paisley's official announcement that he would be stepping down as Liverpool manager, another link to Anfield's distant past was severed when long-serving head groundsman Arthur Riley hung up his spade for the final time. Riley could boast even longer service to the club than Paisley: fifty-four years in total. What was even more remarkable was that, before him, his father Bert had held the job since 1908. Such longevity had become the hallmark of Liverpool Football Club. From the players and backroom staff to the cleaners and tea ladies, everyone employed by the club was steeped in the proud traditions of 'The Liverpool Way'. Newcomers were quickly indoctrinated. Liverpool was a family club and perhaps never more so than under the astute chairmanship of John Smith in the 1970s and 1980s. 'We're a very, very modest club. We don't talk. We don't boast. But we're very professional,' Smith once said. After taking over in 1973 he preached the virtue of continuity. It would be his stock answer whenever he was asked to divulge the secret of Liverpool's success: his one-word response was delivered in his typically succinct style, getting the message across but without giving much away. He applied this philosophy to his own position, too, ending the tradition of electing a new chairman every three years. Change was not entered into lightly. Crucially, this attitude was shared by those around him and it summed up the whole ethos of the club during the glory-laden era. With this in mind, it was perhaps the worst kept secret in football that Joe Fagan would succeed Bob Paisley as Liverpool manager in the summer of 1983. Liverpool were the reigning League champions, and had been the dominant force domestically for the past ten years, so why run the risk of rocking the boat by bringing in an outsider? Keeping it in-house was a policy that had worked when the club last found themselves in this position, back in 1974 when Bob Paisley replaced Bill Shankly. Based on the theory of natural succession Joe was now the rightful heir to the Anfield throne.

When he announced to the world in August 1982 that he would be stepping down, Paisley gave no hint that his loyal righthand man would be next to roll off the Bootroom's managerial production line. However, in his autobiography, published the following year, he revealed: 'I came to the conclusion that it was time for a new manager and I envisaged my successor being one of these three: Joe Fagan, Ronnie Moran or Roy Evans.' Typically, the club also maintained a wall of silence on the subject for the next ten months. At other clubs it would have been easy for an air of uncertainty to arise. The departure of English football's most successful manager would have set alarm bells ringing, and been the cue for mass histrionics from the boardroom down through the shop floor on to the terraces. At Anfield, everything carried on as normal; there was no panic. Almost everyone, be it a player, fan or journalist just expected it to be Joe. It was never really up for debate. A system was in place: it was called the Bootroom. A decade earlier the club had been taken by surprise when Shankly announced his retirement. On this occasion there was to be no state of emergency because Paisley had given prior notice of his intentions. It gave the board ample time to assess their options, but in reality they did not need it. Joe Fagan was always the number one choice and, as Peter Robinson reveals, the only man in contention. 'I had always thought of Joe as a potential manager,' he says, 'but there was a hierarchy in place at the club and the thinking was that everyone must wait their turn.

That meant that the possibility of Joe taking the reins only really became an issue when Bob informed us he was stepping down. It was a case of natural progression and, whereas nine years earlier, when Bill retired, the possibility of bringing in an outsider was openly discussed at boardroom level, on this occasion we very much wanted to keep things in-house.' Robinson's admission that it was always the board's intention to appoint Joe begs the question: why the long wait for confirmation? As ever, with the Anfield leadership of that time, there is a simple solution. As Robinson points out: 'Until Bob had relinquished control, we saw no reason to go public with our future plans. Why give our opponents the heads up on what was going to be happening at Liverpool? Plus, it would only have diverted the focus of attention from what really mattered, and that was the team maintaining their high standards on the pitch during Bob's final season.'

In betting parlance the smart money had always been on Joe and the 'next Liverpool manager' market was as near as you could get to a closed book. But with official confirmation of his appointment put on hold until after the 1982–83 season had ended, speculation was inevitable. The ritual guessing game as to who would follow Paisley began as soon as the news of his impending abdication hit the streets. Compared to the media frenzy that would engulf such a story today, coverage was pretty low-key, especially in the national press. Nevertheless the newspapers immediately got to work on drawing up shortlists of potential candidates. A host of names were openly discussed, though the majority could be dismissed out of hand almost immediately. 'Liverpool's search to find a successor to team manager Bob Paisley by the end of the season will concentrate on two specific areas,' reported the *Daily Post*. 'The first is their own backroom, or rather the famous Anfield Bootroom. The second is a small group of men with strong Anfield backgrounds, whose subsequent successes have enhanced their reputations around the country.' Under the headline 'The Contenders' the same paper listed (in no specific order) Roy Evans, John Toshack, Ian St John, Ronnie Moran, Joe Fagan and Gordon Milne as the front-runners.

Given the general consensus that Liverpool would be 'keeping things in-house', those who pushed the claims of 'outsiders' such as Watford manager Graham Taylor, Southampton's Lawrie McMenemy and Keith Burkinshaw of Tottenham, all of whom were doing commendable jobs at their clubs, were clearly barking up the wrong tree. Winning the odd cup competition and achieving a series of promotions may well have been deemed success elsewhere, but much more was expected at Anfield. Likewise, such were the pre-requisites for the job that doubts were soon placed against the names of the former Liverpool players who had been mentioned. John Toshack, Emlyn Hughes and Gordon Milne, three much-loved sons of the Kop, had all made names for themselves in managerial circles since hanging up their boots. But while they could still claim to be very much part of the 'Anfield family' they had yet to prove themselves at the highest level. Toshack, in particular, had made no secret of his desire to one day manage his former club, and his achievement in guiding Swansea City from the Fourth to First Division in just four seasons, had certainly marked him as 'one for the future'. Unfortunately for Toshack, Paisley's announcement coincided with an alarming dip in fortunes at Vetch Field. Swansea were relegated from the top flight in May 1983, placing the first black mark against Toshack's previously rising managerial stock.

Hughes had suffered a similar fall from grace, albeit on a smaller scale. In his first managerial role, he guided Rotherham United to their highest Football League position when they finished seventh in Division Two in 1981–82, missing promotion to the top flight by just four points. The following season, however, Hughes oversaw their rapid descent towards Division Three. At the same time, Gordon Milne was taking Leicester City up from Division Two in his first season at Filbert Street, adding to the impressive work he had done already at Coventry City. Milne had cut his coaching teeth with Wigan Athletic, then of the Northern Premier League, and he had worked with the England Youth team, who he guided to success in the European Championship in 1972. Two years later he was named on an initial shortlist of potential candidates to replace Sir Alf Ramsey.

One of the more surprising names to be linked with the job was Ian St John, considered by the *Daily Post* to be a 'dark horse', not least because his career seemed to be heading in a totally different direction. Following a brief spell at the helm of Motherwell, the club where he started out as a player, St John was in line to succeed Don Revie as manager at Leeds in 1974 until the Elland Road board made an ill-fated U-turn and appointed Brian Clough instead. With that went St John's chance of managing at the top level. Following an unhappy spell in charge at Portsmouth, where he was forced to work under tight financial restrictions, St John hung up his manager's jacket and established himself as a highly-respected television pundit.

Writing in *The Times*, David Miller was in no doubt that 'the club would like to maintain a line of domestic inheritance'. Closer to home, Bootroom boys Ronnie Moran and Roy Evans were more obvious candidates. Like Joe, both had played major roles in Liverpool's period of dominance and possessed a deep knowledge of how the club was run from top to bottom. Yet the Anfield chain of command that Peter Robinson spoke about meant they would have to wait their turn. Miller also suggested the possibility of a 'stop-gap manager, who would ride on the shoulders of the present team while waiting for a contemporary player such as Neal or Dalglish to acquire managerial/coaching foundations'. Both Neal and Dalglish were approaching the end of glittering playing careers, and as Neal later revealed in his autobiography, John Smith had privately intimated there would be a job on the coaching staff waiting for him. At this stage of their careers, however, inexperience went against them. As it turned out, it would be Dalglish, not Neal, who would go on to manage Liverpool, not once but twice, though not for another three years.

Amid all the conjecture Joe's name invariably featured prominently. Peter Thomas in the *Daily Express* urged the Liverpool board to 'Give it to Joe', while the *Daily Post* wasted no time in installing him as their favourite. 'Anfield's tradition of continuity would be best served by the simple promotion of Paisley's current deputy, Joe Fagan. Fagan is sixty (sic), but age would not necessarily count against him if he wanted the job as his influence on the side is already considerable,' wrote Nick Hilton.

While those inside Anfield's corridor of power remained tight-lipped publicly on the identity of Paisley's successor, behind the scenes they were doing all they could to persuade Joe. Just like Paisley nine years before, Joe was initially reluctant to step out of the shadows. He later admitted: 'When Bob decided to retire, it frightened me that they might ask me to take over. I said years ago that I'd never take on a manager's job, that coaching was my game. But things do change, don't they?' The prospect of filling the void left by Paisley was something Joe did not even deem important enough to discuss with his wife and children. In Joe's eyes it was just a continuation of what had gone before, albeit with a different name on the office door. 'He never had any real aspirations to take the job,' says Stephen Fagan. 'Becoming a manager was never his thing. He was happy to remain in the background, so when the vacancy came up none of us really gave it much thought. I don't remember him telling any of us that he was going to become manager, it was just something that happened. He didn't even tell us that there was going to be an announcement or anything. I don't think he thought it was important for us to know. We were going to find out when the news was announced.'

At what point Joe informed the board of his decision to accept the role is not clear. But on 14 December, 1982, the *Liverpool Echo* were confident enough to run the headline: 'Fagan Ready For Anfield Hot Seat'. Still, there was no official comment from the club, and just as his family had no inkling of what lay in store, neither did his work colleagues. However, when the appointment was made, it did not shock or surprise anyone. 'To me, Joe was a manager long before he was made manager because I'd been brought up through the ranks of the Bootroom with him and knew all about the work he'd been doing,' recalls Ronnie Moran. 'A lot of the players had also worked with Joe for a long time and everyone at the club was well aware of his managerial potential.' It is a point reiterated by the then club captain Graeme Souness, who says: 'Bob had shown that promotion from within can work so I for one naturally assumed Joe would one day follow in his footsteps. I suppose it was just a question of whether the chance would ever come his way because Joe, obviously, wasn't getting any younger and no one knew when Bob was going to step down. When he did announce he'd be retiring then no other name came into the reckoning for me other than Joe.' Alan Kennedy says: 'I think if we're being honest, we all guessed it would be Joe but no one dared ask him. We wouldn't put him under that pressure where he had to tell us a white lie, because he probably knew deep down that he was going to get the job and I think in the end he just accepted it.'

Not that the man himself considered the promotion to be his divine right. Far from it. 'In all the time that I've been at this club, I have always said that whatever the directors wanted me to do, I would do. But I certainly had never given a thought to becoming manager of Liverpool FC. As a matter of fact, if the directors had appointed someone else it would not have made the slightest difference in my attitude towards this club,' he later commented.

At sixty-two, an age when he might have been contemplating the thought of a well-earned retirement, Joe could have probably done without the pressure that comes with managing a club of Liverpool's stature. But as Roy Evans is quick to state, there was one key factor in his decision to accept the board's offer: 'He basically did it to keep other people in a job.' Given the work that Joe, Roy and the other members of the Bootroom had invested in building the club into the 'bastion of invincibility' Shankly had craved all those years ago, the Wise Old Man of Anfield was loathe to stand by and risk seeing the end of the winning formula they had worked so hard to perfect. 'My first reaction at the time was that I wouldn't take it,' said Joe, 'but I thought about it carefully and realised that someone else might come in and upset the whole rhythm. I finally decided to take it and keep the continuity going for a little longer.' Stephen Fagan says: 'All that mattered to him was that the club continued to be run in the same vein as it had done under Bill and Bob. He was very loyal to the club was my dad, I can safely say that. You don't work at a place for all those years like he had done, then stand by and see all the hard work dismantled. It would have broken his heart to see that happen.'

Confirmation of Joe's promotion finally arrived on 23 May, 1983, at a specially arranged press conference in the Anfield trophy room. In the unfamiliar attire of dark suit, white shirt and tie, the new boss sat to the left of his predecessor Bob Paisley, chairman John Smith and chief executive Peter Robinson as the formalities of unveiling Liverpool's sixth post-War manager were completed. For the Fagan family it was a moment of immense pride. Michael Fagan remembers: 'Of course, we were proud. Liverpool was the biggest football club in the world at the time and for our dad to be manager, yeah, it was a great feeling. Because of the way we were, though, the way we were brought up, what Dad did was never a major part of our life. His work at Liverpool was just that – work. It was his job and while it must have been seen as a bit more glamorous than the jobs our mates' dads had, to us it was nothing out of the ordinary because we'd grown up with it and knew nothing else.'

The story made the front page of that evening's *Liverpool Echo*. Under the headline 'Bootroom boys still rule OK!', reporter Ian Hargreaves wrote: 'Joe Fagan is the new manager of Liverpool – and that's official. Bob Paisley's righthand man throughout all the glory years was today confirmed as his successor to end months of speculation.' Joe's promotion was widely acclaimed in the press. *The Daily Telegraph* football correspondent Donald Saunders described the appointment as a 'commendably sensible move' and predicted that 'scarcely a ruffle will be noticed on the Anfield conveyor belt that has been turning out the best teams in the League since the early days of Bill Shankly'. In the *Daily Mirror*, Chris James said: 'Only three things matter in keeping going the Mersey giants' unprecedented success story — stability, continuity and tradition. And the champions remained faithful to them all yesterday by appointing Fagan as Bob Paisley's successor.' Generally, very few doubts were raised about the club's decision to again fill a vacancy from within, or that it was Joe. At his unveiling, Joe said: 'This is something I didn't expect but I am very pleased to accept. In this game of ours you do not expect anything at all. You just work at your own job and do the best you can.'

Despite being only three years shy of his bus pass, and just two years younger than the man he was succeeding, Joe was certainly in no rush to settle down on the sofa with his pipe and slippers. But as sprightly as he may have been, Joe did confess to having some slight concerns about taking the job. 'When the chairman and board asked me, I wasn't too happy at first. It was really a question of my age, but they decided I wasn't too old.' Peter Robinson confirms that age 'never came into consideration'. It was also never an issue among the players. 'You are only as old as you feel and Joe was certainly not your average 62-year-old,' says Bruce Grobbelaar. 'Healthy body healthy mind, isn't that what they say? Well, there's no doubt that Joe had kept himself in good shape, so age didn't come into it.'

It was a view echoed in the press, especially by James Mossop in the *Sunday Express*. 'His promotion is an inspired move. Anyone who suggests that he is too old does not know the workings of Liverpool or appreciate the experience of Joe Fagan,' he wrote. 'Joe Fagan is as tough as the old boots that have hung behind him in the Liverpool kit-room for the last twenty-five years. His face features the clobbered nose of the post-War centre-half. He ambles through life with a rolling, ex-footballer's gait and loves to play the old-timer. It is a good act. For behind the simple humour and modest living there is a mind as bright as Jupiter.' At any other club, appointing a manager of Joe's age would have been greeted with more than a few raised eyebrows. At sixty-two he was a year older than Bill Shankly when he retired. But as *Liverpool Echo* reporter Ian Hargreaves was quick to explain: 'It is testimony to the remarkable respect in which Fagan is held – and also to the efficiency of the Liverpool "family system" – that chairman John Smith and his fellow directors have felt able to take what would, in other circumstances, amount to a major gamble. They believe that Fagan's deep knowledge of the game, his total loyalty and his remarkable fitness, will see him through the challenges that undoubtedly lie ahead, even though they recognise that his appointment must inevitably be a short-term one.'

Joe remains the oldest debutant manager in Football League history. Until the summer of 2010 when Roy Hodgson was appointed Liverpool's twelfth post-War manager, he also held the record as the oldest in Anfield history – just two-hundred and sixteen days younger than Hodgson. In 1983 he was certainly the elder statesman among his contemporaries in Division One. With Notts County's Jimmy Sirrel, thirteen months his junior, having recently 'moved upstairs' to the position of general manager, Joe was way out in front as the most senior. Taking Joe out of the equation, the average age of a First Division manager in the summer of 1983 was just under forty-three, the oldest being 50-year-old Ron Saunders at Birmingham; the youngest was former Liverpool defender Larry Lloyd, the new man in charge of team affairs at Meadow Lane, who was still a few months short of thirty-five.

In familiar Liverpool tradition, Joe had no contract. As with Shankly and Paisley, Joe's acceptance of the position was based on trust. The *Liverpool Echo* reported that the 'length of his contract will depend solely on his health, happiness and performance'. According to son Michael: 'It was never his intention to work beyond sixty-five, and all parties were aware of this.' Therefore, it was widely expected that he would hold the job for no more than three years.

Paisley gave his blessing to the appointment. 'I am delighted it's staying in the family. There will be no break-up. Joe is a seasoned campaigner and he's well enough experienced to know he's got to get on with the job. I don't expect any drop in standards at Anfield – that's how much I respect him. You may have found me mean and thirsty in my search for trophies, but the bad news is the man who is taking my place is hungrier than me. Fagan's the name and I don't think he'll need any help from the Artful Dodger!'

As those who have tried it will testify, the leap from coach to manager can be a daunting one. Paisley had proved it could be done, but there was a long line of failures to argue otherwise. Perhaps the most notable was Wilf McGuinness at Manchester United. McGuinness, a former United player and coach, stepped into Matt Busby's shoes just a year after they became the first English club to win the European Cup. Eighteen months later he had been sacked; within four years United had been relegated. No one was anticipating a similar fall from grace at Anfield, but any change at management level brings with it risk and it would be churlish to suggest that Joe's appointment did not carry some uncertainty. With Paisley remaining on the Anfield payroll as a part-time director, Ian Hargreaves pointed out: 'For several months, at least, a large question mark is bound to hang over the actual decision-making process.' He also flagged up Joe's inexperience when it came to public relations as another potential problem. Graeme Souness says: 'The only possible thing you could have worried about with Joe was the decision making, picking the team and being ruthless.' The enormity of the task was not lost on Joe, who admitted: 'I suppose if I really thought about what I have to prove I'd be climbing the wall.' However, he had the utmost confidence in his own ability and was eager to get started. 'I honestly think nobody else at this stage could have taken over from Bob. I am not being big-headed when I say that, but I know the drill.' In one of his first interviews as manager he went on to explain: 'He (Paisley) is supreme in all he's done, but that doesn't worry me. I start afresh. Bob Paisley and I have worked together for many years and I've enjoyed every minute of it. The Bootroom staff here have always been very loyal and very helpful. That's not going to change. I know I can expect full support from them. I am my own man. I will do the job the way I think is right. That's not to say there will be drastic changes – just little ones. We are up with the game here. There are no fuddy-duddies. No matter what our ages, we always had a young outlook here. That's what has kept us ahead. I am starting with a clean slate because just thinking about following Bob would be mad. That's the secret of our success here. We never look back, always forward.'

Joe's appointment was universally popular, particularly with the club's most important employees, the players. 'There was nobody I knew at the football club who thought anything other than "brilliant",' recalls Kenny Dalglish. Alan Hansen says: 'When Bob decided he was going, I think one hundred per cent of Liverpool players wanted Joe to be the manager. Sometimes it can be a bad thing if the board appoints the man the players want, but everybody knew that Joe was hugely respected. He knew all the ins and outs of the club, and what the players wanted was continuity.' None of them admitted to noticing any change in their daily routine. According to Souness: 'The transfer of power was as smooth as you'd expect.' Grobbelaar remembers it being 'just a case of carry on as normal'. Hansen puts this down to the fact that, for the previous two seasons, Joe had almost been doing the job. 'We knew things wouldn't change much because he already ran the place, the training and the day-to-day workings of the club,' Hansen says. 'Joe didn't change anything for the simple fact that he was part of the think-tank that had always regulated everything. He was a bigger part of that side of things than anybody was. So why would he change it?'

For a man with no obvious ego, it would have come as a major surprise if Joe's elevation had gone to his head. At almost every opportunity he was quick to stress that the club would continue to tick over as normal. However, when pressed by *Daily Express* journalist David Emery on what changes there would actually be, he reluctantly conceded that the players would now have to call him 'Boss'. 'It's tradition, isn't it? And I'm old-fashioned like that,' he reasoned simply. Not that it would be a problem if they had not. Alan Kennedy remembers Joe telling him at the time: 'I'm the boss but nothing changes, OK? And if you call me Joe, don't worry about it.' It is a story backed up by the then Liverpool reserve striker Paul Jewell. 'Just after he took over from Bob Paisley as manager, I was walking past him in the corridor and called him Joe instead of boss. I thought my world had ended, but to be fair he was fine about it. That's the way he was, he was just a very down-to-earth bloke.' He may have been the most powerful man at the most successful club in Europe, but as Ronnie Moran explains, there was no danger of Joe forgetting his roots. 'His relationship with the players may have changed slightly, which it had to because he was now their manager, but with regards to the staff we detected no change in him whatsoever. The Bootroom was always Joe's home and that stayed the same even when he took over as boss. We'd still have our regular little talks as we always had done and he treated everyone the same as always.'

It is clear that Joe's move into management caused very little to change in terms of the day-to-day running of the club. But as the countdown to his first season in charge began the world around him, in football and beyond, was in the midst of considerable hardship. While Liverpool continued to go from strength to strength on the pitch, the increasingly harsh economic climate – best epitomised on Britain's television screens by two classic Liverpudlian dramas of the time, Alan Bleasdale's *Boys From The Blackstuff* (1982) and *Scully* (1984) – was having an adverse effect on attendance figures. Despite the ongoing success of the team, the recession had cast a dark shadow over the Mersey and Liverpool's average League crowd had dipped to 34,836 in the 1982–83 season, a fall of more than thirteen thousand from the figure ten years before, and the lowest since they returned to the top flight. Complacency among the success-spoilt fan-base may have been a contributory factor, but more significantly rising unemployment was biting hard. Many match-going supporters were left with no option other than to forsake their 'spec' on the Kop every other Saturday. Joe, of course, was one of the lucky ones and thankful for that. He was in employment and sympathised with those who had fallen on hard times. Like most Scousers, his political allegiances lay with the Labour Party, and his socialist beliefs, while not as pronounced as those of Bill Shankly, meant he was in touch with the average man in the street. As a club Liverpool did their bit to ease the financial burden by keeping admission prices among the lowest in the country. Entry to Anfield was almost half what Nottingham Forest and Brighton fans, for example, were being charged. Only the previous season, cheap tickets for children and pensioners had been introduced, reducing prices on the Kop from £1.90 to £1.30. For the first time, a combined adult-child ticket in the recently-seated Anfield Road Stand could be purchased for £4.50. 'We are very conscious of the way our fans have been hit by rising prices,' explained Peter Robinson. Similarly, Joe had the welfare of the supporters at heart. Long-time fan Brian Durand, a schoolboy friend of Stephen and Michael Fagan, remembers how Joe always made sure tickets went to the right people. 'Even going back to when we were kids, he'd do his best to look after those who were struggling for tickets, whether because of money or lack of availability,' says Brian. 'We never liked to ask but if he got wind of someone needing a ticket he'd always sort something out. He certainly came to my rescue for the 1974 FA Cup final and again in 1981 for the European Cup final in Paris.' While his native city suffered during the days of the Thatcher Government, the game he loved was also entering one of its darker eras. The escalating sight of open spaces on the terracing at Anfield, and empty seats in the stands, was also becoming a depressingly familiar sight at grounds up and down the country. The announcement during the summer of 1983 that live football would be hitting television screens on a Friday night and Sunday afternoon hardly seemed likely to reverse the decline. Neither would the worrying increase in hooliganism. Minor tit-for-tat outbreaks of disorder away from the ground aside, Anfield had so far been spared the problem. Liverpool supporters were generally considered to be among the best behaved in the League. However, football violence had been a growing concern since the mid-1960s and one that would soon peak with devastating consequences.

*

Until then, though, little could dampen Joe's enthusiasm for the job. On the first day of July 1983 a new chapter in his long association with Liverpool Football Club formally began. In keeping with his character, no real fuss was made. His day began like any other. Up early, quick read of the papers over breakfast before kissing Lil goodbye, putting on his flat cap and, on this occasion, jumping into his modest Triumph Acclaim for the short drive up Arkles Lane to the place he called work. Aside from opting to drive rather than walk, it was what he had done almost every day for the previous twenty-five years, the only other difference being that now the wellbeing of the entire club rested on his broad shoulders. 'Suddenly, I became the man who had to make the final decisions regarding team affairs. And I must admit that inside the first few weeks of taking over I had my eyes opened regarding the way the club was run from a management point of view,' he recalled in an interview for the official *Liverpool Yearbook* later that season. Such responsibility undoubtedly brought added pressure but, as Stephen Fagan remembers, his dad did well not to show it. 'Apart from the fact that we all probably saw a bit less of him there really was no noticeable change. I'd still visit every Sunday as normal, but there was never much football talk on the agenda so it was hard to gauge how he actually felt about the job.' Joe's home life changed very little. 'There was no upheaval as far as our lives were concerned. Everything just carried on as normal,' said Lil. 'That's how Joe saw it and that's how we saw it. To him it was basically the same job he had been doing for years, but with a few more extra responsibilities thrown in, which, of course, he didn't mind if it was for the good of the club.'

Before settling down behind the manager's desk for the first time, Joe popped into the Bootroom to say hello. The old familiar faces were there: Moran and Evans, Bennison and Saunders, casually going about their business as preparations began for another pre-season. He even made the tea and hung around for a quick chat. Then he made his way towards his office, stopping to engage in more conversation along the way, this time with the cleaners in the long, narrow corridor beneath Anfield's Main Stand. In his diary he was moved enough to describe his first day in the job as: 'A significant day in my life', though in typically understated fashion he quickly followed that by adding: 'Nothing startling happened.' With the players yet to report back, there was little for him to do and he filled his time on that first morning by speaking to a couple of press men and posing for the photographs that would appear on the back pages of the following morning's newspapers. 'Don't know whether I said the right things but I tried to! Got to get used to it, but I have said this before – what appears in cold print isn't necessarily what you actually say. Must be careful,' he noted. For such a private, family-orientated man as Joe Fagan, life in the full gaze of the public was something he would have to get used to quickly. He soon adapted. In one of those early interviews he was quick to lay down the law, and told David Emery of the *Daily Express*: 'I'm not one for *bon mots* like Bob, or abrasive quips like Shanks. What I have to offer is one word – honesty. I couldn't be devious if I tried. I know a manager's job can sometimes entail bending the truth, but I don't subscribe to that. Once you start telling white lies you can trap yourself and the players can see through you.' Those chats with the press were novel: between joining the club in 1958 and being appointed manager twenty-five years later, Joe never gave a single interview. Privately he admitted to being 'a bit squeamish' about speaking in public. But, contrary to the public perception of him, Graeme Souness insists that Joe was never out of his depth. 'I'd say the opposite was true. I went to a dinner with him once where he had to get up and give this speech. With him he had all these sheets of paper to read off, or so we thought. He went on to deliver this really great speech, lasting for what must have been a good ten to twenty minutes, and when he finished he turned the paper around to show everyone that they were blank. That was Joe. He gave this impression that he was uncomfortable speaking in front of people, but I think he enjoyed it really.' Journalist John Keith, a veteran of the local Mersey beat, concurs. 'I'd say he actually adapted to this side of the job quicker than Bob did. Bob was never completely comfortable dealing with the media. We (the local press pack) used to call him the great train robber because he never finished sentences! He actually asked four or five of us if we'd finish his sentences for him, which was an enormous responsibility because we had to second guess what he was thinking. In contrast, Joe used to think of witty one-liners to throw at us. That was probably the Shankly influence rubbing off on him. He liked the image he had and secretly revelled in it.'

Dealing with the press was something Joe quickly became comfortable with, especially when among those who covered Liverpool on a daily basis. Ian Hargreaves, then of the *Liverpool Echo*, would see Joe most days and has nothing but fond memories of their working relationship. 'He was always smartly turned out, probably the smartest of Liverpool managers, always in a suit. He'd come up the steps, saying, "How are you, how's the wife, like a drink?" He was totally honest, totally decent and his interviews were hilarious,' Hargreaves remembered. 'We often used to make arrangements to give him a quick call of a Sunday for an update if there'd been any injuries the day before,' recalls John Keith. 'But I remember on one occasion we were all left stunned when he turned around and said, "You won't be able to get hold of me tomorrow, lads, I'm painting the kitchen!" Imagine a manager coming out with something like that nowadays?' A deep and intellectual thinker when it came to football matters, Joe's observations on the game and its players would become much sought-after. But though always cordial in his briefings with the media, Joe was far too long in the tooth to be sucked in by them. Creating headline news was never of interest to him. He was well aware of how easily words could be twisted and was always careful not to give too much away. Hargreaves said: 'He'd always take the initiative. "By jove, that was a good game". He was never involved in bad games, always a good game. "But Joe," we'd say, "you were beaten". He always prefaced things with, "Well, I said to Ronnie beforehand, this is a good side we're up against ..." At the end of it there was not a thing you could use.'

Press commitments aside, Joe's main worries early on in his management career were mostly to do with what clothes he should be wearing and what he should actually be doing. On just his second day as manager he complained: 'I have been here since 9.15 a.m. The time now is 10.15 a.m. and there is no sign of anyone or anything happening! I am also dressed up in collar and tie. It is not my normal gear – but it becomes me!' For a man used to patrolling the training pitch every day, confinement in the manager's office was an alien concept. So was dealing with the directors. In mid-July he attended his first board meeting, and Peter Robinson recalls that this was another facet of the job with which he quickly got to grips. 'He was much more confident in these surroundings than I expected him to be. He was never afraid to speak up if he felt the need to and could be quite vocal at times.' The nine-man Liverpool board contained a string of familiar faces, not least his managerial predecessor Paisley, but it was the chief executive-cum-club secretary with whom he had most contact. 'We'd sit down to discuss things almost every day,' says Robinson. 'He'd ask me questions and I'd ask him. It worked both ways and was usually about players. Our relationship was absolutely brilliant. I couldn't fault it. In business terms we were extremely close.' The pair had been working together, planning for the following season, even as the last ball of the previous one was kicked.

To those on the outside, inheriting a Liverpool team who had finished the previous season as League champions and Milk Cup winners, must have looked like the easiest job in the world. Liverpool had been the most powerful footballing force in England for the previous decade, and could boast a squad containing eleven full internationals and the reigning Footballer of the Year, Kenny Dalglish. They also had, in Ian Rush, Europe's hottest young goalscorer, while Graeme Souness was undoubtedly at the peak of his midfield powers. Yet this normally well-oiled Liverpool machine was in need of some minor repairs if it was to continue running as smoothly and efficiently as it had been. Writing in *The*

Times, Stuart Jones warned: 'Fagan's task is even more awesome than that which faced his predecessor in the summer of 1974.' John Keith, in the *Daily Express,* described the job of keeping Liverpool at the top of the tree as 'the most daunting in English soccer' adding: 'His task is as terrifying as it is tempting.'

The championship pennant may have been flying proudly over Anfield for the fourteenth time, but beneath the paintwork the odd warning signs of rustiness were beginning to show. Joe knew this, his predecessor knew this, and so did the chief executive and chairman. Paisley's last seven competitive games as manager yielded just two points out of a possible twenty-one. It was a worrying run of form that, while not enough to sour the title celebrations, was enough to trigger the ringing of alarm bells within the four walls of Anfield. Robinson openly told the press: 'Our present squad has become dangerously small.' The outgoing manager Bob Paisley admitted: 'There is a lot of work ahead for the club.' Robinson says: 'Our policy in those days was to try and sign at least one outstanding big-money player every year, and one or two players of potential from the lower leagues, as we did with the likes of Ray Clemence and Kevin Keegan from Scunthorpe, or Ian Rush from Chester. It wasn't uncommon back then for players to stay at the club for ten years or more. With time continually catching up on certain players, there was an almost annual need to keep replacing players and freshening things up.'

With Joe very much involved, the club set about rectifying this uncharacteristic slump. Several players had been targeted and just three days after Liverpool had completed the 1982–83 season Robinson was revealing to the local press that firm offers had been made for four players. 'I would like to emphasise that the offers have all been made with the full knowledge and approval of Bob Paisley and his successor,' he said. 'We wish to make sure the new manager starts with as strong a hand as possible.' Indeed, on the day of his unveiling as manager, Joe held talks with one potential signing, Swindon Town's 19-year-old striker Paul Rideout, who had impressed playing for the England youth team. Also on

Liverpool's radar was Everton's England Under-21 midfielder Steve McMahon. His signing would have been a controversial one because no player had crossed Stanley Park in the direction of Anfield since Dave Hickson in 1959. As it transpired, McMahon, no doubt aware of the ramifications such a move would bring, opted to join Aston Villa, where he was eventually joined by young Rideout.

Liverpool's number one target, though, was Celtic and Scotland striker Charlie Nicholas, a player whose style had drawn comparisons with Kenny Dalglish. Nicholas had netted fifty-one times for Celtic during the 1982–83 season and was being chased by all the leading clubs in England, including Arsenal and Manchester United. The transfer story dominated the back pages for almost a month. 'The three clubs chasing him agreed that we would all make identical offers and that none of us would vary from that. It was then up to Charlie which club he chose to sign for,' recalls Peter Robinson. The pursuit of Nicholas continued until 22 June when the Scot unexpectedly opted to join Arsenal in a £750,000 deal. Losing out on Nicholas was a major disappointment for the Liverpool fans, who were relishing the prospect of him linking up with his boyhood idol Dalglish. Ironically, it was the spectre of Liverpool's number seven that played a major part in persuading Nicholas to go elsewhere. 'When it boils down to it, it was a choice between Liverpool and Arsenal. I believe that Arsenal is the right selection because I am not following in people's shadows, like Dalglish followed Keegan at Liverpool,' he explained at the time. 'I think he made a mistake,' says Robinson. 'I remember bumping into him one day a good few years later. He shouted across the road to me and openly admitted that he sometimes wished he'd joined Liverpool instead of Arsenal.'

Another player Liverpool courted and lost around this time was the highly-rated young Denmark forward Michael Laudrup. Robinson says: 'He turned out to be a wonderful player, but I firmly believe we made the right decision at the time because he was demanding terms and conditions in his contract that were

impossible for us to meet …. The main stumbling block was that he
wanted the option to be able to just walk away after a short period
if he felt things weren't working out. From our point of view, this
just did not make any business sense.' The failure to sign both
Nicholas and Laudrup was perceived by some that the lure of
Liverpool was not as strong as it had been. But no one at Anfield
was about to panic. 'It was very disappointing not to sign either of
them because they were two very good young players who we
believed could have done a good job for us,' concedes Robinson.
'Over the years it was very rare for a player to turn Liverpool
down. We were quite confident both players would join, especially
Nicholas, so it was a surprise not to get them. But it wasn't
something we dwelt on. It was just a case of moving on and
identifying another target.'

The focus of attention now turned to Coventry City's promising
young centre-back Gary Gillespie. A Scotland Under-21 international, Gillespie first achieved fame as a 17-year-old at Falkirk
where he became the world's youngest player to captain a professional team. Scouts subsequently flocked to Brockville to monitor
his progress. A move to Highfield Road soon followed and the six
foot-plus Scot continued to develop at an impressive rate with
Coventry. A host of leading clubs expressed interest in signing him,
but Joe completed his first successful foray into the transfer market
by beating off competition from Arsenal. Liverpool paid £325,000
to take Gillespie to Anfield. Though the player admits to not
knowing an awful lot about his new manager at the time, he was
quickly won over. 'For me, joining Liverpool was a very straightforward decision to make, and Joe Fagan had a big part to play in
that,' he recalls. 'As soon as I got to know the man it became
instantly clear to me why Liverpool had been so successful through
the years. It was because of men like him.' Along with Peter
Robinson and Tom Saunders, Joe was part of the welcoming
committee who met Gillespie over lunch at a Liverpool hotel and
concluded the deal very quickly. 'From my point of view there was
nothing really to discuss because I'd been hooked by Joe straight

away. He sold the club to me. He probably didn't need to, but if there was any doubt in my mind it soon evaporated within minutes of meeting him. For the manager of Liverpool to meet and greet me, then take such an interest in my wellbeing, deciding whether to sign or not was a no-brainer. I'll never forget him saying to me after I'd put pen to paper, "Well done, Ga, you've joined a great football club".'

While Joe was delighted to have made his first signing, he confessed in his diary that wheeling and dealing was a part of the managerial role with which he was not entirely comfortable. 'It is hard going. The money side of the game is far too complicated for me. Thank God the chairman and Peter (Robinson) are good at it.' According to Robinson, though, this was yet another aspect of the job to which Joe did not take long to get accustomed. 'The bulk of the negotiating would be down to me, like it always had been, but Joe would be very much involved in the initial meeting with the player and he would do his best to sell the club to them.'

Two men crucial to the process of keeping the Liverpool squad fresh were Geoff Twentyman and Tom Saunders, unsung, but highly influential members of the Anfield backroom staff. Both had served under Shankly and Paisley, and were now operating in the same way as before under Joe. Cumbria-born Twentyman, an ageing left-half at the club when Joe arrived back in 1958, was recruited as chief scout by Shankly in 1967 following spells as player-manager with Ballymena United in Northern Ireland and coaching roles at Morecambe, Hartlepool and Penrith. In the intervening years his record when it came to plucking players from lower-league obscurity was second to none. Among his finds were Kevin Keegan, Phil Neal and Ian Rush, to name just three. Liverpool-born former schoolmaster Saunders was another Bootroom stalwart who, where the search for talent was concerned, originally operated much closer to home. After successful stints in charge of the Liverpool and England Schoolboy teams during the 1960s, he was enlisted to join the staff as youth development officer in 1970. While Twentyman cast the Anfield scouting net far and

wide, Saunders scoured the local playing fields and was responsible
for nurturing, among others, Phil Thompson, Jimmy Case and
Sammy Lee. His role evolved over time and as well as being sent to
spy on upcoming opponents, especially in Europe, his opinion
would be sought on all major transfers. Like Shankly and Paisley
before him, the trust Joe placed in both Twentyman and Saunders
was implicit. Together, says Robinson, they formed the perfect
team. 'The manager would pinpoint the type of players he wanted.
Geoff would identify potential targets and invariably Tom would
then have the last look before it was decided by the manager
whether to push on and put in a bid.'

Having completed the Gillespie deal, Joe knew further strengthening was required before the season kicked off, and admitted as
much in his diary entry for the last day of July: 'Looking through
the pro staff (we have twenty-seven), we have numbers but not
quality. Maybe there are thirteen players who are pretty good but
after that we could do with a good player in midfield and up front.
The temptation is to go out and buy now, but that could be fatal to
the rest of the season if we signed the wrong ones.'

With one or two deals having already fallen through, the search
for an understudy to Bruce Grobbelaar was suddenly made top
priority after Joe realised that reserve goalkeeper Bob Wardle would
not be up to the job of providing cover in the coming campaign.
This was no slight on Wardle's ability. The former Shrewsbury
man had yet to make a senior appearance but had played every
game for the second team the previous season. However, a serious
eye injury was to signal the end of his brief Anfield career. It was
only after much deliberation that Joe came to this conclusion, which
he described as 'a great pity'. The man he targeted to replace
Wardle was Sheffield Wednesday stopper Bob Bolder, who had
recently played a key role in Wednesday's run to the last four in the
FA Cup. Bolder started with his local non-League side, Dover, before
moving to Hillsborough where he made more than two hundred
appearances over six years. Wednesday rejected an initial bid of
£90,000 and it took a tribunal to settle the eventual fee of £250,000.

Having begun his Liverpool career as reserve-team coach, Joe was a firm advocate of strength in depth being crucial to the efficient and successful running of a football club. His promotion to first-team manager meant a reshuffle further down the Bootroom ranks. With Roy Evans stepping up to join the senior squad, a rare vacancy arose within Anfield's inner sanctum. Joe knew what qualities were needed to manage the reserves, and the man he chose to take over this important role was Chris Lawler, a player whose talents he had helped nurture back in the early 1960s. Lawler had played five hundred and forty-nine games for the club between 1963 and 1975, and had been working in Norway before his return to Anfield. He had little previous experience of coaching at this level, but what he did possess was a deep understanding of 'The Liverpool Way'. Quiet, unassuming and, above all, loyal, Lawler possessed all the characteristics required to be accepted in the Bootroom. He was also another local lad, meaning for the only time in Liverpool's history the entire backroom team was made up solely of Scousers.

Lawler was the only fresh face added to the coaching staff as Joe stood by those he had known and trusted for years. But with the extra responsibilities management brought, Joe was forced to take a less active role in training. 'That was probably the most noticeable change,' recalls Kenny Dalglish. 'The fact that Ronnie and Roy took most of the training. It was probably something Joe missed because he used to really enjoy getting out on to the training pitch. It would have been a big thing for him to lose, but it was the right decision. There is so much more to being a manager and that's why it's so important to surround yourself with the right staff.'

Pre-season preparations were stepped up in early August, and while Joe's reduced presence on the training pitch may have kept him out of sight, he was certainly never out of mind. He continued to exert the same strong influence about the place as he had always done. As pointed out by Ronnie Whelan, a key figure on the left side of midfield during the club's triumphs of the previous two seasons, there could be no denying who was boss. 'Joe may have taken more of a back seat in terms of hands-on training, but you sensed that he was always watching you. Even if he wasn't, the backroom team were so close that anything you did, be it good or bad, would invariably get back to him.' One player whose confidence was in desperate need of a boost at this time was centre-half Alan Hansen. Towards the end of the previous season, as Liverpool struggled in their last seven games, Hansen admits to suffering the worst dip in form he had experienced. But within a few weeks of being back in training his self-assurance was fully restored, and for that he had the new manager to thank. 'When we reported back for pre-season training Joe noted my determination to get back on the right track. He praised me almost every time I did something well – even for things that, previously, would have been taken for granted. I was so worried for my future that in one pre-season training match I even treated Joe to the rare sight of me making a full-blooded tackle (albeit on one of the young players). Joe looked blankly at me, and said, "That's different".'

With a hectic run of friendly fixtures looming, Joe faced up to the first big decision of his managerial career. With Hansen and Lawrenson established as the regular centre-back pairing, and the promising Gillespie recently added to the ranks, he could find no place for Anfield veteran Phil Thompson in his 14-man squad for the upcoming trips to Belfast and Rotterdam. Thompson could boast a medal collection to rival the best and was as loyal a servant as you could wish to meet. As the elder statesmen of the central defenders he was also the most vulnerable. It was not a decision Joe took lightly and he described informing Thompson that his services would not be required for the forthcoming games as the 'first unpleasant thing' he had to do. Thompson was understandably irked. In his autobiography he explained how this 'was not how I dreamed my Anfield playing career might begin to wind down', describing his omission as a 'bombshell'. Ever the professional, though, he duly accepted the decision and vowed to battle even harder to regain his place. It was a reaction that delighted Joe.

Another notable absentee from the tour was Ronnie Whelan. Joe was informed by the medical staff that the Irishman would have to undergo an operation to realign his pelvis, keeping him out of his immediate plans. Unlike Bill Shankly, who would famously shun injured players, Joe maintained regular contact with Whelan. 'Joe took a big interest in my injury,' he recalls. 'He'd always be asking how I was doing and what was wrong. He was very keen to make sure I wasn't rushed back too quickly and that it was treated right. It was reassuring to know that I remained part of his plans.'

The blow of losing Whelan reawakened Joe's fears that the coming season was not going to be a happy one. On the outside he may have cut a jovial, confident figure, but privately he was worried that it could turn out to be a mirror image of the 1974–75 season – Bob Paisley's first as manager – when Liverpool last finished without a trophy. 'Everything seemed to go wrong then, including the results,' he remembered. 'Since I took over there are similarities. The storm clouds are gathering – so I must keep a clear head and not panic.' Crucially, Joe did not air these doubts outside the four walls of his office, though as Hansen explains, this fear of failure was what drove the team on. 'Success tends to go in cycles,' he says. 'Some obviously last longer than others, but Liverpool had been at the top of the tree for the previous ten years and were now up on a pedestal to be knocked down. There was always that concern: that sooner or later it had to stop. What no one wanted was it to happen on their watch, even more so with it being Joe's first season as manager.' Every player was determined that this would be a successful season, and no one epitomised this spirit more than club captain Graeme Souness. 'Souey, in particular, was a big, big fan of Joe's,' recalls Mark Lawrenson. 'That pre-season he called a meeting just for the players. He came in and said simply, "Right, we think the world of this fella and this year we are absolutely determined to be successful for him". To a man everyone said, "Yep, you're right". Graeme knew the pressure would be on Joe and that's why he gave the little speech, just to ensure every player was one hundred per cent behind the new boss.'

*

Joe penned his concerns just over a week before taking charge of his first game, a testimonial in Belfast for long-serving Irish FA officer Billy Drennan, against Liverpool's arch-rivals Manchester United. Despite there being nothing but pride at stake, it was a baptism of fire, though one Joe relished. 'It's a tough way to start a new job but we are all used to that sort of thing,' Joe told the local press before making the short trip across the Irish Sea. 'We are looking on this game with United and our pre-season fixtures as ideal preparation for the defence of our title.' His first team selection was pretty straightforward. Of the squad who finished the previous season the only notable departure had been David Fairclough to Lucerne, and he had played only bit parts during the 1982–83 campaign. With no major signings yet, other than Gillespie, the side showed just one change to the XI picked by Paisley in his final match. In front of an expectant crowd of around thirty thousand at Windsor Park the early signs were good. Liverpool took the game to their opponents and raced into a 3–1 half-time lead. Souness had the honour of netting the first goal under Joe's management, giving Gary Bailey no chance with a blistering 20-yard drive after just nine minutes. Two Ian Rush strikes, either side of one by Norman Whiteside, put Liverpool in command. There was no doubt that during the opening forty-five minutes they were the vastly superior side. But Joe's decision to stick with the same line-up for the entire ninety minutes, while his opposite number Ron Atkinson made six changes at the break, was to prove a decisive factor. United's fresher legs clawed back the deficit to set up a grandstand finish and turn the game in their favour, Lou Macari snatching a fortuitous winner with just seconds remaining.

The Belfast crowd were enthralled with the spectacle they had witnessed and despite defeat the press were unanimous in their praise of Joe's Liverpool. 'The final honour may have been shaded by the Old Trafford side, but the greater satisfaction must surely have been with the Reds who battled away unchanged for ninety minutes. In the first half Liverpool, playing for the first time under new manager Joe Fagan, were quite simply magnificent,' reported the *Liverpool Echo*. Joe was less complimentary about his team's performance, though, and was clearly worried about what he had identified as a problem on the left side of midfield. In his diary he noted: 'Not a bad start but still got beat. Played very well first half but when the pressure went on in the second half we had no resistance to it. As they say in other circles – our bottle went. That is no bloody good. The players may have an excuse if that is possible. United put on about seven fresh faces in the second half which I suppose could have made a difference. But that is no excuse for our defence crumbling the way it did. I am afraid with Whelan being out we have a problem at left midfield. Johnston did not look like the answer. I will try him again in Rotterdam and if he doesn't improve I will have to consider someone or something else.'

If facing FA Cup holders Manchester United was viewed as a tough opener, it was not about to get any easier. Next up was a meeting with the reigning champions of Europe, S.V. Hamburg, in the prestigious Rotterdam Tournament. Joe's injury worries heightened on the morning of the game when Ian Rush was ruled out with a slight groin strain. Then, just eighteen minutes into the match, the situation became worse when his replacement, debutant Gary Gillespie, limped off with a thigh strain. As in Belfast, Liverpool were the better team but again came away with nothing to show as the Bundesliga side won on penalties following a goalless draw. Afterwards Joe told the press: 'I didn't really feel as though we lost. I told them not to worry about the missed penalties, but even so we don't like losing. It was a tactical game and a useful exercise for us.'

With Rush's injury proving more serious than first expected, Joe was forced to move swiftly in an attempt to reinforce his diminishing ranks. In between the last two games he had indulged in further pre-season shopping by bolstering his reserve squad with the capture of highly-rated young Irish duo Ken De Mange and Brian Mooney from Home Farm. But it was a player who could go straight into the first team that was needed. The following day he met Brighton's Republic of Ireland international striker Michael

Robinson in the plush setting of the Amsterdam Hilton where a £250,000 deal was quickly concluded. Robinson had reportedly been pursued by Everton, Manchester United and several other clubs throughout the summer. Spanish La Liga club Sevilla also made an attempt for his services, but once Liverpool had made their move there was only one club Robinson was going to join. 'When Jimmy Melia called to say Liverpool had made an approach for me I thought he was joking,' he recalls. 'I was delighted and would have swum across to Holland if I had to. Negotiations took less than ten minutes because I wanted to play for them so much. I didn't want to bicker over details. Mr Fagan started to read out the terms and before he had finished I interrupted him and said I would sign. I didn't really want to leave Brighton because I'd been very happy there, but at twenty-five I didn't want to start all over again in the Second Division. Sevilla would have been something new and the money they offered was terrific. I was ready to move there until Liverpool came in, but once that possibility emerged I never had any doubt. Every player's goal must be to play for a club like this with great tradition, reputation and world-class players.'

While not in the 'world-class' bracket himself, the burly Robinson was an honest, hard-working forward who would provide Liverpool with a more powerful attacking option. He started his career at Preston where his goalscoring form earned him a big-money move to First Division Manchester City in 1979. Burdened by a huge weight of expectation at Maine Road, though, Robinson struggled to make an impact and was sold to Brighton at a loss the following year. On the south coast he re-established his reputation and impressed during Brighton's run to the 1983 FA Cup final, starring against Liverpool in the fifth round, and scoring the winner against Sheffield Wednesday in the semi-final. He shook hands with Joe on a four-year contract but did not sign in time for Liverpool's final game of the Rotterdam Tournament against hosts Feyenoord. Despite being a striker short, Liverpool rediscovered their scoring touch in a six-goal thriller, only to once again finish on the losing side after a penalty shoot-out.

Liverpool headed home with Joe telling the press that the tour had been 'a very useful exercise for us', and that his team had shown 'a good attitude in both games'. Once back in the sanctuary of his Anfield office, however, he concluded that, aside from the performances of several players, notably Lawrenson, Souness, Dalglish and young Steve Nicol, it had not been a very successful tournament at all. With the start of the League season just over three weeks away, the mounting injury crisis was his biggest worry. But he revealed with some pessimism that it had come as no surprise. 'The funny thing about all this happening is that I knew it would! I could have written the script from the moment I took the job. It was a feeling, intuition if you like, that things would not go smoothly. And the curious part is that I am taking it all in my stride as if I was born to it! Life is no bed of roses and I certainly knew that this job isn't either! Patience plus willpower will see it come right some time, but when? Don't ask me. I have a feeling that this is not the end of my feeling for bad times.'

The two pressing problem positions for Joe were centre-forward and left midfield. But there was little time to dwell on them as Liverpool's hectic pre-season schedule meant the squad were back on home soil for little more than twenty-four hours before flying out on their next, less demanding, tour to Morocco and Spain. The game against local side W.A.C. was the first to be played in the recently-rebuilt eighty-thousand all-seat Stadex D'Honneur. In the stifling heat of Casablanca it was to be a significant occasion as it marked Joe's first win as Liverpool manager. His team coasted to a comfortable 3–0 success in a very one-sided match. But the result was deemed so inconsequential that it did not even warrant an entry in Joe's diary. Roy Evans admits it was a game he can only vaguely recall. However, he explains: 'No matter how important a game it is, I know from experience that it's always a relief to get that first win under your belt. It just takes that pressure off. Joe didn't show any signs that he was feeling the pressure but he'd have been a lot happier afterwards, that's for sure. The longer you go without a win the press can pick up on it and it can start affecting the players

Joe *(front row behind the shield)* and the successful St Elizabeth's school team of 1934-35. *Family Collection*

It was as captain of his school team that Joe *(seated)* first showed signs of his leadership qualities and where he developed his insatiable appetite for silverware. *Family Collection*

In the Navy: Joe set sail for Egypt to serve his country in 1941 but later described himself as 'the world's worst sailor' due to regular bouts of seasickness. *Family Collection*

A young Joe *(back row, second from the left)* lines up for one of his first senior games in a Manchester City shirt during the inaugural post-war season of 1946-47. *Family Collection*

Joe quickly established himself as a tough, uncompromising defender and is seen here in the thick of the action during a First Division encounter for Manchester City in the late 1940s. *Coloursport*

The Maine Men: Joe *(centre)* shares a post match bath with City team mates Roy Clarke, Jack Oakes, Dennis Westcott and George Smith. *Family Collection*

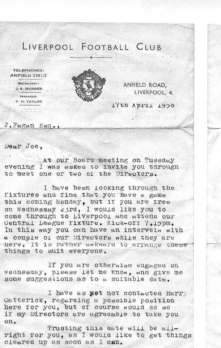

J. Fagan Esq.,

Dear Joe,

At our Board meeting on Tuesday evening I was asked to invite you through to meet one or two of the Directors.

I have been looking through the fixtures and find that you have a game this coming Monday, but if you are free on Wednesday 23rd, I would like you to come through to Liverpool and attend our Central League fixture. Kick-off 7.15pm. In this way you can have an interview with a couple of our Directors while they are here. It is rather awkward to arrange these things to suit everyone.

If you are otherwise engaged on Wednesday, please let me know, and give me some suggestions as to a suitable date.

I have as yet not contacted Harry Catterick, regarding a possible position here for you, but of course would do so if my Directors are agreeable to take you on.

Trusting this date will be all-right for you, as I would like to get things cleared up as soon as I can.

I have no doubt that everything will be O.K. here for you, but I am quite happy that we shall be able to work together without any trouble.

We have as you know a house in Anfield and I would like you to see it, before the game on Wednesday, so if you can get over here early we could get down and look it over. If you would like to bring your wife, all the better.

Best wishes,

Yours sincerely

Manager.

The letter that changed the course of Joe's life. It is from then Liverpool manager Phil Taylor and it outlines the offer of a job on the Anfield coaching staff.
Family Collection

The Bootroom Boys: Bill Shankly, Bob Paisley, Ronnie Moran, Joe and Reuben Bennett, pictured during a pre-season photo-call at Anfield in the late 1960s. *Getty Images*

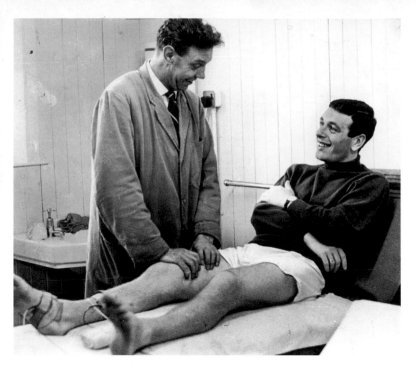

Healing hands: Joe administers treatment to Liverpool's record appearance holder Ian Callaghan. *Daily Mail/Rex Features*

Anfield's three wise men: Bill, Bob and Joe in deep conversation out on the training pitch. *Mirrorpix*

The principles of 'pass and move' were laid down in the famous five-a-sides at Melwood in which the staff team, including Joe and Shanks, would play until they won. *Mirrorpix*

The tension shows as Joe looks on from his regular vantage point in the Liverpool dugout during a home game in the early 1970s.
Family Collection

Life after Shankly: The new management team of Ronnie Moran, Bob Paisley and Joe prior to kick-off in the away leg of the European Cup Winners Cup tie against Ferencváros in November 1974. *Getty Images*

Joe celebrates another title triumph in the Bootroom with Moran, Paisley, Evans, Saunders and Bennison.
Getty Images

July 1983: After 25 years in the background Joe is elevated to number one. *Getty Images*

Merseypride: Joe leads Liverpool out at Wembley alongside Everton manager Howard Kendall for the historic all-Merseyside Milk Cup of 1984. *Mirrorpix*

It's the morning after the unforgettable night before and Joe relaxes with the greatest prize of them all following Liverpool's second Roman conquest.

Getty Images

The original treble winners and the Manager of the Year: *Back row* – Robinson, Gillespie, Bolder, Hansen, Grobbelaar, Lawrenson, McGregor. *Middle row* – Moran, Wark, Whelan, Rush, Nicol, Hodgson, Evans. *Front row* – Lee, Thompson, Neal, Fagan, Dalglish, Kennedy, Walsh. *Family Collection*

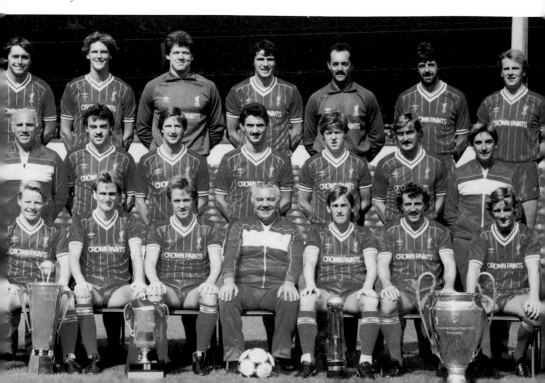

A crying shame: An emotional Joe is comforted by Roy Evans as the Liverpool team arrive back at Speke Airport following the horror of Heysel. *PA Photos*

End of an era: Joe brings the curtain down on 27 years at Anfield by handing over the managerial reigns to Kenny Dalglish. *Mirrorpix*

Joe takes his final bow before the Kop in April 1994, flanked by the wives of his former colleagues Bill Shankly and Bob Paisley. *Family Collection*

psychologically.' It was also an evening to remember for recent signing Robinson who enjoyed an impressive debut. He scored Liverpool's second, a stooping header from Hodgson's cross, after earlier setting up Nicol for the opener. Despite being far from fully fit his persistence and power up front shone through. However, it was Souness, scorer of the final goal, and Lawrenson, who were Liverpool's outstanding performers on the night.

A short hop across the Mediterranean for the La Linea Tournament in Cadiz followed. Liverpool lost to a Hugo Sanchez-inspired Atletico Madrid before beating Dinamo Bucharest thanks to two more goals from Robinson. However, on returning home, Joe was well aware that there remained a lot of fine-tuning to be done. 'We've tried to build up continuity but it has been disturbed by one or two enforced changes. Out of the tour came the hard work of Robinson. The disappointments were Hodgson who will not try more shots and Nicol at left midfield. I wasn't too happy at the last two games he played. Not to worry. We must try and tighten up in midfield. All our midfield players are more concerned with attacking rather than defending. Got to get a happy balance.'

Focus now turned to the season's annual curtain-raiser at Wembley, and a second meeting with Manchester United. Liverpool's record in the Charity Shield was a proud one. Since their return to the top flight in the early 1960s they had contested this fixture on ten occasions and suffered defeat only once – to Leicester City in 1971. They were the current holders, having beaten Tottenham twelve months before, and there was no question of them treating this clash lightly. As an indicator to what may happen over the course of the next nine months nothing much is traditionally read into the result of the glorified friendly. But everyone was well aware that defeat could prompt suggestions of an imminent shift in power at the top of English football. United were widely perceived by football fans on Merseyside to be the darlings of the media. It was a long-held belief that stemmed from the early 1970s when the rise of Bill Shankly's second great Anfield team coincided with the dramatic fall of United's European Cup winners. Despite their contrasting fortunes, United still managed to attract plenty of positive press, and any sudden upturn in fortunes, no matter how minor, would see them touted as potential heirs to Liverpool's throne. Sixteen years had passed since United had last been crowned champions, but fresh from FA Cup success over Brighton there was renewed optimism among their supporters. In its preview to the game *The Times* was quick to note that: 'Liverpool's results during the close season have been far from encouraging.' They cranked up the pressure on Joe's men by declaring that the 'psychological advantage lies with United'.

Joe was unruffled by what was being written. His only concern in the days leading up to the game was the welfare of his players and which of them he would have available for selection at Wembley. Whelan was a long-term casualty, while Hansen wihdrew late from the squad. However, Johnston and Gillespie came back into contention after proving their fitness in a specially arranged practice match behind closed doors at Wrexham. Most interest centred on the possible return to the starting line-up of Ian Rush, who had missed the previous four games with a groin strain. The manager and his coaching staff were keen that Rush play, but the player himself was not too sure. He was concerned that if he came back too soon he could face a lengthy spell on the sidelines later in the season. Having watched him closely in training, Joe was convinced the problem was nothing serious and a touch of cunning psychology eventually convinced Rush that he was fit enough to play. 'I wasn't happy about facing United and told Joe and Ronnie as much,' says Rush, 'but Joe Fagan was already calling on his vast experience with players. "Why not give it a go? It's not worth messing about with it. If the groin's gone it's gone – give it a try and find out", he said. He told me that if I couldn't get through, he'd just leave me to rest the injury until Christmas. So I took his advice and played, and though I was a long way from my best, at least I stayed the course. I believed what he had told me about my nagging groin, that it would clear, and it did.'

By his own admission, Rush was way off his best form against United, and he was not the only one. Despite a bright opening that saw Dalglish hit a post, Liverpool were forced to play second fiddle to the FA Cup holders. A goal in each half from Bryan Robson claimed the first silverware of the season. 'Disappointing to say the least,' admitted Joe afterwards. 'We played well for half an hour, but that is not enough. Still the goals go in against us and that at this time of the season is important. We need to plug the gaps. We are not hard enough or enthusiastic enough to win anything. At the back of my mind I have got this feeling that certain players are going through the motions. They have lost that spark to win more things.'

Joe's claim that his players had lost their hunger is a surprising one based on the evidence of just this defeat and the few friendly games he had overseen. The fact it was an entry in his diary and not a spur-of-the-moment reactionary quote given to the press, adds substance to the thought that he was genuinely concerned about his team's prospects. 'It probably was a bit of an over-reaction,' reasons Phil Neal, 'but it was almost a tradition for us to open the season with a victory in the Charity Shield. I think with it being Joe's first big game in charge he took the defeat more personally. You never lose the will to win, though. We wanted to win every match against United, especially at Wembley and with silverware at stake, but it was just one of those days. They deserved it and we could have no complaints.'

Much of the post-match analysis revolved around Joe's decision, with the score at 1–0, to make a double substitution as Liverpool prepared to defend a corner. He sent on Johnston and Hodgson in place of Robinson and Thompson, and from the set-piece United scored their second goal. The *Liverpool Echo*'s 'Monday Verdict' rated it: 'The howler of the afternoon'. With typical honesty, Joe held his hands up and admitted it was a costly error. But he stressed that it was one he would learn from. 'It was a bit of inexperience ... a combination of things really. I said, "Right, I'm going to put the subs on now", but at Wembley these days it's not just a matter of stepping up and shoving the lads on. You have to go to another referee, who goes and gets the number boards and holds them up and goes through all the procedures. It takes time and when everything was ready they (United) had got a corner. Instead of waiting until the ball was cleared, I went ahead and we weren't quite organised enough, which probably caused a goal. All right, I should have known better after twenty-five years, but in the early stages of command you tend to do these things. It amazes me now, but I won't make the same mistake again.'

The national press were full of praise for Ron Atkinson's side and talked up the prospect of them usurping Liverpool as champions. 'There can be no question that, on the eve of the new season, United showed they are ready to challenge Liverpool's dominance in the First Division,' wrote Richard Bott in the *Sunday Express.* The *Sunday Telegraph*'s Ronald Atkin said: 'So enterprising were United, so solid in defence, so assured in midfield, so threatening up front that Liverpool's championship could be under serious assault this season.' 'The papers were always the same,' recalls Phil Neal. 'It was nothing new for us to be written off, especially after a defeat to United, but none of us ever took much notice of what was written.' Nor did Joe's opposite number at Wembley, who insisted he had too much respect for his hometown team and refused to get carried away on the back of just one result. 'That defeat could be the best possible result for Liverpool because it will sting them into action,' said Atkinson afterwards. 'There will be no danger of them throwing away points through complacency now. I was delighted with the win, but I think I'd have settled for losing or drawing at Wembley, and sneaking a couple of League wins in the last minute.'

In the press Joe brushed aside the loss as an 'inevitable hiccough'. With a week to go until the opening day of the League season, he prepared for some last-minute tinkering. 'I fully expected this sort of thing to happen when I took over as manager. It's the sort of thing that always happens and Bob Paisley had similar problems when he was in my position. If everything had gone off perfectly on

Saturday and we had won I would have been delighted – but a bit surprised. I knew we had one or two problems and now it's up to us to sort them out.'

Though nothing too serious was ever read into Liverpool's pre-season form, Joe Fagan's first summer in the job had been a mixed bag, not helped by injuries to key players and a failure to land any big-name additions to the squad. Bruce Grobbelaar was of the belief that poor results in the close season boded well for the future, explaining: 'When things go wrong so early they are quickly spotted and put right.' However, it was not a view shared by the entire dressing-room. Graeme Souness said: 'We were not as strong as either we had been or as we should be.' Similar doubts were expressed in the postbag of the *Football Echo*. Dave Wiggins, of Liverpool 6, warned: 'There are already signs that Liverpool's dominance of the English game is about to end. I am convinced that having failed to sign Laudrup, Rideout and Nicholas, Fagan has resorted to buying lesser quality players. Don't be surprised to find Liverpool "languishing" in third or fourth place come May. I forecast a poor season for Liverpool by their standards.' Len Griffiths, of Bebington, wrote: 'It is quite clear Liverpool are not going to have it all their own way any more. We had that string of defeats to finish last season, and a far from impressive time on the Continent to start this one. I think the system is running out of steam and the change of boss will not affect us. I think we need new ideas. I hope I am wrong but our trophy-bagging looks over.'

While not necessarily representative of Liverpool's vast fan-base, this negativity was a worrying sign. Three days before the League season opened with a trip to Wolves, Joe managed to put on a brave face when addressing the assembled gathering at the club's ninety-first annual general meeting. In what was a rousing eve-of-the-season speech, he said: 'It is not our style to make outrageous predictions, but even though competition for major prizes is going to be keener than ever, we are ready to meet the challenge. We have set high standards in every aspect of the game and no effort will be spared to maintain these standards.'

As the man entrusted with prolonging the most remarkable run of success in English football, Joe could have been forgiven for feeling the pressure as he prepared for the official start to his first season as Liverpool manager. Sustaining the glory that had gone before was a big enough task in itself, and anything but a foregone conclusion given the problems he had encountered so far. To surpass it was almost asking the impossible.

CHAPTER EIGHT

CHASING A TREBLE

J OE FAGAN'S APPOINTMENT as Liverpool manager aside, the summer of 1983 had been relatively quiet on the football front. Arsenal's capture of Charlie Nicholas had been the most high-profile player move, and AC Milan's £1 million swoop for Watford striker Luther Blissett probably raised most eyebrows. Elsewhere it was announced that shirt sponsorship was to be allowed on television for the first time and, after a four-year absence, *Match of the Day* was to make a welcome return in its traditional Saturday night slot. In other news, there was a Tory landslide in the General Election, while on Merseyside it was reported that almost one in five people were now out of work. Fortunately, there was always the football team to lift flagging morale and Liverpool kicked off the 1983–84 season as *the* team to beat once again.

As always, the League was the number one priority. With a record-breaking fourteen titles already to their credit, Liverpool were the undisputed champion of champions. However, history did not augur well for Joe Fagan as he attempted to cap his first season with number fifteeen and, more significantly, a third title in succession. For all Liverpool's dominance during the previous decade, three-in-a-row domestic titles had always eluded them. To emphasise the scale of the task he faced, only twice before had a side won the championship in three consecutive seasons. The last time was almost half a century before when Herbert Chapman's Arsenal swept to a hat-trick of First Division titles between 1933 and 1935. Huddersfield Town, a decade before them, and also under Chapman's guidance, were the other club to do so. Even a manager as proficient as Joe's predecessor Bob Paisley was unable to emulate Chapman, though he had gone close on a couple of occasions. The back-to-back title triumphs of 1976 and 1977 and 1979 and 1980 had been followed by second- and fifth-place finishes respectively. After Paisley led Liverpool back to the top of the First Division in 1981–82 and 1982–83, the job of completing 'three-in-a-row' had now been entrusted to Joe.

Despite the enormity of the task, Liverpool were unsurprisingly installed as the bookies' favourites to join Arsenal and Huddersfield in the record books. While odds of 9–4 were placed against Liverpool, other sides thought to be in with a chance of the title were Manchester United (9–2) and Tottenham (5–1). Joe's views on what lay ahead were much sought-after, but he refused to make predictions, other than: 'I've not set myself particular targets this season ... just to win the first match, then the second. I know you've heard it all before but it's the truth. I realise what the fans expect and everyone here will be giving their all to deliver.'

Though the doubts he had harboured during pre-season still persisted, Joe was doing his best not to show them. He simply embraced the forthcoming challenge with a nod of the head, wink of an eye and flashed that trademark effervescent grin at the cameras now tracking his every move. His laidback demeanour and cheery persona ensured an air of calm blew gently over Anfield and Melwood. 'Pressure is something you put on yourself,' he said. 'I'm clear-headed at the moment and I intend to stay that way because I enjoy the job. And apart from anything else there are a lot of people in this game who would love the pressure of being manager of Liverpool.' There were a lot of people eager to shoot Liverpool down at the first opportunity, too. 'The suspicion exists that this season could see a slight decline in Liverpool's high standards,' warned *The Times* on the eve of the season. 'Their new manager, Joe Fagan, may find it awkward to pick up their momentum.' With the majority of newspapers in agreement that the title race 'promises to be closer than last season's procession', the vultures were circling, ready to pounce.

Crucially, though, Joe had the backing of Liverpool's fans. 'He was one of us,' says long-time Anfield season-ticket holder Brian Durand. In return Joe was determined not to let them down. 'I just hope I can repay all the kindness of the well-wishers and supporters. They would be disappointed for me if I didn't and I don't want that to happen,' he said. But with the phoney war of the summer almost over, Joe was anticipating a much rougher ride once the real business started. 'There is no pressure yet, that will come when the League season starts,' he had told reporters. But the weight of expectation was building. 'He had played such a major role in creating this winning culture at the club, and because of that the demands on him to maintain the high standards set by his predecessors were enormous,' says Alan Kennedy. 'The fear of failure was one he wouldn't have openly contemplated and not something we as players picked up on, but it must have been there. It's human nature.'

There was still some fine-tuning to do in the last few days and Joe found himself having to iron out one or two minor team selection problems for the opening game at newly-promoted Wolves. Unhappy with the positional play of Craig Johnston throughout pre-season – 'he sounds as if he plays for Roy of The Rovers and has to grow up' – Joe took time out to have a chat with the enigmatic Australian. Then, in a final trial match at Anfield, he experimented by pushing Dalglish further forward to form a three-pronged attack with Rush and Robinson. 'It seemed to work well, Johnston kept his position better,' noted Joe. 'See how it goes on Saturday v Wolves.'

The sun shone for the opening day of the season, temperatures were high and the shirt-sleeved crowd inside Molineux were treated to the quickest goal of the day. Unfortunately for the new-look Liverpool it was scored by the hosts from the penalty spot. Joe had barely settled into his new vantage point up in the stands, where he felt he could take 'a more detached view of proceedings', when Alan Kennedy brought down Mel Eves, and Geoff Palmer scored from the spot. 'That was certainly one hell of a way to mark my first appearance in the directors' box,' he joked afterwards. 'You get involved emotionally when you're down by the side of the pitch, and then this happens! It was a strange experience but, once over the initial shock, I thoroughly enjoyed it.' Ian Rush equalised immediately after half-time. Joe admitted later that he would have settled for a draw before the start, and was satisfied with the point gained. Joe did not have long to wait for his first League win. It came four nights later in a tight encounter against Norwich City at Carrow Road and set him up nicely for his first home game in charge. In his programme notes for the game against Nottingham Forest he reiterated his promise 'to give one hundred per cent effort to bring more success to this great club'. Though it took eighty-two minutes for the Anfield deadlock to be broken, it was to be the first of many Joe Fagan-led victories in front of the Kop. After six games Liverpool trailed early season pace-setters West Ham United by a point. Following an impressive 2–0 away win at Arsenal, Frank McGhee in the *Sunday Mirror* was moved to write: 'Few teams will this season go forward, away from home, more consistently, more intelligently and more often than Liverpool did at Highbury.'

Victory at Arsenal was made sweeter because of the much-hyped meeting between Kenny Dalglish and the summer's transfer target Charlie Nicholas. By his own high standards Dalglish had experienced a rather slow start to the campaign, but he burst into life at the Clock End of Highbury, curling a perfectly-flighted shot past John Lukic to complete the scoring. Even at thirty-two, Dalglish's class was still evident and as Liverpool embarked on their first overseas trip of the season, he hit a rich vein of scoring form to ease them past the Danish part-timers Odense. He scored the only goal in Denmark and then hit two of the five in the return to take him past Denis Law's British record of fourteen goals in the European Cup. Joe admitted his team were 'playing so well that it's almost frightening'. His big concern, the easy win over Odense aside, was the lack of goals they were scoring, a fact he put down to the team's build-up play. 'I don't want it to be too patient,' he confided in his diary. 'In the area around the goal we must look for the opening when it is there and not be too negative. But we must still work for the opening and not just sling the ball in for our front men to wrestle for it.'

Joe was also growing increasingly worried about the form of summer signing Michael Robinson. The forward had yet to get off the mark in a competitive fixture, and though he never admitted it publicly, Joe's early impression suggested that Robinson was 'not yet quick enough in thought or action'. So anxious was he to see his new striker succeed that Joe explored all options to get him firing. One concerned the metal supports in Robinson's boots, which he had been wearing since his days at Preston when he experienced trouble with fallen arches. Aware of this, Joe felt they may have been impacting on his ability to react quickly in goalscoring situations and persuaded him to try taking them out. 'I was frightened to play without them and initially a bit reluctant to do so,' reveals Robinson, 'but such was the faith I had in Joe I agreed to give it a go and it worked.' Playing without the metal arch supports for the first time at home against Odense, Robinson opened and completed the scoring in the 5–0 rout. 'Joe never put any pressure on me,' he says, 'but going so long without a goal had become a bit of a burden.'

No one was more relieved to see Robinson break his scoring duck than Joe, who commented afterwards: 'He was lighter and faster. You could see the difference in his play once the first one went in.' For a while it looked as if those goals had kick-started Robinson's Anfield career. In a crucial away match at League leaders West Ham he further silenced his doubters with a clinically-executed hat-trick. It was an important win. In the previous outing, at home to lowly Sunderland, Liverpool had suffered an uncharacteristic 1–0 defeat. As he tried to fathom just how Liverpool had lost the game, Joe contemplated shaking up his forward line and replacing Robinson with David Hodgson. It was just as well he did not. On a wet and windswept afternoon in East London, West Ham, according to the headline in *The Times*, were 'Swept Away By Hurricane Liverpool'. Joe agreed with the press assessment that Robinson had enjoyed an outstanding game, noting: 'Even apart from his goals, his appetite for work was tremendous.' That treble, along with a goal apiece in both legs of a Milk Cup tie against Brentford, helped put Robinson at the top of the club's scoring list at the end of October. However, his name was to appear on the scoresheet just six more times in a Liverpool shirt.

Dalglish's early-season purple patch in front of goal had dribbled out, so Joe was grateful that Ian Rush was about to make a timely return to the prolific goalscoring form that had helped establish him as one of the country's most feared strikers in the two previous seasons. Without setting the world alight, Rush had turned in a more than respectable haul of six goals in his first eleven games. Against David Pleat's Luton Town on a sun-drenched last Saturday of October, Rush returned to the side after missing a midweek Milk Cup tie to give one of the most clinical displays of finishing ever witnessed by the Kop. In scoring five goals in a 6–0 win, Rush joined an elite band of Liverpool strikers – Andy McGuigan (1902) and John Evans (1954) being the others – to have scored so many in one game. It was all the more amazing because he had not scored in the four previous League games. Against Luton, though, he had scored twice inside the first five minutes, and the matchball was already his before half-time. Dalglish made it 4–0 before two further Rush strikes completed an unforgettable afternoon. The win sent Liverpool to the top of Division One for the first time under Joe's leadership. Naturally, it left him purring with delight: 'What a game for us! Luton were never in it and we played some really first-class football.' Remarkably, on the same afternoon, Tony Woodcock also scored five times for Arsenal in their 6–2 win at Aston Villa. On Merseyside, though, there was only one striker being talked about. 'Everything I touched that day seemed destined to produce a goal,' recalls Rush. On this form he was unstoppable. His goalscoring exploits in the First Division meant his reputation at home as one of the game's deadliest forwards was safely assured; now it was time for him to step it up in the wider world as Liverpool's European Cup campaign began to get serious.

Following the comfortable stroll past Odense the luck of the draw did not go Liverpool's way in round two. On being pulled out of the hat alongside the reigning Spanish champions, Athletic Bilbao, Joe's response was: 'I don't think anyone would have plumped for them as the team they wanted to meet in the second round.' A tough battle was expected, especially as the Basques boasted in their ranks the fearsome Andoni Goicoechea, the so-called 'Butcher of Bilbao', who had achieved notoriety for a tackle that broke Diego Maradona's ankle in a La Liga fixture the previous month. All eyes were on the centre-half as Bilbao arrived on Merseyside with the sole intention of stopping Liverpool from scoring. But in what was a highly disciplined defensive display, Goicoechea's expert shackling of Rush and Robinson kept goalscoring opportunities to a minimum, and played a huge part in ensuring that the Spaniards returned home with their desired clean sheet. At the opposite end Bilbao showed little enterprise and their niggly fouls and incessant time-wasting earned them the wrath of the Kop. Joe's opposite number, future Spain national coach Javier Clemente, had clearly done his homework. 'A frustrating game, in which we had all the play but couldn't score,' was the post-match assessment of the Liverpool manager. It was a result that raised serious questions about Liverpool's European Cup aspirations. In *The Times*, Stuart Jones wrote about 'cracks appearing in the traditional European Cup stronghold', and how Bilbao had 'caught Liverpool off guard'. It was, he added, 'as though Liverpool were lying in the arms of Morpheus. No one could recall a more subdued performance at

Anfield, usually a noisy arena that became as quiet as the city streets at dawn.' Ian Rush, though, remembers Joe remaining remarkably upbeat about their chances. 'Bilbao thought they were all but through and we expected Joe to have a right go at us when we got back to the dressing-room,' says Rush. 'But he was surprisingly calm and he came in after the match saying what a good result it was for us.'

Joe's optimism flew in the face of the available evidence: Bilbao had lost just once in thirty-one European ties at home. For the first time in Joe's brief time as manager Liverpool went into a game as underdogs. However, Joe never wavered from his belief that his team were capable of grabbing an away goal. Amid a cauldron of noise in the atmospheric San Mames Stadium, known locally as *La Catedral*, the rhythmic drum-beating and English-style passion of the crowd added to the intensity of the occasion. But it was a scenario that was to benefit Liverpool, as Graeme Souness recalls: 'The moment we looked at the pitch, the good weather and took in the tense atmosphere we fancied our chances.' Liverpool produced one of their finest European away displays. With Souness pulling the strings, the yellow-shirted visitors gradually asserted their authority and made the decisive breakthough on sixty-six minutes. Alan Kennedy crossed from the left and Rush put an unstoppable header past future Spain number one Andoni Zubizarreta. It was enough to pierce Bilbao's proud record and secure Liverpool's place in the last eight. 'Liverpool are so difficult to handle because they never let you rest, not even for a second,' admitted Goicoechea afterwards. Sportingly, the home fans stayed behind to applaud Joe's victorious players off the pitch. Souness remembers: 'As we left to get on the coach they came up to wish us well and passed around their little leather flasks of wine.' On the flight home Joe was bursting with pride. 'The whole team played as a team,' he noted in his diary. 'They covered each other, backed each other up and worked hard – just great. Our fellows love this atmosphere. Big hearts and big chests stand out on nights like this.'

*

From the melting pot of Bilbao it was straight into the fire and brimstone of a Merseyside derby. Despite being a proud Scouser, Joe could not allow that to affect the way he approached the game. To him, it was a match like any other. Everton were languishing in the lower reaches of the table, and had not won at Anfield for thirteen years. The one hundred and thirty-ninth competitive meeting between the two clubs, and the first to be screened live on television, went very much to form. Once Rush opened the scoring after quarter-of-an-hour there was never any doubt about the result. Second-half goals from Robinson and Nicol completed a comfortable 3–0 success. It was enough for Liverpool to climb back to the top of the table, but Joe admitted afterwards that it was not a match which would live long in his memory. 'It wasn't like a derby game, it was too easy for us so there wasn't much excitement. Nothing much to say, other than three more points.'

That lack of excitement may have had something to do with the sheer volume of games Liverpool were now playing. The international break aside, the team had been involved consistently in two games a week since the start of the season. With progress being made in the cup competitions there was to be no let-up. While the European Cup now took a back seat until March, Liverpool's sights were set on an unprecedented fourth successive win in the Milk Cup, in which they had to play seven ties before Christmas. The League Cup, now sponsored by the Milk Marketing Board, had endured a much-maligned existence since it was inaugurated in 1960, but it was perhaps at the peak of its popularity and importance in the early 1980s. Liverpool had started their campaign along with the other teams from the top two divisions in early October in the second round. The holders were drawn over two legs against Third Division Brentford, with the first game at Griffin Park just days after the surprise League defeat by Sunderland. In typical Liverpool fashion, Joe decided there would be no knee-jerk reaction and named an unchanged team. He was rewarded with a thoroughly professional performance. Two goals from Rush, plus second-half strikes by Robinson and Souness, gave them a 4–1 cushion in a tie that yielded record gate receipts for the hosts. Such an advantage would have provided an ideal opportunity for modern-day Premier League managers to make wholesale team changes. But 'squad rotation' was unheard of then and Hodgson (for Rush) was the only fresh face in the starting XI who cantered to a 4–0 victory, and an 8–1 aggregate.

A much sterner test waited in round three. At one stage in the away tie at Malcolm Macdonald's Second Division high-fliers Fulham it looked as though Liverpool's stranglehold on the competition was about to come to an end. But Rush pounced with his eighth goal in three games to cancel Kevin Lock's earlier penalty and force a replay. It was not an entirely welcome addition to an already crowded fixture list, but was nonetheless greeted with relief by players and management alike. A fortnight later the sides fought another 1–1 draw, this time after extra-time at Anfield. This heightened Joe's mounting concern about his team's increasing inability to finish off opponents. It was a feeling he first aired the previous weekend in the aftermath of a frustrating afternoon against bottom-of-the-table Stoke City. Despite claiming all three points with a solitary Rush goal, Joe believed that even accounting for the visitors' 'smothering tactics', the margin of victory should have been greater. After the first Milk Cup replay with Fulham he complained: 'I'm not happy with our displays at the moment. We seem to be just hanging on. We are just not performing. Too many players just below par. I credited Fulham but our fellows were just not as sharp as they were.' Even Kenny Dalglish, the previous season's Footballer of the Year, and Liverpool's goalscorer in the Anfield draw against Fulham, was not free from the manager's scorn. 'Dalglish has lost his edge. Started off the season brilliantly but now being caught in possession too much.'

After much deliberation, Joe concluded that his tactic of playing a 4–3–3 formation could be at the root of the problem. He wrote: 'Our three-man midfield is being over-run by other teams with four in the middle. The strain is telling on Sammy, Graeme and Steve Nicol.' His response was to revert to 4–4–2 for the weekend trip to

Ipswich, with Ronnie Whelan called up for his first appearance of the season. Despite his concerns over the form of Dalglish, Joe kept faith with his number seven and Robinson dropped out. It proved an inspired choice because Liverpool rediscovered their true form. Dalglish provided the moment of the match, a sublime curling shot into the top corner to equalise John Wark's opener and secure a point from a highly entertaining 1–1 draw. It was Dalglish's ninth goal of the season and more notably his one hundredth in the League for Liverpool. 'A cracker of a game and a cracker of a goal from Kenny,' observed Joe from his vantage point in Portman Road's Main Stand. 'We were the better side, no doubt about that, but at the end of the day the result was right.'

Joe also noted a marked improvement in the performance of his reinforced midfield and despite a couple of enforced team changes, Robinson for Dalglish and Johnston for Whelan, persisted with the same tactics in the latest instalment of the epic Milk Cup tussle with Fulham. The Londoners had won the toss for home advantage in the third meeting and another evenly fought contest followed. Over the three games there had been little to separate the two sides and a fourth meeting looked probable when a further ninety minutes failed to find a winner. The introduction of Whelan at the start of extra-time gave Liverpool some much-needed impetus, and Souness's strike four minutes from the end finally brought the marathon to a conclusion. 'This game is cruel at times and it is cruel to Fulham at the moment. But thank God that round is over!' commented Joe afterwards. The press were unanimous in describing the game as a far from vintage performance by the holders. 'Without the subtleties of Dalglish, Liverpool were more than fortunate to dispose of Fulham at the third attempt,' claimed Stuart Jones in *The Times*. Steve Curry of the *Daily Express* said that it 'needed all the resilience of a side that has campaigned successfully across Europe for two decades'. Joe added: 'I put Whelan on for Nicol at the start of extra-time. All I did was put on a pair of fresh legs to try and break the deadlock. It worked. There was no ulterior motive about it, nothing tactical as one or two of the press tried to make out, just fresh legs!'

The Milk Cup run continued with a trip to Birmingham in round four where a late Mick Harford equaliser, in a 1–1 draw, forced yet another replay. St Andrew's was never one of Joe's favourite venues and he was happy to come away with a draw. 'I always dreaded coming here as a player because we always got kicked out of sight. It is a place most clubs hate to come to. They give you nothing and generally you go home crying. At least we are not crying tonight. We all agree it was a fair result but we must show a fighting spirit in the replay or we are out.' Two nights later the sides met again on Merseyside and, with their annual Christmas party to look forward to at Tommy Smith's nightclub afterwards, the players showed appreciably more fight in a 3–0 win.

Victory over Birmingham meant Liverpool headed into the busy festive period perfectly placed for a four-pronged trophy assault: quarter-finalists in both the Milk and European cups, top of the First Division by a point from Manchester United, and the FA Cup to come. Joe had been too long in the game not to know that medals are not given out before Christmas, and with the help of his coaching staff he drummed this into the players at every opportunity. 'With Joe, our feet were kept firmly on the ground at all times,' remembers Souness. 'There was never a chance of anyone at the club getting carried away after a couple of good results or if we were clear at the top of the League.' Equally, Joe would not lay into the players or openly criticise them after a defeat, unless he felt they had brought in on themselves, which was rare. However, that is exactly what happened at Highfield Road on 10 December, 1983.

After making their best start to a League season since 1978–79, Liverpool's first defeat had come in their seventh fixture, away at Manchester United, Frank Stapleton's close-range tap-in shortly after the break proving to be the match-winner. In truth, there was little between the sides and on the short journey back along the M62 Joe had few complaints. 'On the day I thought United just about deserved to win, but I thought our lads put everything they had into the game and we might have got a draw,' he reflected. It was a similar story the following week when they lost at home to Sunderland. Apart from the obvious failure to score in either game, he could not fault the overall performance of his players. Both results were dismissed as misfortune. Against Coventry, though, Liverpool suffered one of those rare off-days when they could do nothing right. The crushing 4–0 defeat was a result that no one saw coming, particularly as Liverpool went into it on the back of a 15-game unbeaten run. Nicky Platnauer set the tone for the match by scoring as early as the first minute. Grobbelaar was to blame. He failed to hold on to a weak shot by Terry Gibson and the rebound was bundled over the line with ease. By half-time the normally reliant Liverpool defence were in complete disarray. Gibson had helped himself to two goals and Joe prepared to read the riot act. For young reserve Jim Beglin, who had travelled to Highfield Road as the 'thirteenth' man, being in that dressing-room at the interval proved to be an eye-opening experience. 'I'll never forget that day,' he says. 'I was only there basically to take things in and I ended up sitting there not knowing where to look. There were tea cups flying around all over the place and a lot of raised voices. Alan Kennedy, the player I was hoping to eventually displace in the team, came in for a lot of stick and I was thinking to myself, "Do I really want to get into this team?"' Kennedy remembers the occasion, too. 'It was probably the most annoyed I ever saw Joe and unfortunately for me I was the one he picked on! There were others who hadn't pulled their weight but he targeted me. I felt that was slightly out of order at the time and some harsh words were exchanged. But when I look back on it he was probably right.' That was not the end of the nightmare, though. Gibson went on to complete a hat-trick and Liverpool crashed to their heaviest defeat since December 1976. Joe was scathing in his criticism. But after ordering himself 'a pint of whisky', he revealed that it was a result that had not totally surprised him. 'I feared something like this was going to happen because we haven't been playing too well recently. But what a pathetic performance. It's so long since a Liverpool team have needed to be given a blasting I'd forgotten what to say.' The scoreline sent shockwaves through the football world, and as he faced up to the first major crisis of his reign, a shell-shocked Joe admitted: 'I'm confused at the moment. At times like these we haven't got a prayer.' The fall-out rolled over into the next week as Liverpool's critics had a field day. One irate supporter penned a letter to the *Football Echo* explaining how he 'had now reached a stage of pure anger'. He warned: 'This great team is being plunged into a crisis of confidence.' In the national press, Liverpool were suddenly being written off as a fading force, not long after being declared prematurely as all but home and dry in the title race. John Wragg in the *Daily Express* wrote that it was a result that 'might alert the challengers to the fact that the champions are not invincible'.

Reporting in the *Liverpool Echo*, under the headline 'Destroyers given taste of their own medicine', Ken Rogers took a more balanced view. He described it simply as a 'low-key display', and one 'that the Reds will want to forget in a hurry'. Joe, though, had seen it all before, albeit rarely. A look through the record books showed that even some of the great Liverpool teams of the past suffered similar freakish results from time to time. After mulling over the key points of the game with his coaching staff in the Bootroom on Sunday morning, it was agreed that no drastic action was required. He knew his team well enough and simply put it down to a bad day at the office. 'We were becoming a little complacent,' admits Souness. 'We needed to be brought to our senses and that result was just the trick.' The manager demanded a positive response from his players and that is exactly what he got. A week later, Liverpool bounced back with a thumping 5–0 home win over Notts County. In the words of *The Times* journalist Clive White: 'With pens poised to write Liverpool's obituary, the patients jumped out of bed, leapfrogged over their heirs apparent and sprinted off down the road in the direction of the their fifteenth championship.'

At the halfway point of the season, the champions had their noses in front of second-placed Manchester United. Joe paused to take stock of his first six months in the job. Apart from the odd setback, it had been relatively comfortable so far. He attempted to explain how the role had changed him. 'At home nowadays we drink our tea out of cups with saucers, not mugs anymore,' he joked, proving his wisecracking sense of humour had not been dulled. 'It's a different job with a fresh outlook,' he added, 'and, I must admit, it's rejuvenated me a bit. It's better than taking tablets!' On a more serious note he appeared to be revelling in the role, and said: 'I'm learning as I go along, and I've more responsibility, the biggest being man-management. There are some decisions to take but they're mostly regarding the team. In that respect, I need only take a look at the League table to ease the decision-making. I don't do any of the training now and the switch over has gone quite well. I suppose the biggest difference is that the lads call me "Boss". I must say I am enjoying being a manager. That's amazing to me. I never thought I had it in me and I find it stimulating. There is no way that this job will be anything less than a joy.'

There was more joy for Joe over Christmas as three games in six days yielded seven points which were more than adequate to keep Liverpool ahead in the table. They finished the calendar year with a 1–0 win at Nottingham Forest. Adding spice to the New Year's Eve fixture were the pre-match comments of Brian Clough who accused Joe of contributing to the recent sacking of Richie Barker because he had spoken out against Stoke's ultra-defensive performance at Anfield the previous month. Liverpool had won 1–0, but Joe did not hold back when laying the blame for the dourness of the match firmly at the feet of the opposition. 'What a depressing game,' he moaned. 'In all my twenty-five years here I have never been so disappointed by the visiting side's display. Stoke wanted to defend and they did. The enjoyment went out of it for all our spectators and players, just because of their tactics.' Joe wisely refused to get embroiled in a slanging match with Clough and simply let his team do the talking for him. In what was a typically hard-fought encounter, Rush settled matters midway through the first half.

*

The lead at the top had now grown to three points, but with United due at Anfield for the first game of 1984 Joe was remaining cautious. 'People talk about being top as we go into a new year, but as far as I'm concerned nothing is cut and dried. We'd like to be out in front by a mile but the Manchester Uniteds, Southamptons and Forests are still there. Who knows what will happen at the end of the day?' Before the first meeting between the teams earlier in the season Joe had played down the importance of the outcome in terms of the title race. But as they prepared to lock horns again the phrase 'Titanic clash' was predictably trotted out in the newspapers. For once the fixture lived up to its billing. The New Year could not have begun in more explosive fashion in front of a full house of 45,122, Anfield's best of the season. Craig Johnston opened the scoring only for Norman Whiteside to snatch a point for Manchester United with a late equaliser. Of greater concern for Joe, however, was the horrific injury sustained by Kenny Dalglish, who suffered a depressed fracture of the cheekbone following a collision with Kevin Moran shortly before half-time. The United defender was wearing a support brace on his wrist and appeared to catch Dalglish full in the face in an aerial duel. Moran's challenge went unnoticed by the referee and Joe was forced to restrain an absolutely livid Souness from confronting the Irishman as the two teams went off at the break. After dominating proceedings up until that point, the injury seemed to disturb Liverpool and they were forced to settle for a point. Joe noted: 'What can I say? We were home and dry and then they equalise in the last five minutes. But it wasn't the loss of two points that was significant, it was the injury to Kenny. Who knows now what will happen with him out?' Joe had seen many injuries during his time in the game, but this one particularly upset him. While his number seven recovered in hospital Joe would call in to see him on his way to training, bringing in the newspapers each morning. But as Dalglish recalls: 'He always seemed to avert his eyes and never seemed prepared to stay.'

The result against United had been viewed as pivotal in the race for the championship. Victory for Liverpool would have opened a six-point lead and delivered a major psychological blow to their main rivals. Whiteside's late equaliser had given United renewed hope. Souness was incensed at the manner of Liverpool's capitulation and later vented his feelings of frustration towards the manager. 'For the first time as captain, I had words with Joe. They were rather loud words as well as I rather forcibly put over my opinion that Liverpool had gone soft,' he remembers. 'After going a goal up we were not professional enough to see it through and I told him, Ronnie Moran and Roy Evans, in no uncertain terms that I thought Manchester United would win the League and not us.'

Nevertheless, having to face up to the prospect of at least a month without his star man was seen as a massive blow to Liverpool's aspirations. Stuart Jones in *The Times* was one of many journalists predicting that it could prove to be the turning point of the season, and in United's favour. 'When Moran's elbow crunched into Dalglish's head, disfiguring the left side of his face and forcing him to walk away from the game for at least a month, Liverpool's title ambitions were wounded perhaps as severely,' he wrote. In Jones's opinion, Dalglish was 'indispensable because he lends an extra dimension to the enterprise of their attack'. Joe did not need telling: he was well aware of just how big a loss Dalglish would be.

As he slowly came to terms with Dalglish's absence, Joe sought consolation in the fact that Ian Rush's value was going up with every goal he scored, and during the 1983–84 season that was becoming a regular occurrence. In goalscoring terms it was to be his best campaign in a Liverpool shirt. Records were being broken almost every other week and he was to end the season with a phenomenal haul of forty-seven goals. What set him apart from the rest was the variation in his goals: countless close-range tap-ins, yes, but also many well-drilled angled efforts, the odd 25-yard piledriver and occasional header. Anyone who doubted the claims that he was Britain's most natural finisher since Jimmy Greaves were finally convinced on a freezing cold January night at Villa Park when he scored an unforgettable hat-trick. Unfortunately for

Liverpool the television cameras were there to record it and the highlights served only to heighten awareness of Rush's talent, especially to clubs on the Continent who were busily compiling their shopping lists for the summer.

Another player on the radar, particularly of the lira-laden giants of Serie A, was Souness. His value to the team was rated by Joe as even higher than that of Rush and Dalglish. Speaking after the emphatic 6–0 drubbing of Luton in October, when Rush had scored five, Joe commented: 'I have noticed in the papers that Rush and Dalglish get most of the write-ups and quite right too. But for my money Souness is the one player who is doing his stuff week in, week out. He is the best for me.' His captain had certainly been in imperious form, honouring his pre-season promise that he would do everything in his powers to ensure Joe's first season was a successful one. Away from the game, his liking for the good things in life earned him the soubriquet 'Champagne Charlie', but that was in stark contrast to his image on the field where nothing could disguise a steely determination to win at all costs. The influence he exerted on the team was such that when Souness joined Dalglish on the casualty list, limping off with a hamstring injury thirty-four minutes into Liverpool's fourth-round FA Cup tie at Brighton, there were grave concerns about Liverpool's ability to cope. According to John Keith in the *Daily Express*: 'Souness's absence plunges Liverpool into the unknown.' Joe was facing up to the unenviable prospect of selecting a Liverpool team who, for the first time since 1978, could not call upon either Dalglish or Souness. Keith concluded: 'Fagan now has to ponder deeply how best to utilise his resources.'

There was no time to dwell on the potentially damaging loss of his captain. The fixtures were still coming thick and fast, but Joe was confident his squad had enough strength in depth to get by and publicly backed his players to prove their mettle. Three days later, with the injured duo watching from the stands, they did just that against in-form Watford. Ronnie Whelan, whose season had been disrupted by the pre-season pelvic injury, came in for only his third start of the season. He was on the scoresheet for the first time since his Milk Cup final winner eleven months before as Liverpool scored three first-half goals without reply to extend their lead at the top.

Off the pitch, the main talking point that night was the attendance of just 20,746, Anfield's lowest League gate of the season and smallest since April 1961. It was a stark reminder of the harsh economic climate of the time. Falling attendance figures were endemic throughout the country. Earlier in the season just 9,902, the lowest post-War crowd for a competitive first-team fixture at Anfield, watched the Milk Cup tie against Brentford, even though prices on the Kop that night were slashed to just £1 for children and pensioners. For the tie against Birmingham, just before Christmas, Liverpool officials anticipated another disappointing crowd and closed the Kemlyn Road Stand to save on stewarding and policing costs. For a ground so accustomed to packed, vibrant stands, it made for an unusually eerie atmosphere.

Though the recession continued to bite hard on Merseyside, Liverpool fans were still capable of turning out in large numbers and raising the volume when required, and never more so than when Wembley loomed on the horizon. The FA Cup campaign came to a premature end, but not before Anfield had hosted an electrifying night against Second Division high-fliers Newcastle United in round three. In the first tie, other than the final, to be televised live, eight thousand Geordies helped raise the atmosphere and Liverpool responded. 'We revelled in it,' said Joe. 'Instead of the noise helping Newcastle it helped us. Consequently our lads overwhelmed Newcastle and ran out easy winners.' Two goals from Rush and one each from Dalglish's replacement Robinson and Johnston completed a routine 4–0 victory. The game marked the return of former Liverpool players, Terry McDermott and Kevin Keegan. Having been part of successful teams under Shankly and Paisley, Keegan, in particular, was well placed to pass judgment on the job Joe was doing. He did not hold back in his praise when questioned by reporters afterwards. 'Like vintage wine, they seem to get better and better,' he said.

Whether that view was shared by the Liverpool fans after round four, however, is up for debate. For the second successive season, Liverpool succumbed to a giant-killing at the hands of Brighton & Hove Albion. Twelve months earlier, in a fifth-round tie at Anfield, Brighton dumped Liverpool out of the competition at Anfield on the way to their first appearance in the final. Now, in front of the television cameras at the Goldstone Ground, they confirmed their status as Liverpool's new bogeymen. To compound Liverpool's misery, they lost Souness to injury and Robinson spurned two glorious first-half chances against his former club. Sensing that lightning could strike twice, the Second Division side upped the tempo after half-time and two defensive blunders allowed Terry Connor and Gerry Ryan to seal a 2–0 win. Joe accepted defeat graciously. 'We were well beaten in the end,' he conceded afterwards. 'Two mistakes by our centre-halves cost us dearly. We obviously missed Souness but injury is something you have to overcome in football. I hope Brighton go all the way to Wembley now. They were the better side.'

However, while the door closed on the FA Cup, another more familiar route to Wembley was opening up. In the Milk Cup Liverpool were continuing to make heavy weather of ties against lower-division opposition. They were drawn away at Sheffield Wednesday in the quarter-final. On a quagmire of a pitch at a heaving Hillsborough Liverpool were pushed all the way in a thrilling 2–2 draw. Joe described it as 'undoubtedly one of the games of the season so far', and believed Liverpool came through it with a great deal of credit. What pleased him most was the fighting spirit his players had shown. Their grip on the trophy looked to be slipping as they trailed 2–1 with seven minutes to go. But Phil Neal, after missing with a penalty against Nottingham Forest earlier in the season, was successful this time from the spot. In contrast to the earlier rounds, more than forty thousand packed Anfield for the replay, but this was no close-run affair as Liverpool discovered their ruthless streak to win 3–0.

With Everton also in the last four hopes were high for a first all-Merseyside Wembley final. When the two-legged semi-final draw kept them apart the dream edged closer to reality. Liverpool could have been forgiven for believing they had received the better draw when they were paired with West Midlands minnows Walsall. However, the Third Division side had already knocked out Arsenal at Highbury, and with Mark Lawrenson on the sidelines, they had the scent of blood in their nostrils once again. Backed by a large vociferous support, Walsall stunned the Kop by pulling off a 2–2 draw. Whelan twice put Liverpool ahead, but defensive blunders, including an own goal contrived between Gillespie and Neal, allowed the visitors back into the game. For Joe, it was another far from convincing performance. Liverpool's recent frailties were again exposed. With no Souness or Dalglish, it was clear that a crucial spark was missing from their play. The loss of Lawrenson, an intelligent and stylish ball-playing centre-half who Joe rated highly, had left them even more vulnerable. 'We are only an ordinary team now,' sighed Joe. 'Every one of our players was committed but that is not enough now. We haven't got a player with real flair, just honest to goodness effort.'

The following day's report in *The Times* said: 'Without the guile of Dalglish, the vision of Souness and the speed of Lawrenson, Liverpool looked unfamiliar in both formation and method.' During the BBC's edited highlights of the game on *Sportsnight*, commentator John Motson was particularly critical of Alan Hansen's performance. Hansen felt it was harsh, arguing: 'There was nothing in our performance to be alarmed about.' But it all contributed to creating a mini sense of crisis. For the return leg at Fellows Park, Joe was delighted to have a recovered Souness back in the fold, and his presence was to prove significant. Liverpool were in no mood to succumb to a seismic cup shock in front of an expectant full house, and the game was only thirteen minutes old when Rush eased the tension by pouncing for his eighth Milk Cup goal of the season. Four minutes into the second half, Whelan booked a return trip to Wembley with a goal that brought the wall at the front of visitors' terrace crashing down. Scenes of panic ensued as supporters spilled on to the pitch and several Liverpool players, most notably Souness, heroically pulled fans from the resultant crush. Play was held up temporarily and both sides returned to their dressing-rooms. The game was eventually played out to its inevitable conclusion, and Joe was naturally pleased to have reached his first final as manager. 'Wembley here we come,' he roared in a rare show of emotion. 'The game is about getting goals as well as playing football and that is what we did.'

In the other semi-final it would be another two weeks before Everton saw off Aston Villa to seal the dream final. The city was abuzz with anticipation. The municipal bells rang out in honour of its two major teams meeting at Wembley and Joe was beaming with pride at the prospect of being involved in such an historic occasion. But as the frantic clamour for tickets began Joe made sure that around Anfield and Melwood all thoughts of the big match were put aside. With another two trophies to chase he could not afford his players to be distracted by the sideshow. Talk of a possible Treble surfaced now for the first time, but Joe was adhering strictly to the old adage of taking one game at a time. 'It was never the Liverpool way to look any further ahead than the next game,' says Ronnie Moran. 'This had been instilled into everyone at the club since the days of Bill and Bob, and it was no different under Joe. You can only play one match at a time so what's the point in thinking any further ahead than that? This had always been the Bootroom philosophy. If players mentioned a big game that was a couple of weeks away we used to tell them, "Don't worry about that, son. You might not be in the bloody team".'

Before contemplating Wembley, Liverpool had to get past Benfica, managed by future England coach Sven-Göran Eriksson, in the European Cup quarter-finals. Eriksson had visited Melwood as a young coach in the 1970s to study the techniques of Joe and his Bootroom colleagues. Taking a leaf out of Bilbao's book in the previous round, Eriksson's team arrived on Merseyside for the first leg with a damage-limitation plan, and packed their defence in an attempt to stifle Liverpool's attacking options. For the first forty-five minutes it worked a treat. But the outcome of the tie was to turn on an inspired half-time substitution by Joe. Making a welcome return to the bench that night after two months out was Kenny Dalglish. Having played in just two reserve games during the course of his rehabilitation, Joe had intended to ease Dalglish back into the senior team. However, sensing that Dalglish's creativity could be the key to unlocking the stubborn Portuguese rearguard, he was sent on to replace Robinson. It was not long before Dalglish's sorely-missed subtle skills and penetrative passing began to have an effect. Suddenly, the Benfica back-line had more to think about, and they were finally breached midway through the second half when Rush headed home at the far post. Though a number of opportunities were squandered during the final fifteen minutes, Joe was happy enough with the one-goal advantage and even more delighted with the returning hero. 'Dalglish made a difference. Just his presence frightened Benfica! It was a calculated risk that paid off. He gave us a little more skill and won us the game. Being a world-class player he gives problems to other teams, even when he's not touching the ball. I thought it would be hard and it was. To get one goal was a bonus – at least we didn't let a goal in and that will mean a lot in the away leg.'

The return of Liverpool's iconic number seven had given everyone at the club a big lift. It was particularly timely because Joe needed all his experienced players available for the second leg in front of seventy thousand screaming Portuguese in Lisbon. It was undoubtedly the biggest game yet of Joe's tenure as manager and, as Dalglish remembers, he got his tactics spot on. 'He loved these type of occasions, but he was well aware of how big a part the crowd could play. He would always stress the importance of silencing them. "Get on top of them early and their fans will turn", he'd say.' Liverpool's players carried out Joe's instructions perfectly and overwhelmed the hosts with one of the most emphatic European away displays by an English club. 'Joe's prediction came true and his plan for a high tempo paid off,' says Dalglish. Assisted by the eccentric goalkeeping of Bento, first-half goals from Whelan and Johnston put the outcome of the tie beyond doubt. 'Under the stony gaze of their giant eagle, Benfica were reduced to little more than helpless prey,' wrote Stuart Jones in *The Times*. Nene managed a consolation, the first Liverpool had conceded in Europe that season, but further goals from Rush and another by Whelan completed a remarkable 4–1 drubbing. 'What an incredible result,' beamed Joe. Ian Hargreaves of the *Liverpool Echo* believed it 'sounded a warning to the rest of Europe'.

With a European Cup semi-final and a Milk Cup final to come, most managers would have been content. Not Joe Fagan. As Liverpool prepared for the climax of the First Division season, the manager was far from happy with the form of his team in the League. Despite his warnings, after leading the table for so long he feared his team were in danger of taking their eye off the ball. Since drawing with United at the turn of the year, Liverpool had lost only once, a woeful 1–0 home defeat to bottom-of-the-table Wolves. But amid all the drama of the cup games they had also laboured to dour goalless draws at Sunderland and Luton. The scintillating Rush-inspired victory at Villa Park aside, Liverpool had struggled to hit top gear. Only the failure of their title rivals to capitalise kept them in front. At one stage in February Liverpool even extended the lead at the top to four points, but Joe felt they were hardly worthy of it. After a 1–1 draw in the Goodison derby in early March he admitted: 'We are not a good side now and we are just hanging on to top position by sheer guts.' With Dalglish back, he hoped that Liverpool's 'small crisis' was almost over. But even after a notable 3–1 home win over Tottenham, in which Dalglish got on the scoresheet, Joe maintained his mood of negativity. 'I wasn't impressed with our performance throughout, yet the spectators said it was a good game,' he wrote. 'We were too easy-osey on parts of the field, especially Sammy, Ronnie and Craig. For me, they were poor and I felt like an old-fashioned blast to all three. Good job we had Grobbelaar and the two centre-backs. Anyway another three points. I don't think we can go down now!'

However, the prospect of Liverpool being caught at the top was looking increasingly likely. One of the teams on the fringe of the title race were Lawrie McMenemey's Southampton. In front of the Friday night live television cameras they struck a blow for themselves and their fellow challengers when they defeated Liverpool 2–0 at The Dell. Without the inspirational Souness, who Joe had sent back to Scotland on compassionate leave following the death of his mother, they lacked leadership. His replacement, Nicol, lasted only fifty-three minutes before twisting his ankle, so that when Kennedy was also forced off with an injured knee, Liverpool had to play the remaining ten minutes a man down. By this point, they were already a goal down, Danny Wallace having opening the scoring with a spectacular scissor-kick on the stroke of half-time. Wallace scored the second with a late header, leaving Joe deflated and facing up to the possibility that on that evidence Liverpool could end the season empty-handed. 'Not good enough,' was his simple verdict. 'We got beat and deservedly so. We had flashes of doing something, but that was all. We are not the Liverpool of old, not enough personalities, not enough good players. I'm not surprised with the result or the prospect of not winning anything.'

Liverpool's defeat at The Dell enabled Manchester United to regain top spot for the first time since mid-December the following afternoon. Joe knew something had to be done to stop the rot that seemed to be setting in. He responded by splashing out £450,000 to sign Ipswich Town's goalscoring midfielder John Wark, beating United to his signature. To some the signing of Wark smacked of desperation, but Joe was delighted to have captured the player he dubbed 'the pest'. Wark had scored frequently against Liverpool down the years, including one at Portman Road earlier in the season that proved to be his last in an Ipswich shirt. Joe admitted to being a long-time admirer and joked: 'After the way he's played against us in the past I'm just glad we won't have to face him any more.' Wark, though, was ineligible to play in the cup competitions, so was forced to watch from the wings as the first silverware of the season beckoned.

The first all-Merseyside cup final was an occasion fans of Liverpool and Everton had been dreaming of since the two clubs first met in the late nineteenth century. The *Liverpool Echo*'s souvenir paper 'Mersey Masters' dubbed it: 'The final they said could never happen.' It went on: 'What a day it promises to be. Two great teams representing all that is best in football, walking out side by side in their blue and red jerseys.' At a civic lunch at the Town Hall to mark the occasion, council chairman Hugh Dalton said: 'We have a situation in the city where we are facing many difficulties, particularly over unemployment, so it is a great pleasure to be able to pay tribute to the prestige and honour our clubs have brought us.' It was a match every football-loving Scouser was determined to attend, recession or no recession. Both clubs dispensed their allocation of thirty-two thousand tickets in no time; such was the demand, it could probably have been sold out twice over. The city of Liverpool was caught in its own cup-fever bubble. Exiled Scousers returned home from all over the world and talk about the game was so endemic that it even formed part of a storyline in locally-based television soap opera *Brookside*. Red or blue flags hung from the windows of almost every house and building, and an enterprising local off-licence entered into the celebratory spirit by producing commemorative bottles of whisky, labelled Anfield and Goodison. A newly-married couple with split allegiances postponed their honeymoon and planned to spend their first full day of wedded bliss at opposite ends of Wembley. On the day of the game Merseyside resembled a ghost town. A third of the men from the city joined a mass exodus travelling south. Twenty special trains departed from Lime Street Station and another three thousand fans left by coach. Countless street parties took place back home and the unlucky, ticketless fans sat glued to their television sets.

Everton, emerging from the gloom of a 14-year barren spell, were about to enter a glorious new era. Since being so comprehensively outplayed at Anfield in November they had improved considerably, as they showed just three weeks before when the two sides met again at Goodison in a dress rehearsal for the final. Despite taking an early lead through Rush's header at the Gwladys Street End, Everton went close to inflicting a first derby defeat in six years. Graeme Sharp had a second-half penalty saved by Grobbelaar, and six minutes from time former Anfield reserve Alan Harper levelled to give the home side a deserved draw. Local pride may have remained intact, but as a prelude to the final it gave Everton a massive confidence boost. Ian Hargreaves in the *Liverpool Echo* commented: 'Too often in the past they (Everton) have given Liverpool exaggerated respect and paid the penalty for it, but this time at least they got on with playing their own game.'

In a cup final preview piece, David Miller in *The Times* wrote: 'To the rest of the football world, Liverpool versus Everton in the Milk Cup final on Sunday probably seems little more than a provincial and all-too-predictable argument, briefly given some cosmopolitan gloss.' On Merseyside it was billed as the 'match of the century' and keen to avoid any accusations of favouritism the *Echo*'s front-page headline the day before read simply: 'May The Best Team Win'. Given respective League positions and recent history, Liverpool were installed as odds-on favourites. However, Everton manager Howard Kendall was quietly confident that his team could cause an upset. 'I'll be saying we don't have to pay Liverpool *too* much respect. They're expected to win, but this is just one match, and in the last encounter we did well,' he said.

In his diary Joe offered few clues about how he was feeling in the build-up, but he did say: 'To get to Wembley is always a great thrill and a real honour. I'm looking forward to it very much indeed, because it is undoubtedly one of football's great occasions. What's more it's an occasion to enjoy, and I have tried to put that over as much as possible. Of course, you go to Wembley to win, and of course, it's disappointing to lose, but the big thing is to be there in the first place.' As the game loomed the pressure within the city heightened. There was no hiding place for anyone involved.

Kendall stoked the fires by saying: 'I think our players will want to please the supporters more than Liverpool's players will.' It was a claim Ian Rush is quick to refute. 'Our fans would have happily settled for us losing the League and the European Cup as long as we beat our old enemies. That's how important the rivalry is and in the weeks leading up to the game all we kept hearing was, "You've just got to beat Everton".' While Everton's matchday squad contained three locally-born players, Liverpool had just one. But as proud Liverpudlian Sammy Lee insists, that did not lessen their desire. 'I never looked at it that way. We were all one, together as a team,' he says.

On the eve of the final, as convoys of supporters began to head south, Joe and his players settled into the West Lodge Park Hotel in Hertfordshire. Their preparations were briefly interrupted, though, by a late-night intruder. 'At about 4.30 on the morning of the match I was awoken by someone chanting "Everton, Everton",' explains Souness. 'Many of the other lads were woken up as well and Alan Kennedy chased the culprit as far as the lift.' Though a bit bleary-eyed no serious damage was done and the next morning, with pre-match nerves kicking in, Joe did his best to keep everyone calm. 'It's no good going out all tensed up and thinking about nothing except the result,' he told the players. 'You have to enjoy the game and make the most of what is a wonderful opportunity.'

Not even grey skies and incessant rain could dampen the Scouse spirit as one hundred thousand football fans mixed freely beneath the twin towers. Inside the stadium there were unprecedented scenes as red and blue stood and sang side by side on the terraces. 'Families may have been divided for the day but the friendship that embraced the Milk Cup final remained unbroken,' reported *The Times*. Once the talking stopped, and the game got underway, it was Everton who made all the early running. After only six minutes they were claiming vociferously for a penalty. A long punt forward by John Bailey found Graeme Sharp who outjumped the Liverpool defence to send Adrian Heath racing clean through on goal. As Grobbelaar charged off his line Heath chipped the ball goalwards.

Just when it seemed Everton were about to draw first blood, Alan Hansen came to Liverpool's rescue, blocking with what every Liverpool fan will say was his knee and every Evertonian his hand. As the vast Wembley crowd held its collective breath referee Alan Robinson waved play on and the Liverpool half let out a huge sigh of relief. Hansen admitted afterwards that he did touch the ball with his hand, but believes the referee still made the right decision. 'It was never a penalty,' he says. 'The ball rebounded up off my knee and although it struck my hand it wasn't intentional.'

Liverpool looked visibly shaken by the incident and took time to settle into their normal passing game. At the interval, a seething Joe launched into his under-performing players. 'We got the slating we deserved at half-time. Joe told us that it looked as though only two or three of us wanted to play,' recalls Souness. 'He did not single out any one player, but used the Liverpool psychology of letting the players answer for themselves. So even the two or three who had acquitted themselves well would feel unsure and would try that much harder in the second period.' Joe later confessed that 'some industrial language had been used'. He said: 'We could have been 3–0 down. It was basic stuff – not about tactics but getting a change in attitude.'

Liverpool did come out of their shell to some extent in the second half, and it became a more open game. But with neither side able to break the deadlock the match drifted into extra time. However, the break ahead of the additional half-an-hour was marred by a flashpoint for the Liverpool manager. It centred on Craig Johnston who Joe had decided to replace with Michael Robinson. 'Now's ya chance to get Warky on,' snarled a sulking Johnston in reference to the midweek purchase of John Wark. Clearly enraged by what he deemed an act of petulance and selfishness, Joe roared back: 'Do you think the game's all about you, son? Go on, piss off now,' gesturing towards the dressing-room. For the remainder of the game a soaked-through Johnston, a wet blanket draped around his shoulders, cut a forlorn figure on the bench.

Both sides tired in the conditions, though Liverpool gradually gained the upper hand and opportunities came, most notably to Rush who had a couple of gilt-edged chances saved by Neville Southall and another fly over from six yards. 'I think I should have won the game for us,' Rush later recalled. 'I jabbed my foot at the ball too quickly. It hit my shin and looped over the bar. I should have done the simple thing and sidefooted it home.' Southall was beaten twice, but the efforts from Kennedy and Whelan were ruled offside. Given the significance of the occasion, a goalless draw was perhaps the right result. As a spectacle, though, the 1984 Milk Cup final had not lived up to the pre-match hype. But as the two teams embarked on an unprecedented joint lap of honour to salute the fans, it was agreed that 'Merseypride' was the winner. 'Merseyside showed the notoriously cynical footballing world just how it should be done yesterday,' began the match report in the following morning's *Daily Post*. 'Before a worldwide audience of millions the men who proudly wear the famous colours of Everton and Liverpool produced an historic final of momentous proportions.' Howard Kendall said of his team's performance: 'I could not have asked anything more from them. Not many sides could come here and achieve this against Liverpool.' Joe had no complaints. 'Of course, I'd have preferred it if we had won, but at the end when I looked around and listened to all the fans chanting "Merseyside! Merseyside!" I thought, "At least they are all going home happy". On reflection it was a fair result – we didn't play particularly well – no snap, no sparkle – too methodical in thought and action. We seemed to have the win in Benfica on our minds. We tried to play the same way we did out there – like a game of draughts – but there is no way you can do that in English football. We were harried down and it could have cost us the game. Still, we get another bite of the cherry on Wednesday at Maine Road.'

Everton's players and supporters were adamant that their side should have been awarded that first-half penalty against Hansen, a claim backed up by ITV's commentator Brian Moore and studio pundit Ian St John. The general consensus in the press, too, followed a similar theme: that the holders had ridden their luck.

'Liverpool will be grateful for a second chance. But for the oversight of the referee and one of his linesmen, their unbeaten record in the competition, which stretches back over thirty-nine ties, might have come to an end,' reported *The Times*. Monday's *Guardian* said: 'Liverpool will enjoy the luxury of a second chance largely because Everton could not quite muster the knock-out punch.' The verdict of the *Liverpool Echo* was that: 'Everton were certainly not overawed by the occasion', but 'Liverpool's vast experience turned the tide in the second half'.

When the battle resumed in Manchester three nights later a similarly tight encounter was expected. Joe's starting XI was the same as at Wembley and Johnston did not let the bitter taste of Sunday's substitution affect him. This time he completed the full match and played his part on a tense night. It was another memorable occasion, settled by Souness after twenty-one minutes. Receiving a pass from Neal just outside the Everton penalty area, Souness struck a scorching shot low and hard that bobbled on the Maine Road turf and crept narrowly beyond the grasp of Neville Southall. It was enough to win an unprecedented fourth successive League Cup, and the first trophy of Joe's managerial reign. 'Well the lads did it! And well worth it. The man of the match scored the goal and didn't he play well? But let's take nothing away from the other ten – each one deserved their medal for their commitment and attitude. And well done Ronnie and Roy for their help in such an emotional moment,' wrote Joe in his diary. The following morning he comically added: 'What a lovely day whether it is pissing down or not! We won the Cup!'

To get that trophy under his belt was a moment of immense pride and relief to Joe. At least now he would not go down in history as the first Liverpool manager since the 1950s not to win something. 'That win really took the pressure off and you could visibly see the change in him after that,' recalls Bruce Grobbelaar. 'It was as if a huge weight had been lifted from his shoulders. Any man would have been anxious following in the footsteps of Bob Paisley, and

Joe, although he never showed it, was no different. Winning the Milk Cup also gave everyone the belief that more could follow.'

Amid the euphoria of capturing his first piece of silverware Joe had to face up to a problem that had been brewing for some time. It concerned Craig Johnston, the player at the centre of the much-publicised bust-up at Wembley. It was very rare for Joe to fall out with a player. He is widely remembered by those who played under him as a good, fair-minded, man-manager, who knew when a player needed an ear-bashing and when he needed an arm around the shoulder. According to Graeme Souness he was 'a very shrewd character', but his strongest asset was the way he handled people. 'He rarely lost his head and could usually make his point without raising his voice,' says his former captain. 'Under Bob, Joe had acted as a buffer on occasions, taking the sting out of situations before player-manager confrontations, so he was well used to dealing with such problems. If a player had a problem he'd let them have their say and would never hold it against them. He handled things so well that he should have been in the diplomatic service.'

Joe proved he was not one to hold a grudge by selecting Johnston for the replay, but the confrontation at Wembley had threatened to sour an otherwise memorable afternoon. It had never been the Liverpool way to wash dirty linen in public, yet this incident had been witnessed by millions inside and outside the stadium. Johnston's frustration had been slowly bubbling since early in the season when he was not selected in the starting XI for the European Cup tie in Bilbao, despite Javier Clemente's claim that Johnston was 'Liverpool's strongest force'. Joe had been in the game far too long to fall for what he believed to be a cunning touch of Spanish kidology and opted to play Steve Nicol instead. In December, Johnston submitted a written transfer request after discovering he was being dropped to the bench for Liverpool's visit to Highfield Road. His impulsive response was to confront the manager instantly and demand a transfer. Though taken aback by Johnston's reaction, Joe calmly explained his decision to the press and attempted to placate the dissatisfied player. 'Craig has given me a letter asking for a transfer and doesn't feel that I've been fair to him,' he said. 'He has a case. He's played in most of this season's games, done well and I can understand how he feels. He's entitled to his opinion and is quite right to express it. Dropping him wasn't easy and I might find out I've done the wrong thing.' After the humiliating 4–0 defeat by Coventry it was a decision Joe probably did regret. Johnston was subsequently recalled and had been an ever-present since.

With recent signing John Wark now eligible, Joe had a big decision to make ahead of Liverpool's next League match, away at Watford. With Manchester United now leading the table by a point, and having scored twelve goals more than Liverpool, Wark's attacking instinct would provide a much-needed extra goal threat. Johnston was the obvious candidate to make way, but Joe ran the risk of inflicting further damage to their already fragile relationship. 'Craig was a great lad but he was prone to fly off the handle at times if not playing and I feared that Joe was maybe too nice to cope with it,' remembers Souness. 'But I should have known better because he handled it superbly.' After much deliberation, Joe did what he deemed best for the football club, as always. 'It is decision day regarding Wark,' he entered in his diary. 'I am going to put him in for Johnston. I think he may bring more stability to the midfield. Also he can score goals and maybe he can get the ball a bit better than Craig. I am sorry to have to do it but this is the part of the job that I get paid for. It is all right winning Milk Cups but that is not all I am here for. It is to try and improve the first team. Sorry, Craig.'

Joe was well aware it was a decision that could have backfired on him. But he was proved correct as Wark celebrated his Liverpool debut with the opening goal in an important 2–0 victory at Vicarage Road, starting and finishing the move that resulted in him shooting low into the far corner. 'To be honest I was surprised to be playing,' admits Wark. 'The team had won the Milk Cup in midweek and I thought Joe Fagan would keep the same team. But he threw me in at the expense of Craig Johnston and Craig was really gutted about the situation. Whether the decision was right or wrong I don't know, but I scored and we won.' Rush, newly crowned as PFA Player of the Year, scored his thirty-sixth of the season for number two. With United losing 2–0 at West Bromwich Albion it was a pivotal afternoon in the title race as the leading two swapped places.

The Craig Johnston controversy continued to rumble on and Joe admitted: 'I am pleased for John Wark and disappointed for Craig – and this is a statement from the heart. Craig has taken it with quiet dignity. Before when I left him out he came storming in. This time I said to him, "Would you like to be sub?" And he just said, "Yes please". I was almost too embarrassed to tell him he wasn't playing because players have to have feelings and emotions. I sincerely hope he stays with us because he is a very good player.' In his autobiography *Walk Alone*, the player offered a slightly different version of events. 'Whenever I had fronted the boss about my non-selection problems he would fall back on the standard quote of managers and coaches the world over, "I will not change a winning team". I made the mistake of taking Joe Fagan at his word. When it came to me he made exceptions to his own rules. I sat in the team meeting two days after the League Cup triumph feeling confident I had secured my place for another week at least.'

Johnston's unrest would surface again, but with a place in the European Cup final at stake it was sensibly put to one side. At least, from his new vantage point in the dug-out, Johnston had one of the best seats in the house to sit back and enjoy the show as Liverpool turned on the style to destroy West Ham 6–0. It was a ruthless demolition, and described by Joe as 'one of our best displays of the season'. It was also witnessed by spies from Dinamo Bucharest, against whom Liverpool had been drawn in the European semi-final. In terms of stature, the Romanian champions were not among the glamour sides one would expect to be competing in the last four. However, given Liverpool's recent record against Eastern Bloc opposition – they had been knocked out by Bulgaria's C.S.K.A.

Sofia and Widzew Lodz of Poland in 1982 and 1983 respectively –
Joe and his backroom staff were more than a little wary of the threat
they would pose. In the earlier rounds Bucharest had eliminated
holders Hamburg and the formidable Dynamo Minsk. With A.S.
Roma and Dundee United contesting the other semi-final, the
Romanians were considered the dark horses of the last four. Back
in August Dinamo had ran Liverpool close in an evenly-fought pre-
season friendly, but Joe was expecting there to be a much more
competitive edge to this tie.

He was right. The visitors came to Anfield intent on spoiling the
game as a spectacle and the ultra-defensive tactics frustrated
Liverpool. In one of the most bad-tempered encounters witnessed
by the Kop, a succession of spiteful fouls by the eastern Europeans
made it a scrappy, stop-start affair. 'They hacked, kicked and
battered their way through us,' said Ian Rush. Four Dinamo men
had their names taken by Swiss referee Andre Daina. While the
Liverpool players did their best not to rise to the bait, one
Romanian, Lica Moliva, was left with his jaw broken in two places
following a collision with Graeme Souness that went unnoticed.
Souness later explained his side of the story in his autobiography.
'Movila was the worst of the lot. He was a disgrace. He kicked
everything that moved and three times caught me with punches off
the ball. I went completely crazy when he came in late and high yet
again and as he half turned I let loose with the best punch I have
delivered in my life.' It was not a night that will be remembered too
fondly by the 36,941 present. The only bright spot was the rare sight
of the diminutive Sammy Lee heading home the winning goal from
Kennedy's free-kick after Johnston, back in the team because of
Wark's ineligibility, had been scythed down. In Joe's eyes,
Dinamo's performance had left a bitter taste. 'I have never seen
such cynical fouling by a team. It wasn't a football match it was just
them trying to stop us playing. It will be hard over there, but bugger
it – why worry? We can only do our best.' Equally appalled were
the British press and David Miller in *The Times*, wrote: 'Dinamo,
who quite clearly have more ability than they now demonstrated,

produced over the ninety minutes every demeaning trick in the book. They feigned injury, lying on the ground for minutes at a time, and they kicked their opponents indiscriminately.' It did not augur well for the second leg and with just a slender one-goal advantage Miller warned that Liverpool would be 'hard pressed to defend their lead and even more certainly their limbs'.

As soon as Liverpool touched down in Romania for the return leg all focus was on Souness following the incident at Anfield 'The atmosphere was distinctly chilly,' recalls Grobbelaar. 'Going through customs and again as we sat on the coach, first uniformed officials and then men in leather coats made extremely threatening gestures, many of which were directed at Souness.' In the eyes of the locals, Souness was public enemy number one and his every touch during the warm-up was booed. Such a level of hostility had rarely been witnessed in Liverpool's previous seasons in Europe and Joe was keen to ensure his vilified captain did not rise to the bait. 'Don't get too involved,' he told him. 'Deal with it if they come looking for you, but just play your football and don't get sent off.' Souness evidently took note of his manager's advice and proceeded to turn in one of his finest performances in a red shirt. When he came off at the end his socks may have been ripped to shreds, but in the face of great intimidation he kept his cool, led by example and dictated play. Within eleven minutes, Rush's one hundredth goal for the club had doubled Liverpool's aggregate advantage. 'I couldn't have picked a better occasion,' said Rush. 'But when everyone is against you, as it seemed here, Liverpool have a habit of rising to the occasion.' Orac pulled one back before Rush's second, six minutes from time, gave Liverpool another famous European away victory and, more importantly, a place in the European Cup final.

It was a momentous achievement, and brought about a rare show of emotion in the dressing-room afterwards, as Souness recalls: 'We were all screaming, shouting and dancing about in celebration after winning through to the final, then Joe come in and bellowed at the top of his voice, which again was rare, "All of you just shut up and sit down!" We're all thinking, "Bloody hell, Joe, what's up with you?" The dressing-room fell silent. He looked at us all and then screamed, "You fucking beauties!" With that, the whole place just erupted again and the party continued. It showed just how much that victory meant to him. Usually, the Liverpool way of thinking was you get nothing for winning semi-finals, but for Joe it was so satisfying to have won against such odds and amid so much intimidation.' The then England manager Bobby Robson, at the game to run the rule over several Romanian players against whom his team would be playing in a forthcoming World Cup qualifier, rated Liverpool's performance as the best by an away side in Europe he had seen. It was high praise and deservedly so. Joe was rightly proud of his players and reflected: 'Every one of them did their share and more. They didn't seem to have any nerves – I had them all for us! After taking some heavy tackling and not retaliating we deserved to win and go through to Rome for the final.' So elated was Joe that he let his guard down momentarily and, for the first time, mentioned the 'T' word when admitting: 'I am thinking at this moment of the Treble of the League and two cups.'

While supporters began planning for a second trip to Rome, Joe and his backroom team had a massive job on their hands to maintain the players' focus on the immediate task in hand, which was wrapping up Liverpool's fifteenth Football League championship. The battle with Bucharest had been an intense one and in the midst of it all Liverpool had been guilty of taking their eyes off the ball where domestic matters were concerned – a cardinal sin at Anfield. Sandwiched between the two legs of the semi-final the League leaders took just four points from a possible nine, with the damaging results coming against teams in the bottom half of the table. The most alarming was the shock 2–0 defeat at Stoke. According to Joe: 'Too many players had no legs and no zip to carry us through.' It was a worryingly below-par display, typified by the performance of Dalglish, who struggled to get going and was eventually substituted. The manager rated it as 'his worst game in years', and added: 'He looked thoroughly bored and out of touch.' Souness's frustration at throwing away three points, giving Manchester United the chance to catch Liverpool at the top, resulted in him smashing his hand through the glass in the dressing-room door, leaving him with a nasty cut. However, when news came through from Meadow Lane of United's 1–0 defeat by second-to-bottom Notts County, his team-mates' sympathy was replaced by laughter. Against Leicester at Filbert Street, John Wark scored late to salvage a point in a six-goal thriller, while it needed a Ken McNaught own goal to set up Liverpool for a home victory against West Bromwich Albion.

Five League games now remained and just two points separated the top two. While Liverpool were celebrating in Bucharest, second-placed United were coming to terms with a last-gasp defeat in Turin that denied them a place in the final of the European Cup-Winners' Cup. Without the suspended Souness, Liverpool appeared to be suffering from a European hangover when they returned to League action against Ipswich at Anfield. Despite coming from behind to lead 2–1 at the interval, Eric Gates netted his second of the game to seal a 2–2 draw that could still have proved costly to Liverpool's title ambitions. Victory for United at home to West Ham would have seen them move level on points. Amazingly, they again failed to capitalise and were also held to a draw, which left the majority of journalists predicting that the title looked like being 'lost rather than won'. The recurring inability of Ron Atkinson's side to seize the initiative – they could only draw again the following week while Liverpool were being held at Birmingham – eventually allowed the champions to ease towards the finishing line. Joe later admitted that he never considered them a threat. 'You could always read the script with United,' he said. 'I felt there was something predictable about them. I felt that even if we slipped up they wouldn't win it. I felt we could read them more than either Southampton or QPR.'

That is not to say the title was handed to Liverpool on a plate. There was still work to be done and on May Bank Holiday Monday

Liverpool made a timely return to winning ways on what was a pivotal and historical afternoon. After wondering 'where a goal would come from in the first forty minutes', Joe's anxiety eased when Rush took centre stage. The first of his four goals in the 5–0 drubbing of Coventry took him beyond Roger Hunt's long-standing club record of forty-two goals in a season. Rush's third of the afternoon, from the penalty spot, ensured he also became the first player since his boyhood idol Bob Latchford in 1978 to breach the 30-goal barrier in Division One. Joe was well aware of what a special talent Rush was, and though never one to go overboard, in his post-match notes he marvelled: 'It is amazing how this lad Rush is always in the right position to score – but it is nice!' A rare Alan Hansen goal completed the scoring and avenged the heavy defeat at Highfield Road earlier in the season. It left Joe on the threshold of a feat no other debutant manager in English football had achieved. On the same afternoon, Manchester United's 2–1 home defeat by Ipswich meant Liverpool now required two points from a possible six to become champions again. They also had a superior goal difference, and only a very brave punter would have bet against them.

Their penultimate League fixture was away at relegated Notts County. On a bright and blustery afternoon in Nottingham, Liverpool barely got out of second gear. They did not need to. With United drawing at Tottenham, the point gained clinched Liverpool's third successive title. Hordes of Liverpudlians had swamped Meadow Lane in anticipation, and though the dour goalless draw that followed will not be remembered as fondly as the title-clinchers at Molineux in 1976, or Stamford Bridge a decade later, it failed to put a dampener on the post-match party. The final whistle was the cue for fans to swarm across the pitch in celebration of history being made: Liverpool had emulated the legendary Huddersfield and Arsenal teams of yesteryear with three titles in a row.

In typical style, the victorious Liverpool manager celebrated this most momentous of achievements by sweeping the dressing-room floor at Meadow Lane. In his first season as a manager he had just guided his team to the greatest prize in English football and there he was, concerned only with leaving the place as he had found it. If any one moment summed him up it was this. Most other managers in his position would have milked the occasion for what it was worth. Joe's only act of over-indulgence was to give a rare television interview to BBC *Match of the Day* commentator John Motson. It was a piece of TV that perfectly encapsulated the personality of the man.

JM: Joe, nineteen trophies in nine seasons must have brought enormous pressure?

JF: At the end of the day I must say congratulations to all the players, to all the supporters and to everyone at Liverpool Football Club.

JM: Fantastic achievement for the club, the first to do it in three successive years since Arsenal in the 1930s …

JF: Not bad, not bad at all, is it? I don't think we ever think about these things. I think we leave it to other people to sort the erm, the erm …

JM: Statistics?

JF: Statistics yeah. Couldn't say that word, John, and still can't say it! (Laughter)

JM: And the European Cup still to come.

JF: No comment!

With that, he shook hands and was off. By the time the BBC interview aired later that night Joe was celebrating in his own inimitable way, sat in front of the television with a large scotch for company. Joe's diary entry for Saturday, 12 May, 1984, read simply: 'Well the lads did it! We are the champions!! Well done everybody. A lovely day! A nice feeling having won the League and not having to sweat on the last game.'

It was an occasion Alan Hansen remembers vividly. 'The game that clinches the title is always special. We were always in control and near the top that season, but it is like a sense of relief knowing that you have finally won the championship. I remember sitting in the dressing-room at Notts County and thinking, "We've done it again". It was a terrific feeling.' It was also a proud moment for full-back Phil Neal, who was enjoying a record-equalling seventh title success. 'It was a difficult season. We won it by a mile the year before, and came through from twelfth in 1981–82, but this time we had to graft,' he says. Joe was also the proud recipient of a seventh championship medal. With the others having been won while on the coaching staff this meant much more, and he admitted: 'I've got six kids and they've each got a medal, but I'm going to keep this one.'

Liverpool chairman John Smith rated this latest success as the pinnacle of the club's history. Never normally one to give press interviews, he said afterwards: 'It's been my greatest ambition to emulate the great Arsenal side of the 1930s, the last team to win the championship three years in succession. Now we've done it and it's the greatest moment in the history of our club.' Debate about which side was the best predictably surfaced and Smith was quick to add: 'When Arsenal and Huddersfield did it there was no European football and no League Cup.' Ian Hargreaves of the *Liverpool Echo* shared a similar belief. 'Arsenal's overall domination of the English game in the 1930s was similar to Liverpool's present command, but I doubt if even they were so capable of coping with so many problems. In those days there was only the FA Cup to occupy the attention.'

The majority of national newspapers were quick to recognise the scale of Liverpool's achievement. The *Daily Mail*'s Colin Wood stated that it 'must rank among the greatest achievements in the history of English football'. Vince Wilson in the *Sunday Mirror* went one better by declaring 'Joe Fagan's boys' as 'the greatest English club team of all time'. Not all the journalists, though, were entirely convinced and Peter Ball wrote in *The Times*: 'Nothing in their display did anything to dispel the view that this championship has been won as much by the failings of others as by their own efforts.' Graeme Souness readily admits that, by Liverpool's high standards of the time, it was not a vintage title-winning campaign, but insists they were more than worthy winners. 'At other clubs it would have been deemed a great League season, but for us it was no better than a good one. Saying that, we were still better than anyone else. You don't win the title on luck and over nine months we deserved it,' he insists. Ian Rush says: 'We were a better team that season than the previous two. I think some papers were just getting bored of us winning all the time.'

Strangely, apart from Norman Wynne's *Sunday People* report that contained the line, 'It will go down in history as the greatest first season any manager could have achieved', there was little individual praise in the national press for Joe's part in it all. This, of course, suited Joe down to the ground. He would have wanted it no other way. He was always more comfortable handing out praise than receiving it. Instead, he singled out the contributions of his players. 'Souness is my man of the year,' he said. 'We needed Ian Rush's goals, but over the year, for his leadership, performance, attitude and total commitment I pick Graeme. You need something special to be champions and we have that with people like Graeme and Kenny Dalglish. Even though Kenny has not played as well as he can recently, he still makes an indefinable contribution. It's something you can't explain like you can with Ian Rush, who sticks the ball in the back of the net. I have also great admiration this season for our central defenders Mark Lawrenson and Alan Hansen.'

It had been a very satisfactory season for the defence as a whole. Four of the back five had been ever present; only Neal missed one game, at Old Trafford in September. As Hansen explains, such stability at the back instilled confidence in the whole team. 'If you have a settled side and a settled defence then you are in front before you start. We had a lot of regulars in defence that season and that was obviously a big help to the side.'

The remainder of that weekend allowed Joe to reflect in more detail on just what he had achieved. The following Monday he shared his considered opinions on the title race. 'It finished up the right way in the end but it's been a nerve-wracking time. It's just beginning to sink in and I am glad the issue has been settled now. I thought it would go to the final game. I was nearly right but thank God I was wrong. I have had quite enough of the anxiety and tension. There were plenty of times, especially during April, when I wondered if we were going to make it. We lost at Southampton, and then later we were beaten at Stoke, and each time I wondered if we were going to let it slip. Fortunately we got a very good result at Watford, in John Wark's first game for us, and then we managed to beat West Bromwich at Anfield after they had missed a couple of good chances. We never got really ahead. It may have looked as though we were quite relaxed, but I can tell you the tension was there. This season we have played some good football, but it has been a battle all the way through. Injuries to important players upset us a little along the way but we fought through those times and showed a lot of character.'

The official presentation of the Canon League trophy was held over until the final home game of the season against Norwich. Rush's goal secured a 1–1 draw to take Liverpool's points tally for the campaign to eighty. The Anfield fans refused to go home, staying in their places until thirty minutes after the final whistle and waiting for the players and management to emerge from the dressing-room for one final salute.

The loudest cheer was reserved for one of their own. Liverpudlians had a long history of backing their manager through thick and thin, but never before had the man in charge been a fellow Scouser. It was a special moment for all concerned when he raised his arms aloft to acknowledge the Kop. The appreciation was mutual. Even the most die-hard Liverpool supporters would admit to not knowing that much about Joe when he took over as manager. The players who had worked with him for years were obviously well aware of the qualities he possessed. Now the fans had realised, too. 'That was very emotional and something I did not expect,' he said. 'But tonight is not about me, it is about the players, the lads downstairs, the directors and the fans.'

Joe Fagan had finally earned himself a place in the hearts of every Liverpool supporter. Now footballing immortality beckoned. For anyone else, one trophy, never mind two, would have been enough; not for Joe, he was still hungry for more. The greatest prize of them all shimmered tantalisingly on the horizon as all thoughts turned to Rome.

CHAPTER NINE

'I DON'T KNOW WHAT IT IS (BUT I LOVE IT!)'

H IGH UP AMONG the abundant trees on one of the seven hills above Rome, the players of A.S. Roma were forced to endure a monk-like existence in preparation for the 1984 European Cup final. Coach Nils Liedholm wanted nothing to distract them from the task in hand. Shut away from their families to ensure they remained fully focused, their only contact with the outside world was the bus ride that took them to the Olympic Stadium each night to train. Around the same time, fourteen hundred miles away on a beach in Israel, the Liverpool squad were also preparing for the big game, but in their own inimitable way: relaxing in the sun, nursing a hangover from the night before and arguing among themselves about who was going to get the next round of beers in.

To onlookers this could not possibly be a team who in little more than a week's time would be battling for the greatest prize in European club football. It seemed like they did not have a care in the world. Laidback and loose, the Liverpool lads appeared more like a Sunday League team on an end-of-season jolly. More remarkable is the fact that the trip had been organised and overseen with the blessing of manager Joe Fagan, who was there enjoying the break with them. 'It was a trip that summed up just how much he treated us like the adults we were,' says Graeme Souness. 'He imposed no curfews or restrictions on us out there. We were allowed to relax, enjoy the sun and have a few drinks.'

*

Observing Liverpool's antics in the Holy Land was a group of Italian journalists. They had been sent over with the brief of gaining an up-close insight into the Liverpool psyche and to see if their so-called preparations would offer any clues as to how they would line up in Rome. They received none of the latter but the news wires back to Italy were red-hot with stories of Liverpool's 'unprofessional' approach. 'I'd like to say we were the very essence of professionals with our minds fixed firmly on the prize,' says Craig Johnston, 'but I'd be lying. We hit the booze from the outset in Tel Aviv. What the hell! It had been a tough season, we'd already won two trophies and nobody gave us a chance of winning the third with it being on Roma's own patch.'

As preparations for the most prestigious inter-club contest on the Continent go there could not have been a more stark contrast. But the 'crazy Englishman', Joe Fagan, knew exactly what he was doing. The Liverpool squad had flown to Israel on the eve of the FA Cup final, twenty-four hours after taking part in a testimonial on Tyneside for former Anfield idol Kevin Keegan, and twelve days before their date with destiny in Rome. With the Tel Aviv temperature high in the eighties, and the climate similar to that of the Italian capital, it was considered a good conditioning exercise. After a long and hard domestic season, club officials did not try to disguise the fact that it was also an opportunity for the players to let off some steam ahead of the final. Gary Gillespie says: 'It was a long time to dwell on things, and be at home. All you do is monotonous day-to-day training. So it was suggested that we went to Israel for the week, and it was a real blow-out, a real blast. It was all about camaraderie.'

Just as in Italy, all the talk back home now centred on the impending final and whether Liverpool could become the first English team to win three trophies in one season. Getting the players away from the goldfish bowl of Merseyside was certainly not a bad thing. The *Daily Post* believed so and felt that Liverpool came back 'refreshed by the longest break in their marathon season'.

As Ronnie Whelan remembers: 'It was one hell of a bonding session and a great idea because it got us away from the pressure that was building back home. It was complete relaxation, a good laugh, a few drinks and some late nights.'

Of course, there was a bit of football thrown in, too. For the final warm-up match Liverpool were without Ian Rush, who had flown home for international duty with Wales, and Alan Hansen, who sat it out as a precaution after picking up a slight thigh strain. However, Liverpool convincingly defeated the Israeli national team 4–1 with two goals by Whelan and one apiece from Souness and Robinson. The mood in the Liverpool camp could not have been better. Like a prize fighter, their training had been timed to perfection and they were in peak condition, chomping at the bit.

Back in Italy the tension was mounting. The streets of the capital were being decked out in readiness for the locals to party on a scale never witnessed before. Almost everywhere there was maroon red and golden yellow bunting being hung in honour of the *Giallorossi*, and banners prematurely declaring A.S. Roma '*Campeone '84*' were flying high. This was Roma's first appearance in the final of the competition and with home advantage the unthinkable was not even being contemplated. Confidence was heightened as news of what the Liverpool team were up to filtered back from Israel. Little did they realise that the first seeds had been sown for the ultimate European triumph.

A.S. Roma were competing in the Champions Cup for the first time. A star-studded squad included Brazil's attacking midfielder Roberto Falcao, his international team-mate Toninho Cerezo, two of Italy's 1982 World Cup-winning side in Bruno Conti and Francesco Graziani, and one of Italian football's most intelligent playmakers in captain Agostino Di Bartolomei. Thanks to their impregnable home form Roma had overcome the challenge of Gothenburg, C.S.K.A. Sofia, Dynamo Berlin and Dundee United en route to the final, without conceding a goal at home. If facing a team of that calibre in the final was a tough enough task in itself, then the fact the game was being staged on their own ground stacked the odds heavily against Liverpool. Not that they complained. It was not the first time a team had played a European Cup final on their home turf and UEFA were not going to change their mind at this late stage. Anyway, Liverpool could boast a one hundred per cent record on their European travels that season and Joe believed that playing in the opposition's backyard could work to his side's benefit. 'We don't mind,' he said. 'It doesn't mean a thing. We take everything in our stride as it comes along, and always have done. Our chaps grow bigger when the atmosphere is there.'

Of course, Liverpool and the Eternal City needed no introduction. In 1977, a mass exodus of close to thirty thousand Scousers made the pilgrimage for the club's first European Cup final appearance. This time it would be different. Only half that number of fans would be allowed to travel in 1984 and, as those who did make the journey were to discover, the atmosphere would be a lot more volatile. Short on managerial experience he may have been, especially compared to his opposite number Liedholm who had recently celebrated twenty-one years as a manager, but Joe had been there, seen it and done it all during the course of his long career. This particular challenge held no fears for him. What was more, his calm air of authority once again kept everyone at ease. Relaxing on a beach in the build-up to the biggest match of the season may have seemed to Italian eyes like gross unprofessionalism, but according to Ian Rush: 'It was a stroke of genius that would never be allowed to happen now.'

Though never one to bother with meaty dossiers on the opposition, video tapes of A.S. Roma games started arriving at Anfield in early May. Unlike today when every minute detail is analysed, and analysed again, it was not something Joe placed too much emphasis on. He commented in his diary at the time: 'If I go through all this I will feel like we can't play. Too much can bog your own team down and make you forget to let them worry about you.' Joe's philosophy was clear, but nothing was being left to chance with the

European Cup at stake. He went over to Italy himself to watch Roma just four days after the semi-final second leg in Bucharest and saw them defeat Fiorentina. After that he concluded: 'Roma have a lot of stars right through their side and are a credit to the game. I was impressed by Pruzzo who is very strong in the air and also Conti. They were obviously feeling the effect of their game against Dundee United in midweek and tired in the second half. It should be a classic final. I would have liked to see Falcao in action but perhaps there will be another opportunity.'

With Liverpool closing in on the First Division title he never did get that opportunity. However, the job of completing Liverpool's homework was passed on to Anfield's esteemed 'Euro-spy' Tom Saunders. After running the rule over Roma, Saunders delivered the following verdict: 'Having seen them play three times, once away from home, it is fair to say that they perform better on their own pitch. Bob Paisley considered that they were the best team he has seen in the competition so far and we shall need to be at our best to deal with them. My own view is that if Falcao and Di Bartolomei perform as they can do, the battle will need to be won in midfield.'

The scouting report and video tapes confirmed that A.S. Roma were indeed a quality side. The information gathered was priceless in terms of how Joe and his coaching staff prepared for the game, but the manager was wary of relaying too much of it to his team. 'We knew the calibre of players they had in their team but that was about it,' remembers Souness. 'We were shown no video tapes of them, no one spoke to us about their set-piece routines and we were unaware of what formation Roma played. That's just the way it was at Liverpool back then, though, and it didn't do us any harm. Sometimes you can over-complicate matters and worry players. Joe Fagan was never big on pre-match speeches about the opposition. It was all about what we did on the pitch and his attitude was always, "Let the opposition worry about us, rather than us worry about them".'

*

On their return from Israel Joe could sense that his men were ready. Over the course of the last weekend the players were given light training only. 'I remember being within earshot of a conversation between Joe and Ronnie Moran just a few days before we flew out to Rome,' recalls Mark Lawrenson, 'and I overheard him saying that training would have to be toned down. Everybody was so up for the game that the coaches were ordered to hold us back in case we peaked too soon.'

There was one last training session at Melwood on the Monday. Again it was nothing too strenuous, just a few limbering-up exercises, a gentle jog around the perimeter and the usual light-hearted five-a-sides. To finish, the players were ordered to practise penalties and the youth team were summoned from another pitch to help out. Legend has it that the kids won 5–0. Over a quarter of a century on, and memories now a bit sketchy, some players dispute the exact scoreline. But whether it was 4–1, 5–1 or 5–2 does not really matter. Liverpool had never been involved in a competitive penalty shoot-out before, and on the evidence of that final training session at Melwood Joe hoped it stayed that way.

In an attempt to keep preparation for the match as normal as possible Joe was keen that the team did not arrive in Rome too early, and he delayed flying out until the latest possible moment. Despite maintaining his usual outer air of confidence the first sign of nerves seemed to even be affecting Joe at this point. Thirty-six hours before kick-off, as they were waved off from Liverpool's Speke Airport, the manager told journalists: 'Some people may be able to stay nice and relaxed, but not me. I can always see how the other side is going to break through and their players tend to look tremendous.'

The sense of occasion was steadily building and Joe was careful not to ignite further what was already going to be a hostile atmosphere when they reached their destination. Before Dundee United's visit to Rome in the semi-final, manager Jim McLean had enraged the Italians by accusing them of time-wasting and cheating. But with the tactfulness of a special peace envoy, Joe refused to become embroiled in such talk, adding: 'Roma are a very, very good team. So are we and I just hope that between us we can give Europe a game to remember with pride. This final has all the makings of a classic. You have two fine teams who both like to attack and some of the best individuals in Europe. Make no mistake about it, we are going to Rome to try and win that cup and I am sure Roma feel exactly the same. We shall both be playing it fast and tight, and for us the result is almost everything. I think we have a reputation for sportsmanship and skilful play, and that we have earned respect wherever we go.'

When the Liverpool squad touched down in Italy, excitement in Rome was at fever pitch. The city was preparing to party like never before and every Italian was only too willing to tell the Liverpool players they need not have bothered turning up. In their eyes Roma were the European champions-elect, and perhaps with good reason. Roma may have surrendered the Scudetto to Juventus, but they had prevailed in the Coppa Italia and, as Tom Saunders had been quick to note, could boast a formidable record in front of their own partisan fans. Kenny Dalglish admits he rated Roma's class of 1984 as 'probably the best in Europe at the time', while Alan Hansen believes Liverpool 'definitely went into the game as underdogs'.

Joe had other ideas and, when facing the media at his pre-match press conference, tried his best to make light of the daunting challenge that lay ahead. According to *Daily Post* journalist Ian Ross: 'He charmed the world's press in typical fashion.' He paid Roma the respect they deserved, but at the same time was equally eager to get his message across that Liverpool were not worried about the opposition. Smiling and joking throughout, he played it perfectly and, with a glint in his eye, sent startled Italian journalists scurrying excitedly back to their desks with the quote: 'Our team talk will be longer than usual for this one – about five minutes.' It was a classic piece of reverse psychology, one that Bob Paisley used to call 'a bit of toffee'. The local scribes certainly bit and news of Liverpool's apparent complacency was quickly passed on to the already confident Roman ranks.

Joe's low-key build-up ensured an air of quiet confidence had gradually been instilled in the mindset of those in the Liverpool camp. And while Souness was of the belief that 'this will be the hardest game in Liverpool's history', he now believes Joe's management of the situation was pivotal. 'Our preparation couldn't have been any different to Roma's, but we were totally relaxed and that gave us a belief that we wouldn't be beaten,' he says. 'We may have been playing Roma in Rome but the general feeling among the lads as the game approached was that something unlucky would have to happen for us not to get something out of it. Four or five of us would have to have an off-day, and that didn't happen too often, or they would have to play exceptionally well to turn us over.'

With street carnivals already taking place in anticipation of Roma's triumph the players were expecting a difficult night's sleep. Indeed, room-mates Dalglish and Souness were kept awake until the early hours. But as Dalglish remembers it had nothing to do with noisy locals. 'We couldn't get to sleep because of a terrible racket coming from the next room. We banged on the wall, shouted "quiet", but our noisy neighbour still wouldn't turn his radio down. So we phoned down to reception to complain. Within a minute or so, the noise stopped. Reception had obviously called up and told whoever it was to turn his radio off. When we got up in the morning, we found out that it was Joe Fagan's room!'

Earlier that night, at a UEFA dinner attended by a delegation of Liverpool directors, match referee Mr Erik Frederiksson of Sweden was asked who he thought would win, to which he replied, 'Roma have to be favourites.' It was an inappropriate question and an unfortunate answer at an inopportune moment. Though it would be wrong to draw false conclusions, such comments could easily be misconstrued. After all, allegations of attempted corruption in Continental competition was nothing new, especially in Italy, as Brian Glanville and his colleague Keith Botsford highlighted in their 'Years of the Golden Fix' investigation for the Sunday Times. Liverpool had suffered an unhappy experience at the hands of

Italian opposition before, when eliminated from the European Cup by Internazionale in the semi-final in 1965. After a thrilling 3–1 victory at Anfield, Shankly's side crashed to a 3–0 defeat in the San Siro, with two of the goals considered controversial. It was a defeat that still rankled at Anfield and one that Joe admitted in later years almost reduced him to tears. A distraught Shankly later told journalist John Keith that he had been told beforehand that whatever happened his team would not win. He said at the time that the image of Spanish referee Ortiz de Mendibil would haunt him until his dying day. In their published investigation, Glanville and Botsford alleged that this was the second of three occasions in the 1960s when 'Inter made offers to referees in the second legs of European Cup semi-finals to be played at the San Siro'. They also accused Juventus of doing likewise in 1973. However, nothing has ever been proved in a court of law and no action has ever been taken against the clubs implicated.

Roma's victory over the champions of Scotland in the semi-final had also left a sour taste. In the first leg at Tannadice Jim McLean's side had built up a 2–0 lead and hopes of an unprecedented all-British final were high. When the two sides met in Rome a fortnight later Dundee United had their dreams scuppered amid allegations that Roma officials tried to bribe the referee. The hosts comfortably overturned the deficit, running out 3–0 winners. Despite Dundee United's suspicions, no probe was ever launched. Again, nothing has ever been proved. However, in March 2011 Roma director Riccardo Viola, a board member at the time and son of the club's late president Dino, admitted to Italian television company Mediaset Premium that 'Roma gave a middle man one hundred million lire (£50,000) destined for referee Vautrot. That is true and a shameful fact. This was done because we had a difficult game ahead of us against Dundee United. Going out of the competition would have had serious repercussions.'

This atmosphere of suspicion led to assumptions of gamesmanship on the morning of the match when Liverpool arrived for one last light training session. The Italians had arranged a pitch for them on the outskirts of the city. When the Liverpool party arrived it was immediately clear that it was unsuitable, even for them to stretch their legs. 'When he got off the bus Joe just took one look at it and said we'd go for a walk instead. There was absolutely no way he was going to let us train on that,' says Mark Lawrenson. 'You should have seen the state of it, it was terrible. If ever a surface was designed to cause problems, and possibly injuries, this was it. I wouldn't have taken my dog for a walk on it, let alone use it for a team of footballers, it was so badly rutted. The dirty tricks had started and I think some of our lads thought there and then, "Right, we're going to have these".'

As always in situations like this a siege mentality took hold and Joe used this to the team's advantage, repeating more than once as kick-off drew closer: 'They don't want us to win this.' By the time the players awoke from their afternoon pre-match nap and turned on the television sets in their hotel rooms they were greeted by the awesome sight of a Stadio Olimpico that, with five hours to go, was already two-thirds full. 'I've got to be honest with you, it was the most intimidating sight I've ever seen in my life,' remembers Hansen. 'It was frightening how much those fans wanted Roma to win that match. It put fear into me.' Joe was determined to keep a lid on the mounting tension. The team gathered for their pre-match meal, at which point the manager made a timely intervention to lighten the mood. 'I remember Joe having to inform us of a new directive from UEFA instructing players not to run towards the crowd if a goal was scored,' recalls Lawrenson. 'Joe amended that when he read it out to "when we score a goal", and not "if". He went on to add, "When we score our goals do as UEFA say for the first two, but do what you like if we get any more". It was a nice touch because apart from demonstrating his confidence it helped to ease the inevitable tension which was beginning to build up.'

Souness says: 'Just after we'd finished our meal Joe stood up in the dining room of the hotel and asked the waiters to leave the room because he wanted to speak with his players in private. We're all looking at each other thinking this is a first, but then he sort of started mumbling to himself about Roma and how they must be a good team because they'd reached the final of the European Cup. Everyone was glued to what he was saying and expecting this big impassioned speech, but then he just turns round and says, "But they're not as good as us. Now the bus leaves at such a time so make sure you get plenty of rest before then and don't be late!" It was typical Joe and it put everyone at ease.'

As day turned to night the mood on the streets of the Italian capital began to turn ugly, a sad precursor to events in Brussels twelve months later. Liverpool fan Jegsy Dodd, who had followed the club all over Europe since 1977, recalled how he landed in Rome early that morning and could sense the growing air of menace even then. 'Within an hour of arriving, it became apparent we were not welcome. No sooner had we reached the street than it started. It seemed as though the whole city was staring or shouting at us. We kept on walking, regardless, ending up by a kind of open-air market. At first they started chucking bits of fruit at us. Then, next minute, they attacked us. This was not a good sign.' *Daily Mirror* columnist Brian Reade, another well-travelled Liverpool fan, was also in Rome for what was his third European Cup final. 'Riot police laden with guns and CS gas, herded us on to buses which had been assigned armed outriders,' he remembers. 'Speeding towards the ground a soon-to-be-familiar sight greeted us. Youths with scarves covering their faces riding alongside us on Vespa scooters at motorway pace, flashing knives and making slitting gestures across their throats.' As many of their fellow Liverpudlians in Rome discovered, there was no hiding place for anyone with an English accent or sporting a hint of red and white. Tony Evans, now football editor of *The Times* but then a trombone player with Scouse Indie band The Farm, recalls: 'There had been much trouble in the tourist areas, with gangs of locals on scooters chasing down small groups or stragglers among the Liverpool fans and slashing them as they passed. Often at away games there were rumours about stabbings and beatings, but they almost always came from the proto-hooligans. Here they were coming from reputable sources.' By the end of the night up to forty Liverpool fans required hospital treatment, five suffering stab wounds.

The Liverpool team bus was another obvious target. As it approached the stadium rocks and other debris rained down as the noise of sirens and exploding fireworks was heard in the distance. Rather than intimidate Joe and his players it made them even more determined to go out and poop the party. Once inside the modern-day Roman amphitheatre, the players were allowed to go out for a wander while Joe and his staff made sure the kit and boots were laid out correctly. The atmosphere on the terraces, which had been steadily building throughout the afternoon, had reached a crescendo. Impressive and intimidating in equal measure it may have been, but so relaxed and confident were the Liverpool players that they simply took it all in their stride. With the help of a song by a then relatively unknown singer from the North-East of England, they proceeded to wind up the natives. Lawrenson recalls: 'When we walked out to sample the atmosphere there was a game on the pitch so we stood at the side watching for a few minutes, then Souey said, "Come on, let's walk right around and wind them up by showing them we're not scared". As we made our way around, their fans were slaughtering us and the noise was unbelievable. We finally made our way back towards the dressing-room area, but once we got inside the tunnel Davie Hodgson starts singing this Chris Rea song that Craig Johnston had got us all into.' Johnston takes up the story: 'I had given Chris Rea's album a hiding to such an extent that all the players knew the songs off by heart especially "I Don't Know What It Is (But I Love It)". One of us would sing a verse, and the rest would come in on the chorus, clapping and chanting, evoking those images of unity and victory. So as we're going back down the tunnel Davie breaks into a solo rendition of the opening verse. One or two join in and by the time we drew abreast of the

Roma dressing-room everyone of us is singing, "I don't know what it is but I love it … I don't know what it is but I want it to stay …"'

The further Liverpool's players advanced along the tunnel, and the nearer to Roma's dressing-room, the louder the singing got. Nils Liedholm said afterwards that he had heard them while trying to conduct his team-talk and the colour just drained from the Roma players' faces. He knew then they were in trouble. 'This was the super-relaxed Liverpool they'd heard about,' says Johnston. That song had become the team's unofficial anthem and it was not the last time it would ring around the bowels of Rome's Olympic Stadium. Once back inside the dressing-room the players went about their business as the clocked ticked towards kick-off. The mood remained one of calm. 'Alan Hansen was a great story-teller and after going out for the walk around the pitch we were back in the changing-room when he started telling this story,' says Souness. 'I can't for the life of me remember what it was about, but they were usually quite funny and when he started all the lads listened. I'm not exaggerating when I say this, but half an hour before kick-off we're all sitting there with our shirts and ties on still listening to him. Joe then had to interrupt and remind us that we had this big game to play and it was time to get changed. It was a sign of just how relaxed we were.' Behind the ultra-cool façade, though, it was only natural that nerves now began to jangle among some of the players. For five of Liverpool's starting line-up this was their first experience of a European Cup final and Craig Johnston says: 'It was easily the biggest game of our lives for a few of us so, let's make no bones about it, yes, there were a lot of genuine nerves there. Here we were about to enter the lion's den, quite literally, and everyone outside the club was writing us off. If we'd let the tension get to us we'd have been a beaten team from the off. Singing Chris Rea and acting as though we didn't have a care in the world was our way of dealing with it.'

*

Once changed, Joe reached into the inside pocket of his jacket and pulled out three tatty pieces of paper ripped from a notebook. On them were the notes from which he would conduct his team talk. As was the norm, he kept it brief and to the point, heeding the advice of Tom Saunders's invaluable scouting report and drawing on all of the vast experience he had gained during his long career. Formation-wise, it was 'the same one that brought us to the final, with Kenny and Craig in deep-lying inside-forward positions, ready to get it off their midfield men and strike quickly'. He stressed to all the outfield players the importance of never standing still and urged the forwards to pepper Franco Tancredi's goal at every opportunity because he 'can't hold a shot and parries the ball'. Though it was never Liverpool's style to place too much emphasis on the opposition, Falcao and Conti were the Roma players Joe feared most. They had the ability to dictate play, so he urged his men to keep close tabs on them at all times. 'Their front men inter-change,' he explained. 'Conti goes to the left, the right and Falcao ends up in the centre-forward position. Don't forget if he is on the wing – close up on him – he can do a bit. Also, don't give free-kicks away outside the box – you know how good they are at falling down. We are not going to man-mark Falcao, but the nearest man will have to pick him up quick.' With the start of the game fast approaching Joe wrapped up by leaving his players in no doubt that returning home with the cup was all that mattered. 'We shall respect them but we are going to win here – let them do the worrying about us – we are as good as them if not better – all this shit talked about a good match is not on – we are going for the ball, nothing else – get it first then let's play our natural game. All the best, now let's do 'em!' And with that, the bell rang.

'From that moment we grew in stature and it just built from there,' recalls Bruce Grobbelaar. 'We were so pumped up it was untrue.' The players emerged from the dressing-room and formed a line in the corridor. 'Then we waited and waited and waited,' the goalkeeper says. 'The cheeky Italian so and sos. They were trying to pull another fast one by keeping us waiting, but it didn't work.

All of a sudden Sammy Lee, Craig Johnston and Souey started singing the Chris Rea song again. One by one all the lads joined in and it wasn't long before the entire team were belting it out once more at the top of their voices. Every time we got to the chorus I would start banging on the door of the Roma dressing-room as if I was playing the drums! The next thing we know the door opens and a head peeps out, and mutters something in Italian to us that sounded like "You Scouse Bastardos!" When they eventually started to come out Souey looked each and every one of them in the eye and continued to sing in their faces. As they went past one-by-one the singing got higher and higher until it was so loud we couldn't even hear the noise of the crowd outside. These Roma guys were just looking around at each other and must have been thinking, "Just what have we got here?" I don't know whether it was off-putting for them but it certainly put a feather in our cap and we felt invincible.'

It would have taken something out of the ordinary to unnerve this stellar Roma side, but even before a ball had been kicked Liverpool had gained the upper hand. The togetherness that Joe had been keen to foster throughout the season, and more recently in Israel, was paying dividends. As he took his place on the bench that night he did so in the knowledge that in terms of team spirit there was not a team in Europe who could touch his Liverpool. Given their home advantage, Roma began the game as 13–8 favourites. But already the playing field was tilting away from them. The champions of England were no longer lambs to the slaughter and with confidence oozing from every red shirt it was not long before the first objective was achieved: the vociferous home crowd was silenced. In the *Guardian* David Lacey wrote: 'From the start the game went according to the plan Liverpool had laid for it. They had to reduce the tempo to the sort of pace that would prey on the already taut nerves of the Roma players.' Patient passing and tentative probing: that was the name of the game for Liverpool in Europe at this time. Within fifteen minutes it paid off as Liverpool took the lead, courtesy of a veteran from the 1977 triumph in the same stadium. Johnston floated a ball in from the right, Tancredi made a hash of collecting it and after falling to the floor the ball rebounded off his head and straight into the path of Liverpool's number two Phil Neal. 'I can still hear Joe saying, "If you're going to join the attack, stay with it until it breaks down". Well, I joined the attack and all of a sudden it continued, a ricochet falls in the six-yard box, and who's in there? Me!'

At the opposite end the Liverpool defence had looked comfortable thus far. In fact, they had hardly been troubled at all. While not exactly a stroll in the park, what pressure Roma did apply was dealt with easily. It had been a near perfect half, better than Joe and his staff could have imagined. But just a minute before the break Roma hit back with a sucker punch. In his scouting report Tom Saunders had warned of Roberto Pruzzo's aerial threat, but on this occasion it went unheeded. Sebastiano Nela's ball over the top freed Conti on the left edge of the box and though his first attempt at a cross was blocked by Lawrenson, he succeeded at the second attempt. Pruzzo got in front of Hansen and with a flick of his head directed the ball beyond the despairing, acrobatic dive of Grobbelaar to draw Roma level.

As the two teams went in at the break there was not much for Joe to say. The equalising goal aside, the players had done all he had asked of them. He kept his team talk short. It may not have been the most inspirational he delivered, but it was enough to reassure the players that they were doing everything right, and the well-laid plans remained very much on course. 'Don't worry about their goal,' he simply said. 'You're doing us all proud, the city, the club and the fans. Just keep it going, they may have ended the half on top, but let's just get back to basics, like we did at the outset. Start creating chances again and see if we can get a winner.'

Pruzzo's goal had bucked the trend of the previous six European Cup finals, all of which had been settled by a single goal, and were remembered mostly for their dourness. What followed was a typically cagey affair as the fixture reverted to recent type. Amid yet more smoke-bombs, firecrackers and flares, the second half got underway. That was about as exciting as it got until the end of extra-time. Roma opened the second period by enjoying another brief flurry of domination, but as David Miller so eloquently reflected in *The Times* they were 'like a Ferrari confronted by endless policemen' as Liverpool 'produced a typical, anaesthetising phase of more than twenty consecutive rolled passes'. Souness was outshining Falcao in midfield and the natives were becoming restless. 'I remember the ball going out of play behind the Roma goal and hearing Tancredi tell the ballboy to take his time. They were playing for penalties then,' says the Liverpool captain. The longer the game wore on, fewer and fewer risks were taken on either side. The fear of losing hung heavy in the air and it came as something of a relief to both teams when the final shrill of Mr Frederiksson's whistle ended one hundred and twenty minutes of tense, nervous action.

For the first time in the competition's history the destiny of the cup would be decided by a penalty shoot-out. Tottenham had won the UEFA Cup by similar means a week before, but the only other high-profile game to have been decided this way was the European Championship final of 1976 between West Germany and Czechoslovakia. If the nerves had not already been shredded they soon would be. Not Joe's, though. In the heat of the intense battle he managed to maintain his usual ice-cool composure, revealing afterwards: 'I did not feel anything when the game reached the penalty stage. I have seen too much and been in the game too long and have learned to live with these pressures.' In those frantic few minutes between the end of extra-time and the start of the shoot-out, Joe hastily gathered his players together and congratulated each and every one of them. It was yet another cunning psycho-logical ploy that took the pressure away from them. 'I am proud of every one of you this evening,' he said, 'and no matter what happens now that will not change.' In his eyes, they were the true winners. As favourites and on their own pitch, the onus had been on Roma to come out and win it. That his team had prevented them from doing so made Joe the proudest man in Rome that night. He could not have asked any more from them and now it was just a case of fingers crossed that luck would be on Liverpool's side in the shoot-out.

However, with Liverpool about to enter the uncharted water of penalties, no one had been pre-selected to take the kicks. Even though they had practised them at Melwood only two days before, they had not seriously thought it would come down to this. For a moment chaos and confusion reigned in the centre circle. Joe had just a matter of minutes to choose and nominate his men, but like a true leader he stepped up to the plate and took control. In what was the sixty-seventh and final match of an epic season he had just one more duty to perform. The club's two regular penalty-takers during the season, Neal and Souness, though they had missed one each, were his two obvious first picks. Leading scorer Ian Rush was next. His job was to score goals so surely he would not miss from twelve yards, reasoned Joe. That left two more and as Joe looked around for volunteers, one by one heads dropped and others looked nervously away. 'I was petrified about the prospect of having to take one,' admits Hansen. 'If there'd been two hundred players in the team I'd have still been the last one to offer my services.' Joe believed that taking penalties was all about a player's state of mind at the time and he was not going to force the responsibility on someone. Out of the blue, young Steve Nicol, a 72nd-minute substitute for Johnston, piped up. He wanted to take one. It was a brave decision, but why stop him if he was feeling confident? Just one more was required. Preferably someone with experience. Joe turned to Kenny Dalglish, at thirty-three the club's second longest-serving player. 'But, gaffer,' said the number seven, 'you've just substituted me!' It was a comical moment that helped ease the tension once again. Given the pressurised circumstances it was an easy mistake to make. Two options remained: Alan Kennedy and Bruce Grobbelaar. It had to be Barney, though Bruce would also have a big part to play.

This was it. The grand climax of Joe Fagan's first season as Liverpool manager. The job of selecting the order of Liverpool's penalty takers fell to Souness and, to everyone's surprise, first to step up was the most inexperienced member of the team. Nicol blazed over and Liverpudlian hearts sunk. To make matters worse Roma captain Di Bartolomei converted his. For the first time on the night the home side were ahead. It was not looking good. Neal scored to make it 1–1. Next up for the Italians was Bruno Conti. The time had come for Liverpool to play their joker. 'Just before the shoot-out began I remember Smokin' Joe putting his arm around me,' recalls Grobbelaar. 'He gave this little speech, "Now, son, myself and the coaches, the chairman and the directors, the captain and the players and even these fans are not going to blame you if you can't stop a ball from twelve yards. You've done your job, we can't blame you now". I felt a massive weight lift from my shoulders. Then as I walked away he shouted, "But try and put them off!" That was the last thing he said to me. The first penalty, of course, I did nothing. It was only when Conti stepped up that Joe Fagan's words came back to me. Conti was dancing around and I thought I'm not having this so started doing the old crossover legs routine. When he shot over I thought, "Aye, aye, this might just work".'

With what was easily the best penalty of the night Souness casually planted his kick to the top left of Tancredi's net. The pressure was now back on Roma. Ubaldo Righetti levelled, but Rush promptly restored Liverpool's lead. If it carried on like this the game could go on all night. But suddenly it was to turn in Liverpool's favour as veteran Italy international Francesco Graziani made his way to the penalty spot to face Grobbelaar. 'When it came to Graziani I'll never forget him putting his arm around the referee before taking it,' says the goalkeeper. 'I was thinking, "You can't do that, it's ungentle-manly conduct", so I went into the goal and started eating the net. It looked like spaghetti and so when I turned round I just started giving it all the spaghetti legs. I went to the right and my hand was actually touching the floor as I looked up and saw it hit the top of the crossbar. I knew what it meant and just started running around and jumping up and down like a lunatic. It was Joe who'd put it into my mind, though, so he must take some of the credit. When it came to football he was a very intelligent man who knew which buttons to press and on which players.'

The mathematics was simple now. If Liverpool scored with their last kick the cup would be on its way back to Anfield for a fourth time. The huge burden of responsibility fell on the shoulders of Alan Kennedy. He may have been the match-winner in the 1981 final, but he is first to admit that not even his manager had much faith in him in this tense situation. 'When Joe initially asked if I was OK to take a penalty I said "yes", but little did I realise what I was letting myself in for. I didn't even know that I'd definitely be taking one because I thought he'd have ended up getting someone else. If I'm being honest I don't think he was confident in me taking it. He had seen me in the practice at Melwood and also when I took one in pre-season. I was shocking on both occasions, so I don't know why he picked me. What he must have seen was something that maybe the other players didn't have. It definitely wasn't ability, because I was limited in that. I suppose it must have been my bottle. Tom Saunders always said about me: if there was a cavalry charge I'd be at the front saying, "Come on!" And then I would be the first to be shot! What he meant was you knew what you were getting with me, that I wouldn't let them down.'

At this point in Liverpool's history there had never been a more nerve-wracking moment. Liverpudlians everywhere, whether back home watching on television or among the fifteen thousand standing anxiously on the Curva Nord at the opposite end of the Stadio Olimpico, everyone looked to the heavens in the hope of divine intervention. Jegsy Dodd was among them. He remembers thinking: 'If it was Rushie, you'd put your house on it, but with Barney Rubble, anything could happen.' On the television gantry, ITV's Brian Moore cranked up the tension, teasing his viewers by 'daring them to watch'. Out on the pitch the rest of the players chewed on their fingernails, held their heads in their hands or simply stared the other way. Down on the touchline Joe Fagan stood in unison with his backroom staff, like brothers in arms, willing the ball to cross the line one final time. All eyes that could bear to look were on Liverpool's number three. In the words of the *Daily Star*'s Bob Driscoll it was 'the biggest pressure moment of his life', adding: 'As he walked slowly forward, he looked the loneliest man in the world.' Following a brief pause, Kennedy started his run and the whole of Europe held its collective breath. Time seemed to stand still. Then in a flash it was over. The red half of Merseyside erupted in ecstasy. The unlikely hero had successfully dispatched his kick beyond Tancredi and Liverpool were Kings of Europe once again. They had completed the Treble and made football history. And all in Joe's first season as manager.

As Kennedy set off on a spur-of-the-moment jig of unbridled joy, soon to be buried under a sea of delirious team-mates, pandemonium broke out on the terracing at the far end of the stadium, while a deathly hush rolled over the rest of Rome. For the man who had guided Liverpool to this ultimate triumph it was a moment to savour. It was undoubtedly the peak of his career. His first reaction was to embrace the staff who had worked so closely with him. No one appreciated their contribution to the success more than him. Twelve months before Joe had been in their position and he fully subscribed to the theory that football is a team game, in which everyone plays a part. This triumph was as much about them – Ronnie Moran, Roy Evans, Tom Saunders and Chris Lawler – as it was him and the players. 'We were always a tight-knit group and Joe made sure it stayed that way,' says Evans. 'He involved the staff in everything he did. We won together and lost together.'

Before joining the raucous celebrations himself, Souness made a beeline for the manager, further proof of the respect and mutual affection that existed between the pair. He had been so desperate for the club to succeed in Joe's first season, but even he could not have known it would be this successful. It was an emotional moment. The enormity of what Liverpool had achieved was not lost on him, and the renowned hard-man was reduced to tears. 'Joe knew what we were capable of,' Souness says. 'While a lot of fuss was made over the fact that we had to go and play Roma on their own ground I honestly don't think it worried him. Such was the character Joe had instilled into that team, he knew we had a fighting chance against anyone, anywhere in the world. I don't think he was the least bit surprised when we eventually won it.'

The party on the pitch continued as UEFA officials prepared the trophy presentation. Amid the back-slapping and hand-shaking Joe finally came face-to-face with the hero of the hour. 'The first thing he said to me,' Kennedy remembers, 'was, "Did you mean it?" And he followed that up with, "Why did you change your mind? Because I remember last week when we played against the reserves, you went for the other corner". I said, "Boss, you wouldn't believe what I was thinking up there". And then he just shook my hand and gave me his famous wink, as if to say "well done" and that was it. That meant I must have done all right.'

As the giant scoreboard flashed up confirmation that Liverpool Football Club were indeed '*Campeone*', man-of-the-match Souness led the team up the steps to collect their reward from Italian President Sandro Pertini. Nowadays the manager and coaches are part of the presentation ceremony, but Joe had to watch from the pitch as the giant silver trophy was hoisted high into the Italian night sky. A veteran of the club's three previous European Cup wins, Joe admitted that this triumph had been the hardest. Souness went further and rated it as 'possibly the greatest result ever achieved by a club side'. The *Daily Mirror*'s 'Voice of Sport', Frank McGhee, agreed, boldly declaring: 'No English soccer team will ever match what Liverpool achieved in the Olympic Stadium.'

Even in this moment of glory Joe took time out to sympathise with the beaten team. 'My feelings about this are sincere,' he said. 'I am always sorry for any team beaten in a cup final, particularly a European Cup final. I feel for Roma and for their coach. But somebody has got to win and somebody has got to lose – even on penalties. I am just delighted that we managed to do that tonight. We did not allow the leading players of Roma, and Falcao in particular, to play to their potential.' Nullifying the threat of Falcao, a key factor in Liverpool's victory, justified the homework Joe and his staff had done. It was a fact acknowledged by Nils Liedholm who, in his last game in charge before taking up the reins for a third time at A.C. Milan, had been desperate to bow out by delivering the ultimate prize. 'It was a great game but Liverpool were stronger than we anticipated and tactically they played well. The Cup is in good hands.'

The devastation of defeat hit Roma hard. Falcao was left psychologically scarred at being outshone by Souness, and was made the scapegoat by the fans who once idolised him. He played only four more times for the club before returning to his homeland. More tragic is the story of Roma captain Di Bartolomei. A lifelong fan of the club, this was a defeat from which he never recovered. The 1984 European Cup final was his last appearance in a Roma shirt. He played on elsewhere for another six years, but beset by money worries and suffering from clinical depression, he took his own life, aged just 39. He shot himself through the heart on the balcony of his villa in southern Italy on 30 May, 1994, the tenth anniversary of Liverpool's triumph in Rome. While there is no official evidence linking his suicide to what happened in 1984, Italian football expert John Foot, wrote in his book *Calcio*: 'The date he chose to take his life could not have been a coincidence. He could have been the player – the captain – who had lifted the European Cup, in his home city, if things had gone differently.'

As Chris Rea once again reverberated around the visitors' dressing-room, bonfires were lit on the emptying terraces. Outside the stadium tensions were running high and Liverpool fans were forced to run the gauntlet as the disgruntled Roma Ultras rioted. The following morning's *Daily Post* reported how 'riot troops had to move in to save hundreds of Liverpool fans after a series of ambushes near to where their coaches were parked'. According to Liverpool-supporting author John Williams: 'Italian knife gangs lay in wait outside the Olympic Stadium.' George Sharp, one of the five Liverpool fans stabbed, recalled: 'I was with my son Ian when about eighty young Italian fans jumped us. Ian was knocked off his

feet by a fan wielding a chain. I tried to protect him, but suddenly
I felt a sharp pain and realised I had been stabbed. I thought we
were both going to die.' The worst of the violence took place on
Tiber Bridge, where pitched battles took place as Liverpool fans
retaliated in acts of self-defence. Jegsy Dodd remembers how after
his bus came under severe attack, 'there were packs of marauding
Roma fans everywhere looking for stragglers'. The *Observer*'s
Hugh McIlvanney condemned the 'local youths who had decided to
play a jolly game of lynch-the-Brits'. Three Liverpool fans were
arrested following an incident in which an Italian was stabbed, and
an official UEFA investigation later decided that both clubs should
share the blame for the disturbances. Both clubs were fined £1,270.
However, a British Embassy spokesman in the Italian capital said:
'The message we have is that the Liverpool supporters behaved as
everyone expected them to and maintained their good reputation.
It appears they were the subject of unprovoked attacks by a small
minority of Roma fans.' The Mayor of Rome, Ugo Vetere, issued
an apology to the City of Liverpool. On and off the pitch it had
been an unforgettable evening, summed up by the next day's front-
page headline in the *Liverpool Echo*: 'THE ECSTASY and THE
AGONY.'

While Rome burned and supporters nursed their wounds, the
Liverpool squad partied. Their celebrations continued long into
the night at a swish private villa tucked away high up in the hills
that looked down on the scene of their heroic achievement. There,
Joe was reunited with wife Lil and together they celebrated the
crowning moment of his life in football. As he relaxed by the hotel
pool the next morning he told reporters that what Liverpool had
achieved 'probably won't sink in until the middle of next week
when I shout "whoopee", jump up and punch the air'. Relaxing on
a sun lounger, flanked by Italian Carabineri, Joe posed with the
spoils of his Roman conquest for what has since become an iconic
picture.

As the Liverpool squad prepared for their triumphant homecoming, Joe closed the book on his first campaign as manager by

making the following entry in his diary: 'Well, what can I say? We won the big one as they say and rightly so. The better team just couldn't score. Anyway, Alan Kennedy made us the European champions by scoring the best penalty he has ever taken!! In conclusion to the season let me congratulate Ronnie Moran, Roy Evans and all the lads for their magnificent efforts during the season. Well done the lads!!'

A journey that had begun with his official unveiling as Liverpool manager little more than twelve months earlier had reached a barely believable conclusion. All that was left to do now was acknowledge the acclaim of more than three hundred thousand supporters lining the streets of Liverpool on which Joe had grown up. Even by Liverpudlian standards, for whom such occasions were nothing new, the noise and colour that greeted Joe's Treble-winners was a sight to behold. As the cavalcade snaked its way slowly through the throbbing crowds, the evening sun shone down on a massed sea of red, white, and yellow, with a hint of gleaming silver.

On the top deck of the bus the party was once again in full swing as players swigged from bottles of lager while proudly displaying three sparkling trophies. One man, though, was conspicuous by his absence. Never one to bask in the glory or hog the limelight – he had also been last off the plane when it landed at Speke Airport – Joe opted to spend the first hour and a quarter of the parade downstairs. Overwhelmed by the scale of the reception, he sat in reflective mood, taking it all in with a huge smile of satisfaction across his face. Not until near the end of the 16-mile procession did Joe finally succumb to pressure and climb the steps to take his deserved bow.

At sixty-three years and seventy-nine days, Joe Fagan had become the oldest European Cup-winning manager, surpassing the feat of his Anfield predecessor Bob Paisley, who was sixty-two years and one hundred and twenty-four days old when he won the trophy for a third time in 1981. It was an honour he would hold until the 71-year-old Belgian Raymond Goethals led Marseille to success in 1993. 'You couldn't have written a more perfect script,' says Phil Neal, the most experienced member of that team. John Keith in the *Daily Express* hailed Joe as 'the 63-year-old with the Midas touch'. Elsewhere Joe was widely described as the newly crowned 'Emperor of Rome'. To have won three trophies in one season Liverpool had, according to Ian Hargreaves in the *Liverpool Echo*, 'completed the greatest marathon in modern times', with the glory of Rome being 'a fitting climax to what has been a quite astonishing season'.

A year before, Joe had been a barely recognisable figure outside the confines of Anfield and Melwood. Now his beaming smile adorned front and back pages of newspapers across the Continent. With the greatest prize in club football alongside him in those photographs, there could be no denying him this moment of well-earned fame. His astute footballing acumen finally received the overdue recognition it deserved. Leading sports writer Brian Glanville paid tribute to Joe: 'Nice guys, after all, don't always finish last.'

Those who doubted his ability to follow in the footsteps of the great Bob Paisley had been well and truly silenced. Joe Fagan had joined the immortals. His place among the game's managerial greats was forever assured. And try as some people might, the events of Rome 1984, and the completion of an unprecedented Treble, is something that can never be taken away from him. No matter what the future held.

CHAPTER 10

A VICTIM OF HIS OWN SUCCESS

T HE SUMMER OF 1984 was a heady one on Merseyside. Visitors flocked to the city's Garden Festival in their thousands, Frankie Goes To Hollywood topped the music charts and, of course, Liverpool Football Club rewrote the history books by winning the Treble. Even Everton got in on the act, coming out of hibernation to claim the FA Cup, their first piece of silverware in fourteen years. So the Liver Birds could look down proudly as all the major football trophies came home to roost on the banks of the Mersey.

With the friendly final of March still fresh in the mind, the city was on the crest of a footballing wave not experienced since 1966 when Liverpool were champions, Everton last won the FA Cup and both clubs provided players for England's successful World Cup-winning squad. It may not have been the summer of love as such, but Merseyside's success on the football pitch was viewed by many as a two-fingered salute to Prime Minister Margaret Thatcher and her Government whose policies were not met with general approval in the city. As Liverpool supporters basked in the glory of Rome Part II, the man who had made it possible was deservedly named manager of the year. His reaction to winning the accolade was typical. 'Obviously, I'm delighted but I also feel a bit humble because this is only my first season in the job,' was the highlight of his brief acceptance speech. Liverpool's decision to promote from within had once again been vindicated. 'When people talk about the importance of continuity at Anfield they mean more than the process of internal succession that saw Bill Shankly hand over to Bob Paisley and Paisley to Joe Fagan,' wrote Hugh McIlvanney in the *Observer* during the close-season. 'They mean more, too, than the accumulation of Bootroom camaraderie. What has been built up is a set of values that amounts to both a professional wisdom and a professional morality.' Yet this feelgood factor did not have as long a shelf life as it should and Joe Fagan would soon become a victim of his own success. 'He'd set such high standards in his first season as manager that I suppose he was on a hiding to nothing unless we won the lot in 1985,' says Phil Neal. 'So, in that respect, there was a lot of pressure on him before a ball had even been kicked.'

Topping the Treble was always going to be a tall order. It was a task not helped by the departure of Graeme Souness in mid-June. After what had been arguably his finest season in a red shirt, Souness had been courted by a host of top European clubs, most notably those from Italy's lire-rich Serie A. Speculation had intensified around the time of the European Cup final, but no deal had been struck. It was only as Liverpool travelled to Swaziland for two exhibition games against Tottenham Hotspur, that the move gathered pace. In the aftermath of Rome, journalist Brian Glanville asked: 'Can Liverpool remotely afford now to let Souness go?' But as supporters braced themselves for the inevitable, Glanville warned: 'If they do, they will take the heart and mind out of the team.' But recognising that a move would set up the player for life financially, Joe was resigned to the fact that he could not stand in his inspirational captain's way. 'It looks like Graeme Souness is going to Sampdoria,' he conceded in his diary on 12 June. 'It will be a great loss to Liverpool FC, but we can remember the happy times and they were happy times! Thanks Graeme and good luck.' That is not to suggest Joe was happy with the situation, or that Liverpool let go such an important player without a fight. 'Like everyone, Joe was determined to keep Graeme at the club and we did try our best, but English clubs just couldn't compete with the money Italian clubs were paying at this time,' explains Peter Robinson. 'Eventually we just had to hold our hands up and accept defeat. It was quite a blow, but he obviously wanted to play overseas. His mind was made up and there was very little we could do to persuade him otherwise. Serie A was the place to be back then.' On the day the European Championship kicked off in France, Souness completed his £650,000 move to Sampdoria. 'I don't think anyone at the club held it against me,' recalls Souness. 'They knew my reasons for going and Joe was never going to stand in my way. He fully understood. I left with his blessing and he said I was welcome back any time. That meant an awful lot to me.'

Though Souness was never hero-worshipped by the Kop in the same way as Kenny Dalglish, Ian Hargreaves was correct when paying tribute in the *Liverpool Echo* on the day of his departure. 'Graeme Souness has probably contributed at least as much to the Reds' cause as household names like Ian St John, Kevin Keegan and Kenny Dalglish,' he wrote. 'When all is said and done, every Liverpool fan knows only too well how badly they are going to miss the man who probably reached his peak in Rome.' One such supporter was D.J. Gore of Woolton. In a letter to the *Football Echo*, he insisted: 'Graeme Souness is irreplaceable.' Others were just as quick to vent their feelings on the matter, with another 'concerned Red' adding: 'I fail to understand how the departure of one of British football's all-time greats, Graeme Souness, has taken place without any positive action by the Liverpool management. Surely a footballer who was a great leader, rugged tackler and supreme passer of the ball would not be replaced by merely shuffling the existing pack. The only answer is to get the cheque book out and buy a classy, hard-tackling midfield player.' However, Stuart Jones in *The Times* warned: 'There is no ready replacement, either inside or outside Anfield.' The names of Liam Brady and Paul McStay were mentioned, though neither were viable options: Brady had recently moved from Sampdoria to Internazionale, ironically to make way for Souness, and Celtic insisted McStay was not for sale.

As Joe was to discover, there would be no quick fix when it came to filling the void left by Souness. It was just one of several headaches he faced before the start of the new season. The most persistent rumour concerned Ian Rush, who had also become a target of the money men from Serie A. With forty-nine goals to his name the previous season, Rush was a much-coveted striker. His stock was sufficiently high that he would finish runner-up to Michel Platini in *World Soccer's* Player of the Year awards. Before signing Maradona, Napoli reportedly tabled a mind-blowing bid worth £4.5 million. To the relief of everyone at Anfield, the deal eventually collapsed. All this had happened while Joe was away on holiday, and when he returned he spoke to an understandably aggrieved Rush. The player laid the blame for being denied his dream move firmly at the feet of chairman John Smith, and Joe was not unsympathetic. But having already lost the services of Souness he could ill-afford to have an unhappy player on the books. He set about restoring the Welshman's shattered morale. 'Joe called me into his office to ask what had been going on,' recounts Rush. 'He was always straight with me so I was straight with him. I told him that I never wanted to leave Liverpool, but the terms Napoli were offering were simply too good to turn down. He fully understood, but explained that there was no point moping about. What's done was done and all I could carry on doing was giving my all for Liverpool.'

On a more positive note, Joe had been involved in signing a prospective new striker partner for Rush. Luton Town's England international Paul Walsh had put pen to paper on his £700,000 move to Anfield at the end of the previous season, shortly before Liverpool embarked on their pre-European Cup final trip to Israel. He had long been on the club's radar, having originally been scouted by Geoff Twentyman while a teenager at Charlton. He had impressed Joe during a game at Anfield in September 1982 when he helped Luton secure a 3–3 draw. The part he played in setting up Luton's first goal that afternoon, when he turned Mark Lawrenson, stuck in Joe's memory. A skilful front-runner with a keen eye for goal, Walsh's slender frame and lack of height provided him with a low centre of gravity which enabled him to wriggle past players with ease. His style resembled that of Dalglish rather than Rush and there was genuine excitement among supporters at the prospect of him pulling on a red shirt. The fee paid was the largest of Joe's time as manager and it was enough to pip Manchester United for his services. 'This is the way we do things at Liverpool. We like to sign newcomers while we are winning, to keep things ticking over,' explained Joe. Walsh said: 'It is a brilliant move for me. I am joining the best team in the world.'

Walsh was the only new face on the official team photograph taken ahead of the 1984–85 season, but the search was ongoing for further reinforcements, particularly in midfield. When the squad reported back for pre-season training, Souness was not the only Treble-winner missing. Sitting in his office at Anfield, Joe Fagan took a call. On the other end of the line, back in his native Australia, was Craig Johnston, who proceeded to say that he would be staying put until his wife had given birth to their first child, due in October. The news came as a bolt out of the blue and was a severe setback to Joe's plans. However, he was quick to play down any talk of a renewed rift. 'I've spoken to the lad and he's explained the situation. We want him back and he would like to be here, but it's just one of those things! There is no animosity about it.' The pair may not have seen eye to eye over team selection throughout the previous season, but after the trials and tribulations of his battle to hold down a first-team place it was ironic that Johnston was now needed more than ever. No matter, Johnston was sticking to his guns. 'I knew what was at stake, but the bitterness of our previous confrontations influenced my thinking,' says Johnston. 'Staring me in the face was the biggest chance I'd ever have of staking my claim to a permanent first-team place. But as much as I wanted to be there for the birth, it wasn't my only consideration. Had it been anyone other than Joe Fagan on the other end of the line, I might have been able to see beyond the bitterness that clouded my thinking. Instead, I dug in my heels and risked my career.' It meant Liverpool began their preparations without Johnston and, as yet, a replacement for Souness.

Despite being the reigning champions of Europe the only representatives Liverpool had at the summer's European Championship were scouts on the lookout for fresh talent. The home nations had failed miserably in their attempts to qualify for the tournament. On the plus side, Joe was able to welcome a fully re-charged squad back to training in mid-July. The departure of Souness was the big talking point among the players on their return to Melwood and Joe was quick to drum into his players that there was no point crying over the loss. 'I think we were all a bit worried about how we'd cope without him,' says Alan Kennedy. 'But I remember Joe getting us all together on that first day back. "Forget about him," he said. "Life goes on and no player is bigger than the club".' Of course, it was not the first time Liverpool had seen a key player depart. Seven years before when Kevin Keegan left for Hamburg life did not just go on, it arguably got better. Kenny Dalglish was brought in as his replacement and the club went on to even greater glory. So in essence Joe was right. But finding a suitable successor was of paramount importance. When Keegan went the club had been given twelve months' notice, which gave them ample time to launch their search.

While midfield reinforcements were sought, Joe tied up one loose end when he announced that Phil Neal, Liverpool's second longest-serving player behind the soon-to-depart Phil Thompson, would be his captain. Though other names were reportedly in the frame, most notably Dalglish, who had led the side on the odd occasion in the past, Neal's longevity made him the obvious choice. The respect between the pair also stood him in good stead. The manager saw in Neal leadership qualities that reminded him of a young Joe Mercer or Tony Book, successful former captains of Arsenal and Manchester City respectively. Despite countless League and cup triumphs, Neal possessed an insatiable hunger to follow in the footsteps of the great captains he had played under at Anfield. He admits that accepting the chance to become the club's thirteenth post-War captain took him two seconds. 'Being given the captaincy by Joe was the biggest compliment he could have paid me,' Neal says. 'I wasn't getting any younger, so to be given this ultimate honour was just the fillip I needed. Young Stevie Nicol had come through the ranks and he was after my place. I needed to keep at the top of my game and I've no doubt that Joe's decision to make me captain helped me. I'd always had a close relationship with him and I think that was important.'

In time-honoured Anfield tradition, Joe was also quick to remind his players: 'The three trophies we won last year have gone. Now we're starting afresh.' Keeping players' feet firmly on the ground was always a top objective of the Liverpool coaching staff as a season approached. 'It didn't matter what the previous season's team had won, this season's team had won nothing,' recalls Ronnie Moran. 'They (the staff) liked nothing better than bringing us back down to earth with a bump,' says Neal. 'It was the same every year, we'd be lucky if we got a "well done". It was all about the next challenge.'

As the sporting attention switched from football's European Championship to the Olympic Games in Los Angeles, Joe led Liverpool on their annual pre-season tour. It did not take long to get back into the winning groove. At the Westfalenstadion in Germany, for a game to mark Borussia Dortmund's seventy-fifth anniversary, a solitary goal from Ian Rush was enough. Sporting Charleroi of Belgium were then hit for six without reply, while the Phillips Cup was secured in Switzerland, courtesy of wins over local sides Young Boys Berne and Grasshoppers Zurich. The only blot on Liverpool's pre-season copybook was a 2–2 draw against K.R. Reykjavik in Iceland. On the early evidence perhaps Souness was not going to be missed too much after all. Steve Nicol, a bit-part figure the previous season, had enhanced his claims for a regular starting place, and Joe was hopeful John Wark would have a big role to play.

The manager was relatively happy with the form his players had shown during the tour, and all thoughts now turned to the season's annual curtain-raiser at Wembley. The starting XI for the Charity Shield match against Everton showed just two changes to the one who began in Rome three months earlier. Wark and Nicol came in for Souness and Johnston, and Walsh had to settle for a place on the bench. 'I think it is right and proper to give everybody who played last season the first chance,' reasoned Joe. There was a record crowd for the Charity Shield of one hundred thousand, but on a baking hot day it was Everton who claimed the early bragging rights on Merseyside thanks to a bizarre own goal by Bruce Grobbelaar. Liverpool's performance was widely described as 'lacklustre' and most reporters agreed why. 'Without Souness Liverpool are clearly lesser mortals, and the opposition greater ones by this knowledge,' observed *The Times* reporter Clive White. Joe was also quite damning in his post-match verdict. 'We were shocking,' he admitted with some concern. 'We didn't know how to resist or compete against more aggressive opponents. It was bad.'

Watching from the sidelines was 21-year-old Ajax midfielder Jan Molby. The Dane, an unused member of his country's squad during the summer's European Championship, had been training with Liverpool as part of a trial period with the club arranged by Peter Robinson. 'Joe had come to me and said he was struggling to find a suitable midfield player to fill the void left by Graeme,' explains Robinson. 'He'd scoured the British market and nothing had caught his eye, so he asked if I had any contacts in Europe who could help. You've got to remember that this was in the days when foreign players were very few and far between in the English game and there weren't many agents about. It just so happened, though, that I knew an agent in Holland and he recommended Jan to us.'

Joe immediately liked what he saw. Though on the hefty side and sluggish in movement, Molby's eye for a pass and deft touch were impressive. A decision on whether to sign him, though, would not be taken until he had been given a run-out in the first team. That opportunity came just three days after the Charity Shield when

Liverpool travelled to Dublin for a friendly against Home Farm. Molby played and capped an encouraging display with the final goal in a comfortable 3–0 win. He had done enough to convince Joe that he should be offered a contract. However, Molby has a vivid recollection of being forced to endure an agonising wait before he was put out of his misery. 'Joe was a man of very few words,' he says. 'I initially came over on trial and contact with him during this time was minimal. The trial was due to end as we were coming back from the game in Ireland. Nothing had been mentioned about my future so, naturally, I thought that was it and I'd be returning home. Anyway, we got to Manchester Airport and I asked out of courtesy was it OK if I just jumped on a flight straight back to Amsterdam. The response was as blunt as they come. "No", he said. It was as simple as that and it left me none the wiser. But it was typical of how Liverpool operated in those days. It was their way of keeping me on my toes. The belief was that judged on the performances I'd put in I should have been able to work out myself whether I was good enough to be signed up. Later on, when we got back to Anfield, he told me to come in and see him the next morning. So in I went the next day, still not knowing what lay in store. I knocked on his office door and he said, "We've decided that we like what we've seen and we're going to give you a chance. The rest is up to you. Just continue playing well and doing your best to get in the team. If you do that there won't be a problem. There's a three-year contract on the table. Now go upstairs and speak to Peter Robinson".'

While the formalities of completing Molby's £200,000 transfer were being tied up, Joe had a more pressing concern after Ian Rush was forced off shortly before half-time against Home Farm. He had suffered a knee ligament injury which would require an operation and rule him out for the foreseeable future. To lose your main goal threat just four days before the season started was a shattering blow. Coming so soon after the departure of Souness, and with Johnston still in Australia, Joe could have been forgiven for believing that Fate was already conspiring against him. He remained upbeat, though, and defiantly told the *Echo*: 'We've managed before and we'll manage again. If someone is hurt it means a chance for someone else and we still have some good players here you know. There were times last season when we had to manage without Kenny Dalglish and Graeme Souness and we didn't do too badly in the end.' At the club's annual meeting on the Wednesday before the first weekend of the Canon League season, Joe was again cheery in his outlook. 'A lot has been spoken about the departure of Graeme Souness and the Ian Rush injury. But they are just words and we will get over it. We relish the prospect of the coming season. Competition is going to be keener than ever but that brings the best out of us. We will be starting afresh after last season's success, but will redouble our efforts to maintain the high standards we have set. When I accepted the job I promised myself I would enjoy it. Up to now it's not been bad and I intend to continue to enjoy it.'

Despite the setbacks, Liverpool remained the bookies' favourites to win an unprecedented fourth successive title. Considering how the critics had been eager to write them off post-Souness, this made Joe chuckle. 'It's somewhat ironic that while the bookmakers can make Liverpool favourites to win the title again, other people are voicing the view that we have come to the end of our trail, as it were. As always, time alone will tell.'

The champions kicked off at Carrow Road, and just as it had the previous season the opening game got off to a sensational start. Steve Bruce, on his Norwich debut, put through his own net. His blunder was followed by a further five goals. Unfortunately for Liverpool, three of them went the way of the hosts. The six-goal thriller kept the fans enthralled and in the end Joe was relieved to have come away with a point. For Molby it was an eye-opening first experience of life in the English League. 'Before I'd even touched the ball, I remember finding myself in an unusual attacking position down the right wing,' he recalls. 'Phil Neal had played a perfect ball over the top to me and I had acres of space to run into. But instead of taking it on I noticed Kenny running in at the far post so crossed it first time. In raced Steve Bruce to make an attempted clearance, but fortunately for me he headed past his own 'keeper to give us the lead. "Not a bad start", I thought, but Joe was straight over to me at half-time for a quiet word. "I thought I told you not to do anything silly", he said. "Play within the system". I knew he was only joking, but he had a point. I shouldn't have been out of position on the wing, especially so early in the game.'

Liverpool picked up eight points from the opening four games. While Molby took time to settle, Walsh wasted no time in winning over the fans. A goal after just fourteen seconds on his home debut in a 3–0 win over West Ham, suggested he was doing his best to compensate for the loss of Rush. His encouraging start continued with further goals against Sunderland, Manchester United and Lech Poznan in the European Cup. But Liverpool's form dipped and Joe pinpointed a lack of strength in the centre of the pitch as the problem. It was following a 3–1 defeat at Arsenal that the alarm bells began to ring. 'Not enough steel in the midfield,' Joe observed. 'We haven't got one strong player. Molby has got the height and weight but isn't using it.' A week later, after a frustrating home draw against Sunderland, Joe unusually ducked out of the post-match press conference. Was the pressure beginning to tell? The *Liverpool Echo* certainly thought so. 'Over the past thirteen months he had put on a cheerful smile and faced the music even after the most humiliating of defeats. So it was surprising to be told that Joe did not wish to discuss the limited merits of Liverpool's 1–1 draw with Sunderland,' reported the local evening paper. 'Perhaps Joe did not want to be drawn into a public debate about what is wrong with Liverpool at a time when injuries and illness are making matters worse.'

The ghost of Graeme Souness seemed to be haunting the corridors of Anfield. On the same weekend that their former captain scored the winning goal on his Sampdoria debut, questions inevitably began to be asked about how much Liverpool were struggling without him. Molby, the man generally viewed as his replacement, admits it was a tough time for all concerned. 'It was difficult for me at first,' he says, 'but I also think it was a difficult time for Joe. He was under pressure to go out and find a player to replace Graeme Souness, and finding a player of that calibre was never going to be easy. I think most people were expecting him to go out and find a typical British-style central midfield player. Instead he got me, who was anything but that, and was also a relatively unknown foreigner. There's no doubt Liverpool missed Souness. What team wouldn't? There was quite a lot of flak flying in those early months, but I don't know whether this criticism was aimed at me personally and I certainly didn't see it that way. Stepping into the shoes of Souness would have been a big ask for anyone, never mind a 21-year-old just getting to grips with life in a new country. People may have viewed me as a direct replacement but we were different types of players. I was never a leader in the sense Souness was and nor did I pretend to be.'

The manager's mood was becoming increasingly irritable as a run of seven games without a win in the League, including a woeful 2–0 home defeat by newly-promoted Sheffield Wednesday, sent Liverpool dropping like an anchor to the lower reaches of the table. Drastic action was needed. But no one was braced for Joe's next move. He was certainly not afraid to drop players he thought were not performing to the best of their abilities. Reputations meant nothing to him. Indeed, the axe had already fallen on England international midfielder Sammy Lee earlier in the season. However, ahead of a Friday night visit to Tottenham, where Liverpool's frailties threatened to be exposed in front of live television cameras, he made the most controversial team selection of his managerial career. Out went Kenny Dalglish, the club's previously undroppable number seven. Joe described it as 'a terrible job but one that had to be done'. The decision sent shockwaves throughout football. 'I must say we, myself and chairman Sir John Smith, were very surprised when Joe dropped Kenny,' recalls Peter Robinson. 'We'd been over in Germany negotiating the contract to change our kit supplier from Umbro to Adidas and flew straight into London for the match. Normally I'd speak to Joe before he left for a game and more often than not he'd tell me the team. On this occasion I'd not spoken to him for a couple of days so you can imagine my surprise when I arrived at White Hart Lane. Never mind the supporters and the press, I couldn't believe it myself!' Dalglish had been rested before during the seven years since he arrived from Celtic, but had never been dropped. After scoring just twice in twelve games that season, he had no problem with the decision. However, the first he knew about it was when he read it in the press. 'Joe had every right to pick whatever team he wanted,' says Dalglish, 'but he should have informed me before telling the newspapers. After training that morning, Joe called me in. "I'm not going to play you tomorrow", he said. "I know. What can I do? You've picked your team. I've seen it in the paper", I replied. Then I walked out. It wasn't a pleasant moment because I usually had so much respect for Joe.'

The decision to leave out Dalglish was based on the belief that when he played poorly, so too did the team. But with Rush only just returning in a reserve-team game the night before, his omission left Liverpool glaringly bereft of attacking options. *The Times* described it as 'a drastic step', while the *Liverpool Echo* reported: 'The shock news that Kenny Dalglish is dropped for tonight's live televised clash at Tottenham emphasises more than anything else the seriousness with which manager Joe Fagan views the club's troubled start to the new season.' Liverpool went into the game with a worse goal tally than bottom club Watford, and on a miserable night in North London a lack of punch up front once again proved to be their downfall. Trailing to a Garth Crooks goal, all hope of salvaging a point just about disappeared when Walsh, the main attacking threat, limped off midway through the second half to be replaced by centre-half Gary Gillespie. Whether Dalglish would have made a difference against Spurs is hypothetical, but Joe did have the good grace to hold his hands up afterwards and admit that leaving him out was 'the daftest decision I ever made'.

The following week's *Football Echo* postbag was inundated with thoughts on the hot topic. A dismayed P. Mahon, of Anfield, wrote: 'I find this decision hard to believe. There is no sentiment in football but you only replace "off-form" players with others who are better. Is Michael Robinson a better "team" performer than Dalglish? Not in my mind. Dalglish's contribution to the success of this side has been enormous and he still has the knack of spotting openings when other players can't. Mr Fagan has to find a new midfield formula to keep the Reds ticking over. If Kenny Dalglish is not to be included in the team the goalscoring rate will be slow to increase.' What Joe's dropping of Dalglish did prove, however, was that he could be ruthless in his pursuit of restoring Liverpool's winning formula. He had shown that no player, whatever his stature, was too big to escape his wrath if he felt they were not putting in a shift for the team. Ronnie Whelan recalls: 'We were as surprised as anyone that he dropped Kenny. But in a way that was typical Joe: reputations meant nothing to him. He treated all his players equally. No one in the dressing-room questioned the decision, but what it did do was make us all sit up and think, "Well, if a player of Kenny's ability isn't assured of his place then we best pull our socks up or we'll be dropped, too".' As Joe later told Liverpool's former matchday programme editor Stan Liversedge, this was a facet of the job he did not enjoy. 'Managers do have feelings, and they don't want to drop players,' he said. 'But it's a job that has to be done at times. That's when you don't want to get up in the morning and go into the club. There was no such thing as going to bed at night, getting your head down and sleeping through. You went to sleep, then you woke up and began pondering upon team problems. One of the worst things was having to drop a player – I preferred to talk about leaving him out. That's something you never wanted to do. Bill Shankly didn't seem to show the stress he was under, but I think he sometimes put on a bit of an act when it came to telling a player he was dropped. A player used to come out of Bill's office wondering why he'd been axed when he'd just been made to feel he was the greatest player in the world!'

After playing a prominent role for Scotland in their midweek World Cup qualifier against Iceland, Dalglish was promptly restored to the Liverpool line-up for the following week's Merseyside derby.

Perhaps more significantly, so too was Ian Rush. Rush's return after a two-month absence could not have been better timed. With just two reserve-team games under his belt doubts were expressed about whether he was fully fit. Given Liverpool's increasingly sorry predicament in the League, Joe had no hesitation in thrusting him back into the fray. Rush had been expecting to start on the bench and perhaps be sent on for the final twenty minutes. Joe thought otherwise. He believed if Rush was fit enough to be named as substitute he was fit enough to play from the start. Unfortunately, it was the manager's second successive selection gamble that failed to pay off. Not even Rush's eagerly anticipated return could save Liverpool from an infamous derby defeat, best remembered for Graeme Sharp's stunning volley to win the game. It was Liverpool's first defeat by Everton in front of the Kop for fourteen years and one that consigned the reigning champions to seventeenth place, just four points clear of bottom club Stoke.

The pressure was mounting and though Joe was never one to show it publicly, on reflection Stephen Fagan admits that all did not seem right. 'I remember calling in one afternoon around this time just to say hello and he was sitting there with the television off, which was rare, and appeared deep in thought. I asked what was up and he said, "Just got a bit of a problem, but we'll get there in the end, it'll sort itself out". He didn't enlarge on it and I didn't ask him anything else about it, but I sensed that the team's poor start to the season was preying on his mind.'

The mood of despondency now hanging over Anfield prompted talk in the press of a crisis. 'Dark clouds have replaced the once golden sky,' read one report in the *Daily Mail*. Stuart Jones in *The Times* warned: 'The rumour about cracks in the Anfield fortress is no longer a game of English whispers. Liverpool are crumbling visibly and their domestic rule has all but been broken already.' There was no getting away from the fact that the club were now in the midst of their worst start to a season in twenty years. As the long dark nights began to draw in, it was shaping up to be a winter of discontent for Liverpool. For the first time in four seasons they did not even have the luxury of the League Cup to fall back on. The long-time holders had lost only once in the competition since August 1980, but their phenomenal stranglehold on the tournament finally came to an end at Tottenham on the last night in October. They had already been given a scare in round two, where it had taken two legs and extra-time to dispose of Fourth Division minnows Stockport County. This near-humiliation left Joe seething. Afterwards he disclosed in his diary that he believed his team was 'playing without conviction or belief in themselves', and accused them of being 'faceless players who are just going through the motions'. The performance at White Hart Lane was much improved, but not enough. A desperately disappointed Joe believed his side 'deserved another crack at the cherry', but nobly accepted that all good things have to come to an end sometime.

At fault for the goal that ended Liverpool's interest in the Milk Cup was Bruce Grobbelaar. It was his failure to hold on to a shot by Tony Galvin that provided Clive Allen with a gilt-edged opportunity to score the decisive goal. In the wake of the inevitable criticism that came his way Grobbelaar went in to see Joe the following day and asked to be taken out of the spotlight. Joe sympathised with the goalkeeper's plight and, in his diary, noted: 'Bruce Grobbelaar has just been in. He wants to be dropped. I can see his point quite clearly now. He thinks, and rightly so, that he is taking the blame for the faults the back four are making. He has a valid point and although he didn't say it I feel that he thinks I am not sticking up for him as I should. Maybe he is right.' It was not the first high-profile error Grobbelaar had made that season. Joe had been quick to defend him following the bizarre own-goal that settled the Charity Shield, but further blunders, most notably the two which handed goals to Imre Varadi and Gary Shelton in Sheffield Wednesday's shock win at Anfield, highlighted the inconsistencies in his game at that time.

Liverpool's number one admits he was suffering a major crisis of confidence. But Joe knew his good moments outweighed the bad and, as Grobbelaar recalls, he handled the situation superbly. 'A manager can't be seen to be molly-coddling his players. I was a grown man and, quite rightly, I was left to fight my own battles. I actually wanted him to drop me from the team, just to take the pressure off. But he was having none of that and told me in no uncertain terms that I wasn't ducking out of this particular battle. "You stay exactly where you are and work out it out for yourself", he told me.' Grobbelaar played in the weekend visit to Stoke and, a couple of hairy moments aside, redeemed himself with a clean sheet in a hard-fought victory. 'I heeded his advice and by the time I went back I was on top of my game,' says Grobbelaar. 'When it came to psychology the man was brilliant and a great motivator. He later explained all this to me and it made perfect sense. He didn't feel a need to mother me. "You'd been in the Army for goodness sake", he would say and therefore felt I was more than capable of taking a bit of stick in the press. If Joe had come out and defended me in the press, making excuses on my behalf, then I wouldn't have become the goalkeeper that I did. It was from incidents such as this that I learnt most and that made me stronger, both as a goalkeeper and a man.'

Another player who needed Joe's comforting arm during the difficult start to the 1984–85 season was Alan Kennedy. The European Cup-winning hero of just a few months earlier was suffering a serious dip in form and had been privately rebuked by the manager for his below-par performance in the Milk Cup tie at Stockport. 'Kennedy is a strange lad,' confessed Joe in his diary. 'It is all to do with his thinking. He always seems confused, and I don't know why it is, but when he should pass he holds it and when he should hold it he passes! Everything he does is the opposite of what he should do!' When thinking back, Kennedy admits the criticism of him was fair and says he was grateful for the advice that was subsequently given. 'He pulled me to one side after that game and he said, "Look, Alan, you seem to be holding on to the ball when you should be releasing it". He was quite right in what he was saying because my game was instinctive; it was all off the cuff, never rehearsed. I wasn't the type of player who could see what was going to happen. Where the likes of Dalglish and Rush could see ahead, I couldn't. I definitely understood what he was saying and realised he was giving me another chance. In no uncertain terms he'd let me know if I didn't buck my ideas up I would be out of the team because he had a young lad called Jim Beglin waiting in the wings.'

Buoyed by their pep-talks, both Kennedy and Grobbelaar put their early-season problems behind them. With Rush soon back among the goals, Liverpool slowly began to show signs of a renaissance. A week after the defeat in the derby, the reigning champions of Europe, by virtue of not playing until the Sunday, had actually dropped into the First Division relegation zone for the first time since the early 1950s. It was a barely believable scenario, even though their stay in the bottom three was brief. Victory at Nottingham Forest kick-started a mini-revival, but it had served as a chilling reality check for Joe and his team.

For a whole generation of Liverpool supporters the club's troublesome start to the season had been a new experience. Not since the morale-sapping spell in Division Two during the 1950s had the team's fortunes appeared so glum. It did not take a genius to fathom out just where the root of the problem lay. The impact of losing Graeme Souness, the injury to Ian Rush, Kenny Dalglish's loss of form and the need to push Mark Lawrenson forward to bolster an under-strength midfield meant that, in effect, the spine of Joe's Treble-winning side had been severely tampered with. Results suffered as a consequence. Goals from Rush and Whelan at the City Ground offered hope of a brighter future. However, there was still a long way to go before the mood of despondency and pessimism that had shrouded Anfield was entirely lifted.

Before that point, one of the few positives was Liverpool's progress in Europe. Molby was ineligible for the opening two rounds because he had signed after the deadline, but those early games certainly made him sit up and take notice. 'The one thing that really impressed me about Liverpool during my first season there was how they handled playing in Europe,' he says. 'They were ruthless, winning games so easily. I'd never won a game in the European Cup while with Ajax so this left a big impression on me. The key to it was the quality of the players. English teams were dominating Europe around this time: they always seemed to show more effort and fight. Liverpool had this and more. We loved having the ball. When in possession we fought very hard to keep it and when we didn't have it we fought very hard to get it back.' Liverpool began their defence against Lech Poznan of Poland, and in both legs sent out a message of intent. A 1–0 away win was followed by a 4–0 stroll at Anfield. The tie was a personal triumph for John Wark, match-winner in the first leg and hat-trick hero of the second. The goals were a timely boost for him because he, too, had started the season poorly and been on the receiving end of criticism from Joe. Wark was renowned for his goalscoring exploits from midfield at Ipswich, but had scored just twice before his goals against Poznan. Pre-season hopes that he might claim the Souness role had failed to materialise. Though he was capable of putting his foot in, this was never Wark's game and Joe quickly realised that to utilise his talents fully he was better deployed in a deep-lying midfield position. From there he could break forward on the blind side and provide an added goal threat. 'I had played this role so effectively for Ipswich,' says Wark. 'One of my best qualities was being able to contribute goals from the middle of the park. But Joe explained that the timing of my runs into the box had been wrong. I'd been making them too early and this meant it was easier for defenders to track my movement. Delaying my run allowed me more time and space.' It was an inspired move because, by the end of the season, Wark would top Liverpool's goalscoring list with a career-best twenty-seven. Rush, meanwhile, was also determined to make up for lost time. The next round of the European Cup was to provide him with the perfect stage on which to do just that.

Until Wark and Rush began firing on a regular basis, Liverpool's profligacy in front of goal had been a major cause of concern for Joe. After fifteen League games they had registered just eighteen goals. Only four other clubs had scored fewer. The home record made even grimmer reading: Liverpool had won fewer home games than any other club in the division. With just three home League wins, Anfield was no longer considered the fortress it once was. Joe admitted that Liverpool's poor form was now causing him sleepless nights. 'We have to try and find a solution. It's all disturbing my nights at the moment, I'll be honest. It wakes me up. I'm not going to have a nervous breakdown over it. I'm too hard for that. But we are not playing as a team.' However, it was then that a Benfica team who had lost all four of their previous meetings with Liverpool arrived on cue for a midweek European Cup tie. A stunning hat-trick from Rush sent them packing again. With Sammy Lee recalled, and Lawrenson moved into midfield to add a bit more bite, it was a morale-boosting night. It was also a notable occasion for Craig Johnston, who made his first senior appearance following his long-awaited return from Australia. As he had promised, Johnston jumped on the first flight back to Liverpool the day after the birth of his daughter. Given Liverpool's situation, his return was warmly welcomed when he re-entered the fray against Benfica as a half-time replacement for Wark. His first touch of the season was greeted by resounding cheers from the Kop, and he did enough to convince the manager that he was a worthy first-team starter for the next two months. 'With a new contract and a place in the winning side, I was confident about my position,' Johnston says. 'As far as I was concerned the hatchet had been buried.' For the time being it seemed that way, but the saga was far from over.

Despite a narrow defeat in the second leg in Lisbon, Liverpool's ticket for the last eight was safely booked, and thoughts of Europe could now be put aside until March. The contrast between Liverpool's domestic form and their performances in Europe had Joe labelling them a 'Jekyll and Hyde' side. The gap between the champions and League leaders Everton was not insurmountable at that stage of the season, even though there was plenty of ground to make up. What continued to concern Joe was his failure to find an adequate replacement for Souness. The manager was running out of solutions within the club to resolve it. 'Nobody in the midfield is forcing themselves to say to me, "I'm good enough",' he mused. While Lawrenson had excelled in the role against Benfica, as Liverpool's most dependable defender his presence was required on a permanent basis at the back. Molby was still struggling to adapt to the faster pace of English football. Off the field he settled in fine, famously developing an accent that was more Kirkdale than his native Kolding – an attribute that quickly endeared him to the locals – but on it Molby believes he suffered as a result of his ineligibility for the opening two rounds in Europe. 'If the lads had a good result in Europe, which they invariably always did, then Joe would keep the same side for the following weekend and I'd find myself back at square one, fighting to regain my place. It was a constant source of frustration for me at the time,' he says. Against Chelsea in December, Molby scored his first goal for Liverpool. In time he would become a valuable asset at Anfield. Unfortunately for Joe, it was not until after the 1984–85 season that the Dane fully adjusted to life in the First Division and that Liverpool fans saw the best of him.

With Sammy Lee the latest Liverpool player to undergo surgery, in his case on a knee ligament injury, Joe's quest to bolster the midfield stepped up a notch. But with Geoff Twentyman and his vast army of talent-spotters working overtime, Joe confided several times in his diary that he was becoming increasingly alarmed at the lack of top-quality candidates on the market. 'Trying our damndest to get a player or players who have outstanding qualities but they are nowhere on this island … I wish there were players to buy but there isn't – not in our class anyway … Obviously we need a player or two, but where are they? No one is good enough to improve our team. It's all very depressing.' Unearthing a player in the Souness mould was always going to be a tall order, and Joe became resigned to the fact that a direct replacement would not be found. Instead, in mid-November, the club splashed out £400,000 to sign 23-year-old Leicester captain Kevin MacDonald, who they had been tracking since the summer. Joe had watched MacDonald in action three weeks before and was suitably impressed by his starring role in Leicester's 5–0 demolition of Aston Villa. His wiry frame and ungainly running style may have deterred some, but to the more discerning observer MacDonald's intelligent distribution of the ball and strength caught the eye. As the player recalls: 'I remember having a good spell for Leicester just beforehand and there was some talk in the newspapers of a bigger club coming in for me, but I didn't really pay much attention to it. Next thing, I was made aware of Joe's interest. We had talks and the rest is history. You don't turn down a club of Liverpool's calibre, do you?' Like Molby before him, MacDonald was instantly tagged as the new Graeme Souness, a comparison both manager and player were quick to play down. 'It was certainly mentioned in some newspapers, but no one at Liverpool ever said I was there to replace Souness. And how could I?' says MacDonald. 'We were two totally different players, anyway. No matter who you are replacing in the team, there's always pressure to perform at a club like Liverpool. But this was where Joe was great because he didn't put any added pressure on me to be the new Souness.'

Due to a suspension hanging over from his time at Leicester, MacDonald's Liverpool debut was delayed until late December when he took the place of Johnston in the 1–0 home win over Luton. He was an unused substitute on two occasions before that, the first being in Tokyo for the World Club Championship match against Independiente of Argentina. Before flying out to Japan Liverpool secured a 3–1 League win over Coventry at Anfield, and had sneaked up to sixth place, just six points behind the leaders.

As the record books show, the World Club Championship is traditionally a competition treated more seriously by the South Americans. They had a one hundred per cent record in the intercontinental clash since it had been switched to a one-off contest in Tokyo. Liverpool had nothing but bad memories of their last visit in 1981, when they crashed 3–0 against the Zico-inspired Brazilians of Flamengo. Furthermore, the Argentines arrived in Japan several days earlier than Liverpool and were a lot more thorough in their preparation. Speaking ahead of the first sporting clash between England and Argentina since the Falklands War, Joe made all the right noises about taking the game seriously and explained that their defeat three years before would act as motivation. 'That won't happen again,' he insisted. 'It was the staff's fault. We were worried about them getting involved too much physically. It turned out to be just another game after a long flight. The British teams have never approached these games in the right manner. It's always been too light-hearted. But this is one we really want to win.' In reality, however, he was desperate to get the game over and done with. Beating Independiente and taking the prestige of being hailed the best team in the world was important, but so too was making sure his players stayed free from further injury. Lawrenson had already been ruled out of the match after pulling a hamstring in training.

Liverpool certainly gave a better account of themselves than three years before. They dominated for long periods and had two legitimate penalty appeals turned down. But on a bone-hard and bumpy surface that was almost devoid of grass, a goal after just six minutes by Jose Percudani was enough to settle matters in the Argentines' favour. Joe declared himself satisfied with the performance but disappointed with the result. Though victory would have fulfilled the ambition of Joe's old pal Bill Shankly, whose idea was to see Liverpool 'conquer the bloody world', on the arduous 18-hour flight home he confessed in his diary that it was a defeat he would not be losing much sleep over. 'People get excited about losing this game. I can't. I wish it wasn't played. Too many things about it upset me. I want to forget the last few days. I don't like going halfway around the world for a football match that we are not prepared for. It is nobody's fault but players need more than two days to get acclimatised. To me, we needed at least a full week. I know it is not possible because of our League programme. I still say that the two different hemispheres can never be bridged. It is all to do with climate, customs, different ways of thinking, different attitudes; it has nothing to do with any one thing but a variety of reasons. Playing surfaces for just one. I don't see how we can adjust from our pitch to a pitch such as it was in Tokyo, especially in a game that appears so important to everybody but me.'

On reflection it is hard not to conclude that this was a missed opportunity for Joe and his players to give their stuttering season a massive boost. Writing in *The Times*, Gerry Harrison certainly felt so. He said: 'Liverpool were the better team for most of the match', and added that 'the nature of defeat was so unsatisfactory'. Jan Molby maintains Liverpool 'gave it their best shot' and that 'the result was never going to make or break the season'. But he accepts it would have been a great honour to be the first English club to win the trophy. Peter Robinson admits: 'Looking back now, yes, there is a hint of regret that we so narrowly missed an opportunity to be world champions.'

Another one-off game Joe viewed as a distraction was the European Super Cup against Juventus. Liverpool had competed twice before, winning against Hamburg in 1977 and losing to Anderlecht the following year. Traditionally it was a contest played over two legs. In 1985, due to a crowded fixture list, there had been talk of a winner-takes-all match in Monte Carlo, as would become the norm in future years. When those plans fell through, Liverpool officials agreed to concede territorial advantage and a one-off game was played in Italy. Five weeks after the clash with Independiente, the European champions flew into an ice-bound Turin where the Arctic conditions almost forced the game to be postponed. Eager not to have made a wasted journey, Liverpool were keen for the match to go ahead and on a blanket of snow at a packed Stadio Communale slithered to a 2–0 defeat. Poland international Zbigniew Boniek scored both Juventus goals. For the second time in five weeks Liverpool had missed the chance to add another trophy to their already bulging cabinet. Again, though, few tears were shed. Despite the treacherous conditions Joe admitted that the Italians deserved to win. 'Beaten by the better side,' he conceded.

'The pitch wasn't ideal, but I have no complaints about it because it was the same for both sides and it caused us no special problems.' Joe viewed it as nothing more than a glamorous friendly. With both clubs going strong in the European Cup it would not be the last they would see of each other.

In contrast, a competition the Liverpool manager was placing much more emphasis on was the FA Cup. With so much ground to make up in the title race, the Cup took on even greater importance in 1985. Liverpool had not reached the final for eight years, and since being knocked out in the semi-final in 1980, had not enjoyed a significant run. At the start of the 1985 campaign hopes were high that Joe could succeed where his predecessor failed. The quest to reach Wembley kicked off with a home tie against Aston Villa and two goals from Rush, and another from Wark, carried them through to round four. With the goals flowing once again, and MacDonald bringing much-needed steel and finesse to midfield, there was renewed optimism around Anfield. 'We are no longer an easy touch,' wrote a satisfied Joe in the aftermath of the win over Villa. 'I have always maintained that our football is good, passing, movement etc. What we weren't doing was winning the ball from our opponents. Today we did.' Liverpool could not have been handed a sterner test in the fourth round than a televised home tie with high-flying Tottenham. But on a snow-covered pitch they avenged the Milk Cup defeat thanks to Rush's early strike. 'Our supporters are dreaming of Wembley,' wrote Joe, 'but there's a long way to go yet.'

The reward was a fifth-round tie at York City, who had just knocked out Arsenal. With the previous season's exit against Brighton still painfully fresh in his mind, Joe was taking no chances and prepared his team thoroughly. 'If anybody says that Liverpool should beat York easily I will scream,' he stressed. 'No team, anywhere, has the right to beat a team in the lower divisions just like that.' The difficult playing surface was only passed fit on the morning of the match and was covered by tons of straw to reduce the effects of severe frost. To counteract this Joe adjusted his tactics. 'We played York the way York didn't realise we could do – up and under. It foxed them,' he later explained. The teams had to settle for a draw after Ricky Sbragia equalised Rush's opener. More than forty-three thousand turned up for the replay four nights later. It was to be a memorable night as Liverpool brought York's gallant run crashing to a merciless end. Two-nil up at half-time, they racked up another five in a second-half goal blitz. Wark completed his second hat-trick of the season.

The seven-goal show may have lit up Anfield, but there remained one unhappy face in the Main Stand that night. Once again Craig Johnston was disgruntled. Having forced his way back into the team with a run of thirteen consecutive starts in November and December, Johnston had spent the past two months on the sidelines as MacDonald took the number ten shirt. Johnston's last appearance had been on Boxing Day when Liverpool slumped to a third home League defeat of the season, losing 2–1 to Leicester. Afterwards, Joe confided in his diary: 'We tried hard enough without having the craft to break the opposition down. I can make many changes and at the moment I don't know what to do. I am hoping for a miracle.' Liverpool had fallen back to tenth place, nine points adrift of joint leaders Tottenham and Everton. Changes were made. The axe fell on Johnston and he had figured on the bench only twice since. In the wake of the York victory he finally admitted defeat and slapped in another transfer request. 'It was apparent the old nightmare had returned, bigger and uglier than ever,' he says. 'When I wasn't in the team I took it very personally. I was never in it for the money. Anyone who saw me play will know I used to give one hundred and ten per cent every time I pulled on that red shirt. So when I wasn't playing it was almost like a knife through my heart to see the lads run out on to the pitch without me. That's just how I was back then. I remember around this time I was playing outrageously well in the reserves and was just so desperate to contribute.' The *Daily Mirror* ran the story of Johnston's unhappiness under the headline 'I Don't Like You Mr Fagan'. Underneath

Johnston was quoted as saying: 'Over the years the manager has made it obvious he does not like me – and I like him even less.' The following day another tabloid reported: 'Craig Johnston's turbulent career at Liverpool ended yesterday when he launched a scathing attack on manager Joe Fagan.' When given a right of reply, Joe was diplomatic in his response. But he was clearly tiring of the on-going saga. He finally agreed that it might be in the best interests of all parties if Johnston did indeed seek a new challenge elsewhere. 'I have no personal axe to grind,' the manager said. 'The poor devil is not in the team. He is a good player and he has done his best for Liverpool. It is all right for him to say things about me as long as he doesn't degrade the club. I have been expecting him to ask for a move and I think it would be better for all concerned if he went somewhere else.'

Johnston stands by his actions but admits he regrets how the story broke. 'Eventually my frustration got the better of me and I made no secret of letting people know how pissed off I was with the situation. It was nothing personal against Joe Fagan this time. It could have been any manager in the world. I was just so desperate to play. I felt I wasn't being given a fair crack of the whip and so I asked for a transfer. It broke my heart to do so but for the sake of my career I had to be playing. That headline in the newspaper was wrong and I wish it had never come out that way. It really hurt both of us because I had more respect for Joe than that. I did have a private conversation with him to explain this and thankfully he understood. But I honestly believed at the time that my Liverpool career was over.' Johnston's days were far from over even though he would start just one more game under Joe.

Johnston was not the only discontented player in the Liverpool ranks. After deputising admirably for the injured Lawrenson throughout much of January and February, Gary Gillespie was irked at the way he was frozen out once Lawrenson had recovered. He, too, asked to be put on the transfer list. As in the case of Johnston, Joe was sympathetic towards Gillespie's plight, but noted in his diary: 'I said yes but that does not mean right now! We have

too many commitments and he is too valuable to Liverpool FC.'
Another member of the squad showing signs of unrest was Jan
Molby. Like Johnston, he had also not figured in the first team since
Boxing Day, and with the World Cup just over a year away he was
concerned about his prospects of representing his country in
Mexico. 'I was thinking this could be the only time we ever get there
so there was no way I wanted to miss out. I felt I'd adapted well to
the English game and was showing good form for the reserves, so
being out of the team really frustrated me. In my eyes I was playing
as well as I had been at the start of the season when I was in the
team, but now I just couldn't seem to get a game, no matter what I
did. I made my mind up that the best thing for me would be to
leave,' he admits. Joe's powers of persuasion, however, eventually
convinced Molby that staying put was in his best interests. 'I
believed I was good enough. Joe, on the other hand, didn't and said
he'd pick me again when I was ready. He explained in simple terms
that I shouldn't be in such a rush. He assured me that the club liked
what they'd seen of me but that it was normal practice for players
to join Liverpool and then spend six to twelve months learning their
trade in the reserves. "Keep doing what you're doing, your time
will come". If I heard that once from him I heard it a million times.'
Though his first-team appearances between then and the end of the
season remained limited, Molby accepted the situation. 'When I
look back now I suppose I was acting hastily. If it wasn't for Joe's
advice I could have made one of the biggest mistakes of my life
because who knows how my career would have transpired if I have
walked out on Liverpool at such an early stage? But I wasn't
thinking that at the time.'

With the crucial stage of the season approaching Joe could ill-
afford to lose players of the quality of Molby or Gillespie. Strength
in depth had always been the bedrock of successful Liverpool teams
and with competition for places fierce his squad seemed well-
equipped for the challenges ahead. Despite his dislike of having to
inform players they were not in the team, Joe was well aware that
keeping all of his players happy was impossible. It was a task that

had been reduced slightly by the departure shortly after Christmas of Michael Robinson. Despite having played a valuable role in the Treble the previous season, Robinson had failed to establish himself as a first-team regular and had figured only sporadically since the arrival of Walsh. A popular figure in the dressing-room, he went with everyone's best wishes and completed a £100,000 move to Queens Park Rangers. Phil Thompson also ended a distinguished Anfield career when he moved permanently to Sheffield United after a loan spell.

While Robinson and Thompson were packing their bags, Joe was busy overseeing a deal he hoped would safeguard Liverpool's future. Initially spotted by Tom Saunders, Oldham Athletic's 17-year-old striker Wayne Harrison was one of the most sought-after youngsters in the game and Liverpool had to beat off competition from Everton, Manchester United and Nottingham Forest to sign him. He had initially impressed Saunders when starring for Oldham in an FA Youth Cup tie at Anfield. Joe was informed about the precocious talent and immediately submitted a record bid for a player so young. It required £250,000 to complete the deal, and took Joe's spending since taking over as manager to just over £2.7 million. Joe was adamant that it was money well spent. 'You hear reports about a special player perhaps once in twenty years,' he said. 'That's why we bought him.' As part of the agreement the player was promptly loaned back to Oldham to continue his development, but after just one further senior outing he was recalled to begin his Anfield education in Chris Lawler's reserve team. A succession of injuries would eventually curtail Harrison's career before he had a chance to play in Liverpool's first team, but two goals in the final five reserve games of the season seemed to bode well for the future.

Liverpool's progress to the last eight in the FA Cup had coincided with an unbeaten eight-game run in the League that took the reigning champions to fourth. It was their best run of results of the season and the top three were suddenly looking over their shoulders. Joe pinpointed the return to form of Dalglish, fresh from collecting his M.B.E. at Buckingham Palace, and scoring on his three-hundredth Liverpool League appearance, as one of the reasons behind the team's resurgence. But with Dalglish serving a suspension in Europe, having been shown a red card away against Benfica, it was his replacement Paul Walsh who helped Liverpool take another giant stride forward in their defence of the European Cup. Having had his season interrupted following knee surgery in October, Walsh came in for only his second start of the calendar year in the away leg of the quarter-final against Austria Vienna, in which Nicol's late goal secured a crucial 1–1 draw. A fortnight later Walsh produced his finest performance yet, scoring twice as Liverpool waltzed into the semi-final with a 4–1 win. But the match ended on a bitter-sweet note for Walsh. He fluffed his chance of a hat-trick when he missed a late penalty, an incident which incurred the wrath of his manager. With three regular penalty-takers – Neal, Wark and Rush – still on the field, Joe felt Walsh acted unpro-fessionally in his attempt to claim the matchball. Joe described the incident as 'diabolical', and made a stern note in his diary: 'Never mind hat-tricks, let's get as many goals as possible.' Phil Neal remembers that he also came in for an ear-bashing afterwards. 'He had a go at Walshy, but I think really he blamed me. As the captain he felt I should have stepped in and made sure Warky took it. It was a valuable lesson and thankfully there were no dire conse-quences. I shudder to think how he'd have reacted if there had been. He'd never have let me forget it.'

There were no such incidents in the semi-final against Panathinaikos. Anfield was lit up with an impressive pre-match firework display from the raucous Greek supporters, but they were soon silenced as the fluency of Liverpool's football hit heights that had not been scaled since the previous season. Following Wark's first-half opener, two goals in as many minutes by Rush just after the break killed the tie as a contest. Five minutes from time Dalglish's free-kick was powered home at the Kop end by European debutant Jim Beglin to complete the scoring. Beglin, a 21-year-old full-back, was the last signing of Bob Paisley's managerial reign. He had served his

Anfield apprenticeship in the reserves and was now starting to establish himself as a first-team regular after replacing the injured Alan Kennedy. He had made his senior debut six months before in a 1–1 home draw against Southampton, filling in for the injured Whelan in an unfamiliar left-sided midfield role. 'Joe generally liked to name his team twenty-four hours before so I knew on the Friday that I'd be playing and I was a bag of nerves,' he recalls. 'I was given no specific instructions other than the odd standard words of advice. Basically, it was a case of "just go out and play". I wasn't entirely comfortable with playing in a new position, but I gave it my best shot. I don't think I did too badly, but the whole emotion of the day eventually caught up with me late in the game and I ran out of steam.' When he returned to the first team in early April Beglin was better prepared. Looking back he believes Joe handled his transition from the reserves perfectly. 'In bringing me through slowly Joe had been preparing me for this moment,' he says. 'There were certain standards that I now had to maintain. If I didn't then I knew I'd be out. I felt the pressure as soon as I made my debut, but it was a fantastic pressure to have thrust upon you.' Scoring against Panathinaikos had been a dream ending to what was only the Irishman's second senior outing at Anfield. 'The funny thing was,' remembers Beglin, 'when I watched it on television later that night the commentator (Barry Davies) sounded so surprised that it was me popping up at the far post. But it was actually a tactic we'd been working on in training so it was great for Joe and the coaching staff that it paid off.' Ronnie Moran insists it was rare for Liverpool to work on particular set-piece routines, but admits this was a move designed solely for European competition. Eight years earlier, en route to the club's first European Cup triumph, Phil Neal had scored a similar goal in the semi-final tie at F.C. Zurich.

Beglin's first senior goal had established what looked like an irreversible first-leg advantage. Not in Joe's eyes. In typical Bootroom fashion, ahead of the second leg in Greece he refused to accept that a place in the final was guaranteed. A touch of Shankly-style psychology from his opposite number Jacek Gmoch ensured sixty thousand passionate home fans in Athens thought likewise. Joe's decision to resist temptation and not play Rush, who was one booking from a suspension that would have ruled him out of the final, hinted at what he really thought. 'The lads were so relaxed. Joe even permitted us a spot of sightseeing,' remembers Dalglish. 'Go and see the Acropolis,' Joe urged his players and it did them no harm at all. Despite a spirited opening from the hosts, Liverpool cruised into the final. A solitary Mark Lawrenson goal put the seal on an emphatic 5–0 aggregate win, the club's best winning margin at this stage of the competition since 1977. Reaching a second successive European Cup final enabled Joe to emulate the achievement of Bob Paisley. It also went some way to making up for the bitter disappointment of having had their dreams of a cup double dashed the previous week.

While Liverpool had mastered the art of European competition, the FA Cup proved elusive again. A day out at Wembley in May was long overdue. After Barnsley had been clinically disposed of in the quarter-final, thanks to Rush's second-half hat-trick, the dream was still alive. For the majority of Joe's squad an FA Cup winner's medal was all that was missing from their collections. The semi-final draw pitted Liverpool against arch-rivals Manchester United who, a fortnight before, had struck a psychological blow by winning at Anfield in the League. Goodison Park was the neutral venue chosen for this eagerly-anticipated re-match. With the stakes so high, the atmosphere was even more tense than usual and, given the enmity between the two sets of supporters, an air of hostility filled the air. It was a typical blood-and-thunder encounter, but with a howling gale blowing around the stands there was little in the way of good football played. As in the League game, which United had won 1–0, Joe felt the sense of occasion got to his players. However, Liverpool refused to be beaten and despite twice trailing never gave up, fighting back with goals from Whelan and Walsh at the end of normal and extra time respectively, to force a replay at Maine Road.

Mark Lawrenson admitted: 'It was like Monopoly: we got out of jail twice.' Mike Langley in the *Sunday People* wrote: 'United can feel aggrieved about being required to play again. They were the superior side here. But you don't pack a trophy room as Liverpool have done by lying down and swooning at every setback.' In Monday's *Daily Mirror*, Frank McGhee said: 'The champs had only three attempts at goal in two hours, yet scored twice to earn extra-time and then a second chance. Acceptance of defeat has become unthinkable to any Liverpool team.'

Having escaped with a draw to keep the FA Cup dream alive, Joe's frame of mind should have been dominated by a sense of relief, but he was not happy. 'Some of our players don't want to know – in other words they shit it on the big occasion,' he raged in his diary. 'They can't think straight, they go slower in movement – they shrink to five-footers. What a thing to say ... but it is true. Without Grobbelaar and Dalglish we would have been out of the Cup. Grobbelaar made three magnificent saves and Dalglish set the last goal up through his determination not to give up.' When reflecting more on the dramatic events at Goodison the following day, he described his mood as 'as dull as the weather'. It was not often that he dwelt on a result for too long, and as a rule never normally took his work home with him. On the rare occasions he did, he would sit quietly with a pen and paper in hand, which signalled to Lil and any of the children who had popped round for Sunday lunch that something football-related was on his mind. There was clearly something worrying him ahead of the replay. Rush, having picked up a knock, was facing a race against time to be fit. But the continuing problems in midfield were of particular concern. 'I am seriously thinking of making changes,' he wrote. 'This fella MacDonald is not quick enough or good enough to hold his place; he is as slow as a carthorse. I took Wark off after 75 minutes but not because he was doing badly, more to try and get a goal out of Walsh. I could have brought MacDonald off but his position in front of the back four was vital. He did at least prevent Robson from coming through on those surging runs of his.'

In the days leading up to the game Joe continued to agonise over his team selection. He noted in his diary: 'I'm having second thoughts about the team. I'm going to play both Nicol and Walsh no matter if Rushie is fit. I'll play him and Walsh with Kenny behind them. I'm sorry to leave John Wark out but I feel they have cottoned on to his play – I must have more options in that midfield. If MacDonald doesn't improve during the game I will put Gary Gillespie on and throw Lawrenson into midfield.' As it was, Nicol and Walsh did play, Rush failed to prove his fitness and Wark retained his place. But Joe's plans were thrown up in the air when Dalglish was forced off with a knee injury thirteen minutes from time. Despite taking the lead through Paul McGrath's own goal just before half-time, United hit back after the break with goals by Hughes and Robson. MacDonald once again struggled, but the injury to Dalglish forced the manager's hand. With that enforced substitution all hope disappeared, and on an all-round bitterly disappointing night Liverpool's FA Cup run came to an end.

Though other players were guilty of not performing against United, MacDonald found himself cast as scapegoat by supporters who were calling for him to be substituted before Dalglish was injured. On reflection he openly admits: 'I played poorly in both games.' Since breaking into the side at the turn of the year the Scot had been one of the main driving forces behind Liverpool's improved run of form, bringing a calming influence to the centre of midfield. Against Barnsley and Panathinaikos, just before the FA Cup semi-final, he had been particularly outstanding. He offers no excuses for the ineffectiveness of his performances against United and accepts the flak which came his way afterwards. 'I was at fault and make no bones about it,' he says. 'I'd love to turn back the clock and put that right, but I can't. We were on a good run and my confidence was high going into the United games, but for some reason it just didn't happen for me. It was certainly one of the lowest points of my time at Liverpool.' When Bruce Grobbelaar's form had come under similar scrutiny earlier in the season Joe stood by his goalkeeper and refused to drop him, believing he had the strength of character to ride out the storm. In the aftermath of the semi-final, though, Joe decided it was in the team's best interests to take MacDonald out of the firing line. Initially it appeared to be a knee-jerk reaction based on two games, but Joe's diary suggests otherwise: it confirms that his patience had been wearing thin for some time. Following a 3–0 victory at Sunderland earlier in the month, he wrote: 'One worry is MacDonald. He is providing the stability in midfield for others to break, but his running off the ball and passing is not yet up to our standard.' MacDonald was to make just one more appearance that season, at centre-back in a makeshift back four against Watford. The promising start he had made to life at Anfield had been curtailed, but he insists it did not affect his relationship with the manager. 'I remember he didn't say much to me after the semi-final. But he knew how to handle players and on occasions like this when things weren't going too well he was always there with a comforting arm around the shoulder and wise words of advice.'

Going out of the Cup to United was a massive blow for everyone at the club and Joe, like his predecessor, was fated never to win the competition as manager. Still, Liverpool now had the consolation of the European Cup final to look forward to. While supporters started planning their trip across the Channel, Joe and his players set about completing the formalities of wrapping up the League campaign. Before losing at home to Tottenham in mid-March – Spurs' first win at Anfield since the Titanic sank – Liverpool had been the form team in the country. Tentative talk in the press suggested that maybe Everton's expected procession towards a first title in fifteen years was not going to be as straightforward as first imagined. Given the ground conceded before Christmas it was always going to be a tall order for the reigning champions to retain the crown, but to their credit, they kept plugging away until it was mathematically impossible.

Despite Liverpool's best efforts the title passed across Stanley Park in early May, leaving Clive White in *The Times* to ponder: 'If the race were extended who knows, Liverpool might even have caught up with their young successors Everton.' It was a purely hypothetical train of thought but one shared by Jan Molby. 'In the end we went really close and if the season had been a bit longer then maybe we would have caught them,' he says. Joe sportingly congratulated Everton on their achievement: 'They won it fair and square and they were the best team over the whole season, there's no doubt about that,' he said. Liverpool were now free to concentrate on their preparations for the match in Brussels. Five League fixtures in the space of a fortnight remained and with runners-up spot still attainable the games were anything but meaningless. On the eve of the FA Cup final, Liverpool concluded their home programme with a seven-goal thriller against Watford. They fought back gamely from 2–0 down to move within three points of second-placed Tottenham, who had completed their season. The Watford win stretched Liverpool's unbeaten run since bowing out of the Cup to eight games and the fixture backlog was providing Joe with ample opportunity for fine-tuning. Victory at West Ham three nights later confirmed second spot, but doubts persisted in Joe's mind about whether his team would be good enough to beat Juventus. He admitted his worries in his diary and was particularly concerned with the form of his defence. 'Maybe I'm being too harsh but both Hansen and Lawrenson were bloody awful,' he wrote after three goals had been conceded at home against Chelsea. MacDonald and Beglin came in for similar condemnation when another three were leaked at Anfield in the Watford game. However, with the most important match of the season fast approaching Joe was careful not to knock the players' confidence by handing out an ear-bashing. 'For now we have to get the best out of them. I don't want anyone to get their head down,' he added. 'We need everyone pulling together – not being sickened by words that mean nothing at this stage of the season.' While having to play so many games ahead of the final may have been useful in terms of players maintaining match fitness, the risk of injury always loomed large and a dislocated shoulder sustained by Lawrenson in a 1–1 draw at The Dell hardly helped Joe's pessimistic outlook. Further injuries to Molby and Walsh saw the queue for the treatment table lengthen at the most inopportune time.

The League campaign came to a close just six nights before the European Cup final as first met second at Goodison. Having seen the trophy that had been their own personal property for the previous three seasons taken across the city, Liverpool were determined to restore some lost pride with a morale-boosting derby win. However, it was Everton, winners of the European Cup-Winners' Cup in Rotterdam the previous week, and narrowly beaten by Manchester United in the FA Cup final at the weekend, who were celebrating once again. Liverpool contributed to their own downfall. The normally reliable Wark, the club's leading scorer for the season, screwed a second-half penalty wide. Thirteen minutes later Paul Wilkinson scored his first goal in Everton colours to settle the match.

For a team who had been written off earlier in the season, and who had slumped as low as twentieth back in October, finishing runners-up in the League was a commendable achievement. Just one defeat in eleven games was indeed title-winning form, but Liverpool had paid the price for their slow start. The departure of Graeme Souness played a huge part, as did the early-season injury to Ian Rush and loss of form suffered by Kenny Dalglish. But Joe did not seek excuses. He branded it a failure and was quick to remind anyone who thought otherwise that 'as always, our bread and butter is the League and we weren't good enough. For this club, finishing second is never a success'. Such were the standards that he and his predecessor had set that the 1984–85 campaign would never be remembered fondly. Dalglish pulled no punches when describing it as 'a dreadful season'. While Ian Ross in the *Daily Post* was a little less harsh, preferring to call it 'uncharacteristically mediocre', there was genuine concern among fans that Liverpool's reign as top dogs was under threat, both locally and nationally.

Yet with one game to go, the greatest prize of all beckoned once again. For Liverpool and their many thousands of supporters it was off to Brussels for another European Cup final. As it was twelve months before, it would be an occasion that would live forever in the memory, but for vastly contrasting reasons.

CHAPTER ELEVEN

HEYSEL

JOE FAGAN TRAVELLED with his team to Brussels harbouring a
deep secret. The 1985 European Cup final was to be his last
game as manager of Liverpool Football Club. When the final
whistle sounded at the Heysel Stadium his long career in football
would be over. He hoped to bow out on a high by leading Liverpool
to a fifth European title against Juventus, and cementing the club's
position as the undisputed heirs to Real Madrid's once untouchable
mantle as Kings of the Europe. He also hoped to leave behind a firm
foundation from which his successor could build. What followed
was the most unimaginable nightmare. 29 May, 1985, would become
a date ingrained in history as the night Liverpool's twenty-one
years of exemplary participation in Continental competition came
to a chilling end. However, the myth that Joe's decision to step
down stemmed from the tragic events which were to unfold on the
crumbling terraces of Belgium's national stadium, is untrue.

   The reality is that his mind had been made up for some time.
Indeed, it was after just one season in the job, as Anfield basked
in the glory of the Treble, that he first broached the subject of
retirement with his wife Lil. According to son Stephen: 'Knowing
Mum she'd have probably just gone, "Oh, yeah, OK, do you
want a cup of tea?" That's the way they were.' From that moment
his tenure was never going to stretch into a third year. Another
twelve months in the hot seat would be enough. 'It was definitely

nothing to do with Heysel,' says Stephen. 'The decision was taken months before, but this seems to have been lost in the mists of time. It annoys me to constantly hear or read that it was because of the disaster that he quit. It wasn't and I'd really like people to know that.'

Joe's time as Liverpool manager was always going to be a short-term project. Though the Anfield board hoped he would complete three years in office before handing over the reins, it was never his intention to go beyond the then statutory retirement age. With his sixty-fifth birthday looming, the time was right. In February 1985, when the prospect of reaching another European Cup final was still a long way off, Joe informed Peter Robinson and John Smith of his intention to step down at the end of the season. While they were reluctant to accept his resignation, Smith and Robinson respected Joe's decision. 'We pleaded with him to stay on, but once his mind was made up there was no changing it,' recalls Robinson. 'He felt it was right that he gave us enough time to decide who would replace him. Again, this was typical of Joe – always putting the club first. We wanted him to do another year at least. We believed he was more than capable of steering the club to further glory, but he just felt he'd had enough and thought it was the best decision for everyone.'

Joe had enjoyed his first twelve months in the job more than he had imagined. Who would not after completing an unprecedented haul of three trophies? But Liverpool's poor start to the 1984–85 season certainly had not eased his state of mind. 'I think he did start to feel the pressure during that season,' says Jan Molby. 'Because of what they'd achieved the season before you could sense he was getting frustrated. It took a long time that season to get the team working at the maximum level it was capable of, and by that time it was too late. Everton had run away with the title and we lost crucial games in the cup competitions, notably the FA Cup semi-final replay against Man United.' Other players noticed a visible change in the manager during that second season and Mark

Lawrenson says: 'Something happened to Joe, and it happened long before the Heysel Disaster. I think he just got tired of the job and of the daily routine, and was happy to get out.'

The stresses and strains of life at the summit of English football had taken its toll, of that Lawrenson is in no doubt. 'This bubbly character had not looked his age in his first season, but looked considerably older in his second,' he says. There was not an older manager in the country at the time. But while age obviously had a bearing on his decision, on reflection Peter Robinson believes Joe was never truly comfortable in the manager's chair. 'I did ask many years later about his reasons for this and, while there were no doubt other factors, what he said to me was that the one part of management he found very difficult was dealing with players who were not in the team. He wasn't comfortable with them knocking on his door, asking why they weren't playing. Having to tell players they were, for one reason or another, not good enough to play in his team was something he found extremely difficult. This maybe had something to do with the close relationship he once had with so many of the players when he was a coach.'

It was agreed by all parties that no official announcement would be made until the last ball of the 1984–85 season had been kicked. While Joe went about his business as normal, leading Liverpool to second place in the League and a second successive European Cup final appearance, tentative plans were being put in place to find his successor. Nowadays it is difficult to imagine the press not getting wind of such a major story. But Joe's imminent departure remained a closely guarded secret. The plan was for the club to go public only after Liverpool had returned home from Brussels, hopefully with a fifth European Cup to add to their trophy cabinet.

Two days before the final, *Daily Express* journalist John Keith took a phone call at home. On the other end of the line was what he describes as 'a very reliable source close to the club'. During the course of the conversation this source informed Keith that this was going to be Joe's last match in charge and that Kenny Dalglish was the man to succeed him. With a major scoop in his notebook, Keith flew out to Belgium with the team the following day. When he checked into his Brussels hotel room he excitedly filed the bomb-shell story. His newspaper duly ran with it the next morning and, once his fellow scribes became aware of it, a number of other tabloids followed suit in their later editions. It was the *Express*, however, who led the way with a bold front-page headline that screamed: 'FAGAN QUITS LIVERPOOL'.

At first, Joe refused to confirm or deny the news. 'Wait and see,' he told journalists who hounded him for a quote to back up this sensational story. With Anfield officials also tight-lipped, confusion reigned. When the papers hit the newsstands talk of Joe Fagan's imminent resignation reverberated across Europe. As the news was digested, supporters, players and other journalists alike dissected the veracity of the story. But Keith stood by the words he had written. 'I had one hundred per cent confidence that what I'd been told was true,' he says. 'My information had come from a very good source. I had no reason whatsoever to doubt him.' The identity of Keith's informant has never been revealed, but Peter Robinson remains adamant that 'only a select few people' knew of Joe's intention: himself, John Smith and Tom Saunders plus, of course, Joe and his soon-to-be-announced successor Kenny Dalglish. In his autobiography, Dalglish wrote: 'Somebody within Liverpool, who knew what was going on must have marked the journalists' card. The press wouldn't have made me hot favourite to replace Joe without inside information. Maybe the person who leaked the information did it to build me up as a candidate, to make it less of a shock when Liverpool announced that I was following Joe.'

Coming on the morning of the most important match of the season, Keith's world exclusive could not have been more ill-timed and Joe was understandably upset that it broke that way. 'I genuinely believe Joe was shattered when he saw the newspapers on the morning of the game,' says Phil Neal. 'From a reporter's point of view though it couldn't have been better ... the most sensational Liverpool story since Kevin Keegan announced he was going to quit the club for Hamburg but with even more poignant timing. This time, though, the story was disturbing in that it created an atmosphere of uncertainty. The fact that it first appeared on the day of the game proved a serious threat to our concentration.'

Neal continues: 'As usual there were plenty of sports journalists milling around the players, some welcome, some not so. Some of the players joined groups of reporters from time to time but generally they were gossiping rather than handing out any state secrets from the Liverpool camp.' Back home, the local press on Merseyside had been caught unawares and with no official quotes to back up the story the *Daily Post* erred on the side of caution, reporting only that: 'Liverpool *may* be lining up a new manager.' Its story added: 'Speculation is rife in Brussels that the current boss, 63(sic)-year-old Joe Fagan, is ready to retire and that tonight's European Cup final with Juventus will be his swansong.' By the time the first editions of the *Liverpool Echo* went to print, at around midday, there had still been no confirmation from Brussels. But beneath a front-page headline of 'Will Joe Go?', Ian Hargreaves wrote: 'The odds are now strong that Fagan will step down as manager whether Liverpool win or lose.' Hargreaves, though, went on to dispute claims that Kenny Dalglish was to take over and instead tipped Alex Ferguson, then at Aberdeen, to be Joe's replacement.

Keith acknowledges that what he had written could have had a damaging effect on Liverpool's preparations, but explains that in situations like this professional integrity as a journalist take over. 'Of course, I'd got to know Joe well during my time covering the club,' he says. 'I had nothing but the utmost respect for him, but I was just doing my job and I hope he'd have understood that.'

The big game was now just a matter of hours away and talk of Joe's future was threatening to overshadow the build-up. It had been such a closely guarded secret that not even those closest to him were aware of his pending retirement, including his children. Son Stephen was in Brussels as part of the travelling support and he recalls: 'I had no intimation whatsoever that he was about to leave. The first I heard about it was when I picked up a paper on the morning of the game. I wouldn't say it came as a surprise but at the same time I wasn't expecting it either. He'd obviously made his mind up, though, and once he'd done that then there'd have been no changing it. He was my dad and I'd have backed his decision one hundred per cent, whatever it was.'

The news also took his trusted confidants in the Bootroom by surprise. 'I was sharing a room with Joe and knew nothing about it, none of us did,' recalls Ronnie Moran. 'I didn't find out until the morning of the game and it came as a massive shock. John Bennison (Liverpool youth coach) told me. He said it was all over the papers. But my initial reaction to him was, "Don't believe everything you read in the papers". I dismissed it as the press trying to cause mischief on the morning of an important game, which was nothing new. The night before, as we always used to do before big games, all the staff had been in our room talking about the game and having a little drink. I remember it would get to a certain time and Joe would say, "Go on now bugger off, we've got a game tomorrow so let's get some sleep". On this occasion he got the whisky back out and we had one more each, but still he didn't let on about him leaving. That was typical of Joe, though. He was so loyal and faithful to the club that if he'd been told to keep quiet he would.'

The players, too, knew nothing. The first room-mates Phil Neal and Mark Lawrenson knew was when they turned on their television sets in the hotel and saw it was being reported on an English-speaking news channel. 'We didn't know whether to believe the story or not,' says Lawrenson. 'Nothing had been mentioned about him leaving, but we soon sensed something was going on and drew our own conclusions.' Phil Neal said: 'It would be easy to say it didn't affect us, but it was such a bombshell. None of us expected Joe to go on as manager for a long time, but I, for one, had no inkling of this. We'd been thinking about nothing but the game. We did our best to keep it that way, but with all sorts of rumours flying around it was difficult not to be distracted.'

The mounting speculation, and the possible detrimental affect it was having on his side's preparations, prompted Joe to eventually come clean. Journalists had been besieging the team hotel since the news first broke and during a mid-morning press briefing he admitted for the first time that the story was indeed true. It came just in time to make the Stop Press section on the back page of the *Liverpool Echo*. He then explained: 'We decided through my express wish that I would relinquish the position of team manager after the last game of the season, and they (Smith and Robinson) didn't try to change my mind. It hasn't been done hastily or behind anyone's back. I gave them plenty of time and if they had asked me to go in February, I'd have gone with no recrimination. The decision is something I feel is right for Liverpool. My two main reasons are that I feel too old and a little bit tired. I think there is a need for a man with a younger brain and energy. I knew a manager's job was not eight hours a day, but twenty-four, and I knew that starting at sixty-two, two years would be enough. I want to stress that I'm not retiring – I'm not sixty-five yet – but relinquishing the position of manager. I might still be connected with the club next season, perhaps in a scouting capacity, but I certainly wouldn't go anywhere else in football.'

According to Keith, Joe appeared 'relaxed and a little relieved' to have finally shared his secret, but he was still keen to ensure that his players and staff remained fully focused on the task in hand. Given the circumstances, that was no easy task. 'We still didn't know if he was leaving, retiring or being moved upstairs, so, yes, it created a bit of uncertainty straight away,' remembers Lawrenson. After lunch Joe called the squad together and told them in no uncertain terms to completely ignore what was being spoken about him on television and written in the newspapers. He was not telling them it was untrue, but he could not stress enough that the only thing they needed to be thinking about was that night's game. His future was not important; beating Juventus and bringing home a fifth European Cup was. There would be plenty of time to discuss the future afterwards. The professionalism that ran through the Liverpool ranks was such that no questions were asked. But as the players headed back to their rooms he quipped: 'After tonight you can call me Joe again.' Considering they always referred to him as 'Boss' it was a telling comment.

The countdown to kick-off could now begin. As he had done the year before, Joe was keen to keep everything as normal as possible. That meant Liverpool's 18-man squad arrived in Belgium the previous afternoon. With only five substitutes allowed Joe knew he was going to have to break the hearts of two players. But he gave nothing away about team selection until after a further training session in R.S.C. Anderlecht's Constant Vanden Stock Stadium on the eve of the final. His worries on the injury front had eased slightly. Lawrenson, Gillespie and Johnston had all proved their fitness when given a run-out just a few days before with a Chester XI in a benefit game played in aid of the Bradford fire disaster. There was a slight scare surrounding Ian Rush, who injured his wrist after being struck by a shot from Dalglish in training at Melwood on the day of departure. But as Joe was quick to point out to inquisitive reporters: 'Rushie doesn't need his hand to score goals.'

That left just Paul Walsh, who had a stomach strain, as a doubt. Having scored four goals in his last six games, Joe was desperate for Walsh to be passed fit. To give him enough time to recover, Joe delayed naming his team until the last possible moment. In the event, Walsh was declared available well in advance and took his place in an adventurous three-pronged attack alongside Rush and Dalglish. At the back there was disappointment for Molby and Gillespie as the fit-again Lawrenson returned. Among the substitutes, Joe could find no place for Liverpool's European Cup-winning hero of 1981 and 1984, Alan Kennedy, who had only recently recovered from injury. Instead he kept faith with Beglin, who had started the previous four matches. Kennedy was understandably distraught, but Joe's philosophy was: 'The lad's (Beglin) taken his chance well and deserves to be in the team.'

Another selection dilemma centred on whether to risk going without a back-up goalkeeper. The regular reserve Bob Bolder had broken his ankle in the final second-team game of the season, at Bradford. That left Chris Pile, who had only recently turned eighteen, and who had only three reserve outings under his belt, as cover for Grobbelaar. Joe certainly knew about Pile's capabilities. Twelve months before, the Huyton youngster was the youth-team goalkeeper in the shoot-out at Melwood which preceded the final in Rome. Joe's decision was swayed by the memory of what happened to Aston Villa in the 1982 European Cup final against Bayern Munich when Jimmy Rimmer was forced off through injury after ten minutes and untested rookie Nigel Spink came off the bench to deliver a match-winning debut, aged twenty-three. At eighteen years and fifty-five days Pile became the youngest player to be part of a European Cup final squad. A lifelong Liverpool supporter, he had begun the season as fourth-choice goalkeeper. But in typical Liverpool fashion no fuss was made about his promotion. 'I was never officially told that I'd be in the travelling party to Brussels,' remembers Pile. 'I used to play club cricket in the Liverpool Competition, but when Bob got injured I was told to give it up, so I knew then that there was a chance I'd be going. Joe was great, though, and not saying anything was his way of keeping the pressure off me. It was an amazing experience just to be around these players who a year or two before I'd been supporting from the terraces. My nan actually had a premonition that something awful was going to happen, but I had no nerves whatsoever. If needed, I'd have jumped at the chance to play. Although I'd never have wished an injury on Bruce, the experience of Nigel Spink with Villa was always at the back of my mind.'

After naming the following starting XI – Grobbelaar, Neal, Beglin, Lawrenson, Hansen, Whelan, Wark, Johnston, Dalglish, Walsh and Rush – Joe told the *Liverpool Echo*: 'This was the team I would have selected weeks ago. I feel very confident indeed. The lads are bubbling and can't wait to get out on to the pitch.' Despite their relatively disappointing campaign at home the mood in the camp echoed that of the manager. It was one of determination to succeed and optimism that they would. Captain Phil Neal, a veteran of the club's four previous European Cup finals, was bursting with pride at the prospect of leading the team out at Heysel and was anticipating nothing but 'another night of glory'. What better way to silence the critics whose response to Liverpool not winning a domestic honour for the first time since 1978 was to taunt them with barbed comments ranging from 'spent force' to 'yesterday's men'.

Yet here was Liverpool Football Club, ninety minutes away from the most coveted piece of silverware in club football. The season hung on a knife-edge. Win and the troubles of the past nine months would be forgotten in an instant; lose and the stigma of a first trophy-less campaign for a decade would fall heavily on the shoulders of all involved. The thought of failure, however, was not one that was contemplated by Liverpool. Those of a superstitious nature may have pointed to the fact that no English side had won a European trophy in Brussels: West Ham in 1976 and Arsenal four years later had suffered defeat in Cup-Winners' Cup finals. But Peter Robinson reiterates that there was an unerring sense of self-belief running through the Liverpool squad who travelled to Belgium. 'I had honestly never seen them in such confident mood,' he remembers. 'True, we'd had one or two setbacks during the season, but Joe always ensured that heads never dropped.'

Juventus, too, had not enjoyed the best of seasons domestically. Despite having the psychological advantage of January's Super Cup success, confidence was not sky-high as they made their way to the Belgian capital. An alarming slump in form in Serie A following their European Cup semi-final victory over Bordeaux meant Italy's 'Old Lady' had to settle for sixth place, their lowest finish in twenty-three years. The spectre of two previous European Cup final defeats (1973 and 1983) also hung over them. Indeed, in spite of the millions of lire pumped into the club by the Agnelli family, owners of the Fiat car company, Juventus's team of 1985

were considered weaker than the one who had lost to S.V. Hamburg
in Athens two years before. Legends such as Zoff, Gentile and
Bettega had not been adequately replaced. On a scouting mission to
Turin after the semi-final Joe admitted to not being too impressed
with what he had seen. 'They are not as good as people make out.
Only one or two are good players, the rest are ordinary,' was his
verdict after seeing them held 1–1 at home by Graeme Souness's
Sampdoria. One player who had made a big impression on him,
though, was the French midfielder Michel Platini. Joe commented:
'We shall have to find some way of stopping that fellow Platini
hitting 30-yard passes all over the place.' Despite Joe's dismissive
view, Juventus were clearly still a formidable force, widely regarded
as the most technically accomplished team in Europe. They were
packed with world-class talent including the Pole Zbigniew Boniek
and a quartet of World Cup-winning Italians: captain Gaetano
Scirea, full-back Antonio Cabrini, midfielder Marco Tardelli and
striker Paolo Rossi. In addition, they were coached by the highly-
regarded former Italy international Giovanni Trapattoni, who was
attempting to become only the second coach, after the German Udo
Lattek, to win all three major European club titles.

With so little to separate the two teams, the English press were
split in their opinion of who would come out on top. In *The Times*,
David Miller wrote: 'My feeling is that Juventus are potentially
good enough to win by a two-goal margin but that they will fail.'
The *Daily Mail*'s Jeff Powell took the opposite view: 'If Juventus
keep their heads this time, I suspect that Fiat mogul Gianni Agnelli's
long and expensive quest for the golden fleece of European football
will be rewarded at last.' The Juventus line-up showed just one
change from the one who defeated Liverpool back in January,
Stefano Tacconi replacing Luciano Bodini in goal. Though evenly
matched on paper, Peter Robinson believes the pressure of trying
to end the club's long wait for success in the European Cup weighed
heavy on the Italians' shoulders. 'In contrast to the relaxed mood in
our camp, the Juventus players appeared so nervous it was untrue.
It ran right through the club. I'd got to know some of the Juventus

officials from playing them in the Super Cup, and this was clearly evident ahead of the game and when they arrived at the stadium. To this day I still firmly believe we would have won that European Cup had it not been for what happened on the terraces before kick-off.'

Hooliganism at football matches had been steadily on the increase since the 1960s. It was a problem that stretched the length and breadth of Europe, yet on the Continent it was labelled 'the English disease'. Considering that fans of Tottenham Hotspur and Leeds United had ran riot in Rotterdam and Paris at the finals of the 1974 UEFA Cup and 1975 European Cup respectively, perhaps there was some justification. Followers of Manchester United and West Ham had also been involved in disturbances while following their clubs away in Europe, and trouble always seemed to follow the England national team during this time. Liverpool supporters, on the other hand, could boast an almost unblemished reputation on their European travels, stretching back to the mid-1960s. In 1977, they formed what was then the biggest mass migration of football fans from these shores to see Emlyn Hughes lift the club's first European Cup in Rome. They returned with their good name not only intact but enhanced. 'It was certainly true that Liverpool and its fans had had a "good" record at football abroad, especially when compared to the violent and sometimes racist trashing dished out by other English crews over many years,' writes John Williams, director of the football research unit at Leicester University and an expert on fan culture. Since 1977 the younger element of Liverpool's support had become more renowned for the designer sportswear they brought back from their trips to the Continent than the mindless sprees of violence associated with other clubs' fans. These 'shopping' trips may not always have been conducted legally, and would occasionally bring bad publicity to the club, but 'hooligans' was very rarely a term attached to Liverpool's followers. The Liverpool 'scallies', as they would become widely known, kept a much lower profile than the organised mobs from their domestic rivals. However, they would come out in force if retribution was required, or for the big games against their traditional rivals from Manchester, Leeds and London. Essentially, this new generation of Liverpudlians were more interested in enjoying their Channel-hopping escapades than wreaking havoc. Just a month before Heysel, though, the violence around Goodison Park at the FA Cup semi-final against Manchester United, is remembered as among the worst to involve Liverpool fans.

It was a worrying sign of the times, not just for Liverpool but football in general. In the FA Cup, Millwall fans had infamously rioted at Kenilworth Road, Luton, which led to the Government setting up a football hooliganism 'war cabinet'. On the same day as the Bradford fire disaster, a 14-year old boy was killed after violence erupted at St Andrew's before, during and after the Division Two fixture between Birmingham and Leeds. It seemed 1985 was shaping up to be English football's *annus horribilis*.

Peter Robinson had been a busy man in the weeks leading up to the final. With Liverpool having been involved at this stage on four previous occasions it was not an entirely new experience for the club's experienced administrator. He was now more than familiar with UEFA's protocol when it came to organising such events. As usual he and a small delegation from Anfield travelled to Belgium in advance of the final to visit the stadium and attend meetings with officials from European football's governing body, the opposition club and local dignitaries. The purpose of the trip was to iron out any potential problems and Robinson immediately flagged up his concerns over the ramshackle state of the stadium. 'It wasn't right to stage a game of that size,' he recalls. 'We were shown the dressing-rooms and executive areas. I asked to go out on to the ground and we looked at the fan divisions – which were little more than a chicken-wire fence. It would not have got a ground licence in England at that time.' Opened in 1930, and initially known as the Stade du Centenaire, it once boasted a capacity of seventy thousand and was afforded the honour of staging the European Cup finals of 1958, 1966 and 1974. Three Cup-Winners' Cup finals had also been held there, and it also played host to the climax of the 1972 European Championship. No other ground on the Continent had staged more European finals at the time. It was, however, no longer in the best of condition. Arsenal fans who attended their club's clash with Valencia described Heysel as 'a dump'. Furthermore, with the capacity now lowered to fifty-two thousand, it was considered by many too small to host a match of this importance. Interest in the game was such that Robinson was informed by Belgian officials that it could have been sold out four times over.

Journalist and seasoned footballing Europhile Brian Glanville was under no illusion that it was a poor choice of venue. 'That Heysel was ever chosen for the game was a shocking commentary on the folly of UEFA and the idleness of its team who were meant to inspect the stadium,' he said. 'The word was that the day they came, it was very cold, and that they scarcely bothered to emerge from the warmth to see what should have been obvious to them – that this stadium was not fit to stage a game of such magnitude.' According to author John Foot: 'The stadium was crumbling and grass sprouted from the concrete terraces.' Brian Reade, the *Daily Mirror* columnist, described it as 'an ancient, dilapidated tip'. After inspecting the ground on the day of the match, Juventus president Giampiero Boniperti's verdict was: 'It was old, decrepit and looked like a scrap yard.'

Both clubs received an allocation of fourteen and a half thousand tickets for the final. As was the case for any big game played at a neutral venue, each club was given a designated 'end' of the ground where the majority of their supporters would be housed. However, as Liverpool fan Peter Hooton clearly remembers, it was instantly obvious that all was not right. 'When I bought my ticket at Anfield the first thing I noticed was that one of the sections, which turned out to be Z, was crossed out with a felt-tip pen. This immediately struck me as strange. Why the need for a neutral section? It didn't take a genius to work out that these were going to fall into the hands of Juventus fans.' The potential security risk of having a 'neutral' section at the Liverpool end of the ground was another major worry of Robinson's. Tickets for this section had been put on general sale in Brussels, a city renowned for its large Italian population. Robinson made known his concerns about this to the Belgian authorities. 'It worried me that the neutral area was in the middle of the Liverpool tickets and I expressed concern that if those tickets fell into the hands of Juventus supporters it was a recipe for problems,' he says. 'I asked why we couldn't have a complete end. But they were adamant the outlined system was the only way they could comply with UEFA regulations. They said they were well used to handling large crowds and said ticket sales had been totally controlled in Belgium. But I went back to Merseyside with great reservations.' Liverpool's uneasiness with the arrangements heightened in the weeks leading up to the final when it emerged that thousands of counterfeit tickets had become available on the black market, and the club repeatedly voiced their growing concerns. 'On the Monday before the game Sir John Smith, our club chairman, even arranged for the British Minister of Sport to send a telex to UEFA,' says Robinson, 'with a copy to the relevant football bodies in Belgium, requesting their assurance that UEFA's own rules and the provisions of the Council of Europe's recommendations on spectator violence would be vigorously implemented with regard to the match.' No reply was received.

Upon their arrival at the Heysel stadium Liverpool's players embarked on their customary walkabout. They liked to sample the pre-match atmosphere and ease any big-match nerves, particularly among the younger members of the squad. The longest-serving player was Phil Neal and nights like this were nothing new to him. An England international and veteran of more than six hundred games for the club, he had played in some of world's best arenas. His first impression of Heysel was that, compared to the Rome's Stadio Olimpico, Wembley and Parc des Princes in Paris, it was 'certainly a poor relation'.

As the first Liverpool players emerged from the tunnel the late evening sun was still shining, the stands were slowly filling up and a junior game was taking place on the pitch. The atmosphere initially seemed affable enough. As usual, the Liverpool fans appeared in good voice, working their way through the Kop's vast song book. Each player was saluted with an individual chant. As they waved back to acknowledge the support, some players kicked around a ball thrown down from the terraces. Others chatted and joked among themselves at the many humorous home-made banners draped over the perimeter fence. The mood throughout the sun-drenched day in the Belgian city had been friendly. Supporters of both clubs swapped scarves and engaged in good-natured banter in and around Brussels' Grand Place.

Only as afternoon turned to evening did the atmosphere among a minority of these fans slowly begin to turn for the worse. One Liverpool fan was stabbed, while several incidents of looting and sporadic outbreaks of violence were reported as the strong local beer began to take its toll. With just over an hour to go until kick-off the excitement was building steadily. But there was still nothing to suggest the horror that lay ahead. However, supporters arriving outside the ground at the Liverpool end could not believe their eyes at the sight that greeted them. Security was almost non-existent. Brian Reade has never forgotten how 'for the first time in my life I turned up at a football ground and there was no one to take my ticket'. A huge hole in the outer wall allowed supporters to come and go as they pleased. 'I laughed in disbelief at what I saw,' says Reade. 'Flimsy, eight-foot high breeze-block walls, the type you used to see around council playing fields, had been kicked down, so that a twenty-foot gap had opened up next to the turnstiles. Actually, the turnstiles may well have been kicked down, too, because I couldn't see any. Fans just walked over what was left of the wall, ticket in hand ready for inspection, with nobody to inspect. The few bored police who were around looked on unconcerned.'

It was a balmy spring evening, reminiscent of the club's four previous finals. But as the team continued to look around the stadium, it suddenly occurred to several of them that all was not as it should be on the terracing at the end reserved for the majority of Liverpool's support. With the Liverpool party as they slowly embarked on their pre-match walkabout was a well-travelled Liverpudlian known as 'George The Fish', a friend of a number of the players. He had managed to sneak in with them. Craig Johnston remembers how George was first to spot the potential for disorder. 'There's going to be trouble here tonight, look at that fence over there,' George pointed out to Craig as they stood near to the players' entrance. 'A lot of tickets have gone into the wrong hands.' As feared by Peter Robinson, this so-called neutral area had become occupied by Juventus fans. As the players set about making their way back inside Alan Hansen recalled that debris began to rain down on them as they passed this section. It was a haunting portent of the trouble that would soon follow.

Once back in the changing-room, just fifty yards from the ill-fated Sector Z, Liverpool's familiar matchday routine kicked in. Unbeknown to Joe and his players, missiles were now being exchanged between the two sets of supporters in Y and Z sectors as the mood outside began to turn. 'What made the tinderbox situation infinitely worse,' recalls Brian Reade, 'and showed how out of their depth the Belgian authorities were, was the barrier they erected to separate Blocks Y and Z – a run of thin chicken wire protected by five police officers.' It was not long before Reade's fears were realised. Liverpool fan Terry Wilson, then eighteen, was later jailed for his actions at Heysel. He was in Y section and vividly recalls his version of events. 'No one wanted any trouble and it was great at first,' he says. 'But as we were singing our songs our attention was drawn to what was happening in Z section. There was a young lad in a Liverpool shirt, he must have been aged between eight and twelve, and he was just getting destroyed by Italian men.'

Seeing the young Liverpool fan being attacked, and with memories of the harsh treatment they received at the hands of Italian supporters in Rome the year before, a group of Liverpudlians, including Wilson, charged towards the Juventus supporters. 'We were getting angry watching this and our immediate reaction was to pull the fence down and get over there to the assistance of our supporters,' he says. Peter Hooton was in the far side of the terrace in section X and admits to thinking nothing of it at the time. 'It was the type of skirmish you'd seen a hundred times before at grounds back in England. The type twenty police from the Anfield Road End would have sorted out in thirty seconds.' It was at this point that BBC Radio reported: 'The Belgium police had already lost control.' The panic-stricken Juventus fans retreated, causing a stampede, only to find there was nowhere to go. Guido Corini, a Juventus-supporting builder from Milan, has never forgotten. 'I tried to escape but seeing as my feet weren't even touching the ground I couldn't and I fell,' he recalled. 'Dozens were trampled underfoot or crushed against barriers,' reported *The Times*. Guido was one of the lucky ones. 'I heard someone saying, "They're charging again", and in my desperation I grabbed the wall and dragged myself over it without even looking,' he said. 'There could have been a fifty-metre drop on the other side for all I knew.' As supporters desperately tried to flee the crush, a wall at the far end of the terracing gave way. According to the *Daily Express*: 'The screams of the dying went unheard amid the cries of panic as thousands of people ran over them to safety.' Thirty-nine people who had turned up to watch a football match were never to return home. They were trampled on and suffocated by those trying to get away. Police records show that half an hour after the wall collapsed the death toll stood at sixteen. An hour later it had risen to thirty-five. By the end of the night it had reached thirty-eight. The thirty-ninth and final victim passed away after sixty-six days in a coma. Of the thirty-nine, thirty-two were Italian (only two from Turin), six Belgian and one Northern Irish. A further five hundred and eighty people were injured. Liverpool Football Club's reputation lay in the gutter.

To everyone who witnessed the horrific scenes at close hand, or watched on television, the match no longer mattered. Not everyone, though, was aware of what had taken place. Back in the changing-rooms conflicting reports drifted in about the severity of the trouble on the terraces. With paramedics and riot police rushing about, chaos and confusion reigned. No one knew what to believe. Players, who had heard the wall crash down, flitted in and out, eager for more information. Tony Chinn, a former European karate champion and martial arts expert, had travelled with Liverpool to Brussels as the club's personal security guard. He had carried out a similar role the year before in Rome. There, all he was basically required to do was make sure the trophy came to no harm amid the raucous celebrations. At Heysel, Chinn was witness to the most horrific scenes. 'There was this noise, like a quiet thud,' he remembers. 'Then came the screams and people were pouring over the wall like water. It was my job to look after the players so I pulled myself back from it. I'm not saying that's eased my conscience. I walked away from them because I had a job to do. It's the type of decision I don't ever want to make again.' Sensing there had been a serious incident, Joe immediately ordered his players back inside and made sure the door remained locked. The man entrusted with the job of doorman was Chinn. 'It was mayhem, absolute mayhem,' he recalls. 'The Liverpool changing-room was just yards away from where the wall had collapsed. There were bodies everywhere and the situation very quickly turned nasty. We didn't know what was going on, apart from the fact that there'd been some trouble, and Joe's first concern was for the welfare of his players.'

Accompanied by Chinn and an official from the Belgian Football Association, Joe took it upon himself to try and quell the unrest. First he used the stadium's antiquated public address system and then appealed personally to the Liverpool fans behind the goal. As he made his way across the running track towards them, he tore off his dark suit jacket and white shirt to display a Liverpool top with the number thirteen emblazoned across the back. 'This is a football match. It is my last game as manager and you are spoiling it. Get back and be sensible,' he pleaded. Amid all the pandemonium it was sadly an appeal that fell on deaf ears. Chinn remembers the emotion of it all began to get the better of Joe. 'He started crying, sobbing.

He was saying, "Please, please, let's just have a game, let's enjoy the day". He was pointing to his shirt as if to say, "Look, I'm the same as you. We are Liverpool, please stop the violence and let us get on with what we've all come here for". But he couldn't get his message across. It was so frustrating. He couldn't be heard, the noise was at full volume. The powers-that-be just couldn't control the situation. It was just expanding and snowballing. Joe was in total shock.'

Joe was still unaware of the deaths and his mind was in turmoil. Once back in the safe haven of the changing-room, he somehow managed to put on a brave face in front of the team. He instructed everyone to keep their minds firmly on the football. Only when the team was changed and ready to walk out did a UEFA official deliver the message that kick-off had been delayed. Some players passed the time with a game of cards. Proud Liverpudlian Sammy Lee was in tears. Kenny Dalglish, who had been suffering from flu and was dosed up on Lemsip, rested on the treatment table. 'Because of the delay we were at a loss as to what to do,' recalls Ronnie Whelan, 'and I just remember Joe constantly coming around trying to gee us up and keep us on our toes for when the call came to get out there. I must admit it was hard to keep focus, but he kept reminding us that all we could do in such a situation was "be professional".'

Only as time wore on did it become increasingly obvious that something really serious was afoot. With many of their family and friends seated in a section of the main grandstand close to where the wall had collapsed, there was genuine concern for their safety. Paul Walsh's girlfriend was forced by a group of angry Italians to look at the dead bodies that were being piled beneath the stands. Others were verbally abused and spat on. In their autobiographies, Bruce Grobbelaar and Phil Neal claim they had heard unconfirmed reports of fatalities. Some, like Dalglish, beg to differ. Even now it is not clear just who knew what and to what extent. 'It was a very confusing situation and I don't think anybody can say they knew all the facts at that stage as we hadn't been told anything officially,' says Roy Evans. 'It sounds terrible to say it, but my overriding anxiety was that we had a European Cup final to play, and I had to get myself ready for it,' admits Alan Hansen. 'I succeeded in getting myself so psyched up for the match that what was happening on the terraces was pushed into the background.' Joe stated later that while he and his players knew there had been serious trouble on the terraces, they were unaware of the full extent of the tragedy. 'We knew that there was a lot of trouble out there, but none of the players knew about the deaths until after,' he said. 'I had heard something about it, but that was as far as it went and it was nothing official.' Similar contrasting stories have since emerged from the Juventus camp. Club president Giampiero Boniperti said he did not want the players to know. He told the coach to keep them in the dressing-room and concentrate on the game. Amid all the confusion that followed those plans went out of the window. Distressed supporters sought refuge in and around the dressing-room area, and some players ventured outside in an attempt to find out what was going on. Striker Paolo Rossi said: 'We only had a vague idea of what happened.' Full-back Antonio Cabrini claimed: 'We knew everything.' Over a quarter of a century on and it remains difficult to uncover the true facts on either side. Had Joe known, his son Stephen is in no doubt that he would not have agreed to the game going ahead: 'I'm sure his opinion would have been, "Come on, we're going home, football is no longer important".'

With no official information available it is debatable if even those apparently 'in-the-know' knew the full extent of the tragedy at this point. There was no public announcement inside the stadium and the majority of supporters were oblivious to the fact that people had died. Only those watching on television were getting the full picture. They were now looking at images of riot police trying to contain Juventus fans at the opposite end of the ground to where the tragedy had occurred. Those fans seemed hell-bent on charging at the Liverpool fans to exact revenge. Some were ripping concrete posts out of the ground, others held aloft a banner with the words 'REDS ANIMALS' daubed on it, one even brandished a gun, later discovered to be a starting pistol. As helicopters hovered overhead, a line of police horses formed a divide across the centre of the pitch.

'It was just a surreal scene and by now we were all beginning to realise something terrible must have happened,' recalls Mark Lawrenson, 'and if anyone from UEFA had come in and said the game was off we'd all have been very relieved.'

What we do know is that senior officials of both clubs also now wanted the game to be postponed and they only agreed to play under duress from the Belgian authorities and UEFA. 'I wasn't happy about the match being played,' admits Peter Robinson. 'But it was decided it was the only way of getting the security forces they needed.' The decision for it to go ahead was taken at a hastily arranged meeting in the V.I.P. hall beneath the main stand. Also in attendance was Gianni De Michelis, the Italian Government's Foreign Affairs Minister, and he later told the *Corriere della Sera*: 'I immediately realised there was a situation of absolute uncertainty.' Discussions lasted for almost an hour. With no one apparently willing to take charge, De Michelis eventually asked the Mayor of Brussels: 'Would you please tell us if you can guarantee a safe evacuation from the stadium?' The answer, which came from Robert Bernaert, head of the Belgian gendarmerie, was negative. He made it clear that to prevent the threat of further violence the show must go on. That way extra troops could be drafted in to handle the eventual dispersion of those fans still in the stadium. Getting them back to their transport and out of Brussels safely was now of paramount importance.

Another question raised as the meeting drew to a close was, how seriously would the game be taken? Juventus director of sport Francesco Morini, takes up the story: 'Our president, Mr Boniperti, wanted to know, "Is it a real game? Will it count?" And the Liverpool people said, "If we play we want it to be a real game". And the heads of UEFA said, "Yes, whatever the result is it counts".' When informed of the decision, the players on both sides accepted it. 'Some people thought it would have been a mark of respect to those who died not to play the game,' says Kenny Dalglish. 'But UEFA decided it had to be played for fear of even greater trouble and at the time it was understandable.' Juventus captain Platini was clear. 'If we had not played,' he said, 'it would have been the end of football.'

At approximately 8.40 p.m. English time, and with the stadium still resembling a war zone, the respective team captains, Phil Neal and Giaento Scirea, were asked to relay UEFA's decision to the supporters over the public address system. Unfortunately for Neal the P.A. box was situated towards the end where the majority of Juventus fans were now apoplectic with rage and threatening to spark a full-scale riot. The Liverpool captain was visibly shaken by the battle-scarred scene that confronted him. 'It wasn't the best of passages to make your way through, particularly when you've got a Liverpool tracksuit on,' Neal remembers. 'In fact, it was one of the most terrifying experiences of my life, with the Italian fans throwing missiles and hissing and spitting at me. I just remember some UEFA official handing me a statement. I took one look at it, screwed it up and just spoke from the heart.'

A similar request was made for the two managers to do likewise, forcing Joe to run the same gauntlet of anger. 'At this point the stadium was a very dangerous place,' remembers Tony Chinn. 'The Italian fans were baying for blood. Anything could have happened to Phil or Joe. There's no way I could have let them go out there on their own.' In the Liverpool sections of the ground, as the red and white flags continued to flutter in the evening breeze, there was an air of confusion. 'Nobody around us knew of the deaths,' says Brian Reade. 'Of far more concern was why some Italians had come streaming at us from the opposite end of the ground looking for trouble. That must have been why the kick-off was put back. "Animals", we thought, and started yelling abuse at them. That's how insane it was that night.' Back in Liverpool, Joe's family could only look on helplessly while he was subjected to another torrent of abuse. Watching from his seat in the stands, Stephen Fagan believes that 'having to walk across that track and talk over the public address system must have been one of the most difficult things Dad ever had to do. It must have been a horrendous ordeal and watching him have to go through that made me realise just how serious a situation it had become.'

For the millions of viewers glued to their television sets across Europe and beyond, the gruesome images of innocent people dying at a football match had unfolded right before their eyes. Yet, some ninety minutes later than planned, two and a quarter hours after the wall collapsed, the two teams entered the arena. Liverpool were sporting their new Adidas-sponsored kit for the first time. An eerie atmosphere greeted them. It was now a game nobody cared about. The *Guardian* reporting that it went ahead 'alongside hideous scenes, as corpses in green plastic shrouds were carried to a makeshift tented mortuary outside the main entrance'. Jeff Powell in the following morning's *Daily Mail* described it as 'a grotesque, macabre, de-humanising experience'. Both sides went through the motions. 'I have no recollection of it whatsoever,' says Sammy Lee, one of three unused Liverpool substitutes on the night. 'All I remember is a feeling of numbness. I couldn't even tell you what our team was. It was all a complete blank.'

For the record, the thirtieth European Champions Club Cup final was settled by a Michel Platini penalty after fifty-seven minutes, controversially awarded after Boniek was tripped by substitute Gary Gillespie just outside the box. Swiss referee André Daina judged the infringement had taken place inside and Platini duly sent Grobbelaar the wrong way, sparking wild Italian celebrations. Given what had gone on, no Liverpool player was in the mood to argue. However, twenty years later, Bruce Grobbelaar revealed how determined he was to save it. 'I just got this rush of adrenalin,' he recalled. 'I thought they had tried to cheat us so I was going to do my best to stop it because it was just wrong.' At the opposite end, fifteen minutes later, Liverpool were denied an obvious penalty when Whelan was fouled. Again, no one protested. Neal and Dalglish have both since claimed in their autobiographies that they 'heard from a number of reliable sources', there was no way

Liverpool were going to be allowed to win the match. There is no tangible proof to confirm this, and given what had occurred it does not really matter. Wark went on to spurn Liverpool's best chance of an equaliser when Tacconi saved superbly. But despite a more spirited late rally, Liverpool surrendered their crown without much resistance. 'It was the only game, right from being a kid, when I wasn't bothered whether we won or lost,' says Ian Rush. 'As a professional, I approached every game, even friendlies, with a fierce determination to win. That time, I honestly did not care. The game itself seemed almost unreal.' The first-half losses of Lawrenson, who dislocated his shoulder for a third time that season, and Walsh, who suffered a recurrence of his stomach injury, had been a blow to Liverpool hopes. But when pressed for a comment on the match afterwards, Joe simply shrugged his shoulders and graciously accepted the defeat. 'They played a good game and I thought Juventus's goalkeeper was very good indeed. It was a bit of a blow losing Mark Lawrenson so early but Gary Gillespie came in and did very well.'

Though nobody really cared, according to Ian Hargreaves in the next day's *Echo*, Liverpool had given one of their best performances of the season. 'Though it was hard to concentrate on football, in the knowledge of what was happening off the pitch, the courage of the players and their efforts to provide some kind of entertainment in the European Cup final has to be admired,' he wrote. 'It is sad that the club who have been Britain's greatest ambassadors over the years, should have become involved in such a dreadful disaster that made a mockery of everything that has gone before.' In the *Daily Post* Ian Ross reported: 'Liverpool's dream of bringing the European Cup back to rest at Anfield for all time, perished in Brussels on a night of shame for both football and Merseyside. Mighty Juventus, outplayed by Joe Fagan's battlers for the most part, claimed the most meaningless of titles amid the tears and tragedy which descended on the famous Heysel Stadium. It was a heartbreaking end to the two-year reign of Gentleman Joe but his players really couldn't have done any more than they did to try and provide a sliver lining to his Anfield swansong.' Other match reports were lost amid the endless column inches dedicated to what happened on the terraces before kick-off. In the eyes of the *Guardian*'s David Lacey: 'Professional football as a spectator sport lay mortally wounded.' Stuart Jones in *The Times* told how 'football weeped'. The *Daily Express* described in detail: 'The most horrifying outbreak of soccer violence the world has ever seen'. Headlines like 'Sickening,' and 'Bloodbath in Brussels', were commonplace as Liverpool prepared to return home and face the shame.

The trophy was heading to Turin for the first time, but it had been a hollow victory. In Italy, *La Gazzetta dello Sport* reported: 'Juve win a cursed Cup.' The official presentation of the trophy took place behind the closed doors of the Juventus dressing-room. Afterwards some of the players went back outside for a lap of honour which caused controversy back in their homeland. Cabrini described it as 'simply a release of tension'. He added: 'For me that cup will always be covered in blood. The Cup of Death.' Joe and his team had disappeared without trace. For them there was no official presentation of their runners-up medals. Instead a UEFA official knocked on the door and handed Joe a box with them in. As the players changed the manager slowly went around each one of them, thanking them individually and giving out the least cherished mementos of their career.

For youngster Chris Pile it had been a sobering experience, one that his soothsaying grandmother had feared. But he still remembers how Joe, even in his darkest hour, found time to console him. 'When he got to me he just said, "Here you go, son, all the best for the future, you've made a good start, now go on and become the next Ray Clemence". After what had gone on he didn't have to do that, but it was something I really appreciated at the time and which I've never forgotten.' Once changed, Jim Beglin, the youngest member of Liverpool's starting XI that night, says the horror of what he had just experienced began to sink in. 'The enormity of Heysel hit me like a train after the game,' he admits. 'Dejection over losing the

European Cup final to Juventus quickly gave way to disbelief when I learned that people had died. I walked with my Liverpool team-mates to where the wall had crumbled and the Italian fans were crushed. The remnants of people's lives, handbags and shoes, scarves and spectacles, were strewn among the rubble.' Phil Neal remembers: 'I can talk freely about it now, but it was horrific. It was as if it was something that happens to other people, not in front of your own eyes.'

Ever since the final whistle Joe and his players had only one thing on their minds and that was to get showered, changed and out of the stadium as quickly as possible. Unfortunately, UEFA etiquette meant that before escaping, Joe had first to face the full glare of the media. Ashen-faced and barely able to keep a lid on his emotions, he took to the stand as if on trial for the atrocities himself. The horrific images had by now been flashed to every corner of the globe and the eyes of the world were on him. Never in his wildest nightmares could Joe have envisaged his career coming to an end in this way. With his usual dignity, Joe managed to compose himself for what was a torturous experience. Now fully aware of the tragedy, he spoke with remarkable solemnity in the cramped lecture hall beneath the Main Stand, which was bursting at the seams with press men and cameras.

'I won't be able to forget my last game of football for the rest of my life. It is tragic. It was really horrific. I broke down and cried,' he said in the post-match press conference. 'I felt I was part of the supporters and I was letting everybody else down in Liverpool and everyone in the football world. I felt really bad about it. There was nothing much I could really do. It's something when the game has come to this. It's not the way we hoped things would have worked out. My heart just wasn't in it. Tonight upset me very much but it wasn't over the result. What is a game of football when so many are dead? The match itself just fades into insignificance.'

A dark shadow had been cast over Liverpool Football Club. But Joe diplomatically refused to start pointing the finger of blame. He added: 'I'm not going to accuse anybody. Football fans all over the world are behaving like this now. I just don't understand some of the fans' mentality. It is beyond belief. I only wanted them to quieten down. We just wanted to play football. The problem of soccer hooliganism is getting worse. This is my last match and my last press conference and maybe it's about time I got out of the game – but what a sad way to go.' It was his last act as Liverpool manager.

A full two hours after the final whistle the crestfallen Liverpool squad were finally allowed to depart. As the coach pulled away, distraught Italian supporters banged on the side and shouted obscenities. At the front sat the forlorn figure of Joe, still struggling to comprehend the scale of the tragedy he had just witnessed at close quarters. 'He looked a broken man,' recalled Alan Hansen. 'Of all the men at Liverpool who went through the ordeal of Heysel, Joe was the one for whom I felt most sorry. It was his last game in charge and he deserved good memories, no matter what the result. Whenever I think of Heysel it's the expression on his face that first springs to mind. It was the night that the game which had been his whole life no longer meant anything.' Despite what they had been through the Liverpool squad still had to face the protocol of the post-match banquet. But it did allow them to be reunited with family and friends. It was a subdued affair. 'Win, lose or draw, we usually had a party after a big game. But the atmosphere at our base in Brussels was very sombre,' remembers Beglin. 'We just swapped stories. Several of the wives and girlfriends were distressed by what they'd seen and the players all felt numb. We just wanted to get home.'

Instead of the planned homecoming parade the following afternoon Liverpool flew back into a city shrouded in shame. Council leader John Hamilton had declared a day of mourning. During the team's Aer Lingus Boeing 707 flight, chairman John Smith spoke over the microphone to thank Joe for all he had done during his time at the club. A highly emotional Joe then said a few words himself. 'He was in tears, explaining this was it, goodbye, game over,' remembers Kenny Dalglish, the man about to replace him as manager. 'I love this club and I love football,' said Joe, 'but I feel if I carry on any longer people might not love me any more.' When the plane finally touched down at Speke Airport it was a heartbroken and tear-stained Joe Fagan who disembarked. 'He was at a complete loss about the whole episode,' says Roy Evans. 'He simply had no more words to say. He didn't understand and took it very badly. He broke down again.' As he made his way slowly across the tarmac Joe appeared to be carrying the burden of blame for the actions of a mindless minority. Wracked by emotion and having to be helped along by the comforting arms of Evans, his return was cruelly captured by the full glare of the waiting media. It remains a poignant image. For some, it is sadly the lasting one they have of him, a man who deserved a much more gracious send-off than this. With Liverpool back home, the inquest into the horror of Heysel began and, as it did, Joe slipped quietly away, back to the anonymity he craved. The final curtain had been lowered on a long and illustrious career in the game. But for it to end this way was, indeed, a crying shame.

EPILOGUE

THE HEYSEL DISASTER had a deep and lasting effect on Joe Fagan. The events of that tragic night in Belgium were completely incomprehensible to him. How could it be that people had gone to watch a football match and never returned home? In his years as a player, coach and manager Joe had seen almost everything football had to offer. He was devoted to the game, but men of his generation had a heightened sense of perspective because of their Wartime experiences. Football was not the real world. Neither, despite the famous quip of his old friend Bill Shankly, was it a matter of life and death. No matter how important football seemed, Joe never lost sight of the fact that it was still only a game. That people would die at a match in such a manner was unthinkable.

When Joe returned home from Belgium the wind had been taken from his sails. Always an enthusiastic man, he was now filled with sadness and a sense of incredulity. That it was 'his club' undoubtedly made it harder for Joe. Through no fault of his own, the manager had become personally entwined in the nightmare of Heysel. This was a burden he found difficult to bear. 'He never really talked about it, to be honest,' says son Stephen. 'He did become quite introverted for a period afterwards. Given his long association with the club and the fact he was manager on that night he may have felt a sense of shame. But, of course, there was nothing he could have done to prevent what happened. It was a terribly sad way for him to bow out of football.'

Joe's youngest boy Michael remembers asking his dad if he was all right when he came back from the airport. 'He just said, "Yeah, I'm fine, son", and that was it. He never spoke another word about it. He was just absolutely gutted that supporters of his team had been involved in such an appalling tragedy. He couldn't understand why people would do such a thing over a football game.' On the Friday after the final all the players and staff attended a requiem mass at Liverpool Metropolitan Cathedral. Joe was still distraught and needed his wife's help to enter the church. Though his pain was nothing compared to those who lost loved ones in the tragedy, as Roy Evans says: 'He carried it with him for the rest of his days.'

The shame of Heysel hung like a dark cloud over the city of Liverpool. The team's return to Merseyside was met with such blanket media coverage of the tragic events in Brussels that, not surprisingly, there was little mention of Joe's retirement. Whether Joe might have reconsidered his decision to step down had things gone differently is unclear. Bruce Grobbelaar, who also contemplated turning his back on the game post-Heysel, believes he may have done. 'He should have been Liverpool manager for ten years and I honestly think if it hadn't been for Heysel he could have been. I know he'd already made his mind up, but I believe it would have been very hard for him to walk away had it not been for Heysel and if we had won that night.'

It is unlikely that Grobbelaar's reading of the situation is correct: Joe had decided to go and he was not a man to change his mind. He would not have wanted to mess Liverpool around when they had already started planning for his departure. Besides, even thinking about another game of football, another League campaign, another 'serious' team talk, seemed ridiculous after Heysel. Though he did eventually move on, Joe never forgot and he never really released the great sadness he felt. When Joe would visit Peter Robinson at Anfield after he retired, the pair would talk at length about the players and how the team were getting on, but Heysel was never discussed. Joe's way of dealing with the horror was to bottle it up inside.

On-field matters were almost forgotten during the summer of 1985 as incriminations flew around. In the immediate aftermath there were widespread calls for English clubs to be banned from Continental competition. Pre-empting an official announcement by UEFA, the Football Association heeded Prime Minister Margaret Thatcher's advice by withdrawing the six clubs who had qualified for the following season's European tournaments. Days later UEFA suspended all English clubs for 'an indeterminate period of time', and imposed an additional three-year ban on Liverpool, though that was later reduced. It was five years before an English club team played a competitive fixture in Europe again; Liverpool returned a year later.

Following lengthy investigations in England and Belgium, fourteen Liverpool supporters were found guilty of involuntary manslaughter in 1989. Seven were given three years in prison, while the rest received three-year suspended sentences. Captain Johan Mahieu, the police officer in charge of security at the ill-fated Block Z, and Albert Roosens, secretary of the Belgian Football Union, were both convicted of criminal negligence. The lingering stigma of Heysel, however, will never leave Liverpool Football Club. Along with the Hillsborough Disaster of 1989 it remains the lowest point in the club's history. A permanent reminder of the tragedy was added to the wall of Anfield's Centenary Stand on the twenty-fifth anniversary in 2010. The names of the thirty-nine victims are displayed in the club museum.

At Kenny Dalglish's official unveiling as Liverpool player-manager on 30 May, 1985, Joe put the horror of Heysel to the back of his mind briefly, smiled for the cameras and shook hands with his successor. On the same day chairman John Smith revealed that Joe would still have a part to play at the club. 'An elder statesmen role in its broadest term,' Smith said. In reality it was nothing more than the odd bit of scouting.

Many football men find it impossible to step away from the game to which they have devoted so much time, energy and emotion. Bill Shankly, for instance, could not stop himself turning up at Melwood for months after he retired. This led to some confusion, not least because the players still referred to Shankly as 'Boss', leaving Bob Paisley undermined. In the end Shankly had to be asked to stay away to avoid a thoroughly awkward situation escalating. Joe was never going to allow something similar to arise once Dalglish took over. He considered it best for the club and, characteristically, put that before any concern for what was best for him personally.

Joe wrote to wish his successor luck before the 1985–86 season began and having been invited to Dalglish's first match, at home against Arsenal, he sought out the manager for a pre-match handshake. 'All the best, Kenny,' was all that needed to be said. Joe had huge respect for Dalglish, not only as a player but also as a strong and independent character. 'Kenny is very much his own man,' he would say. 'He has his own ideas and makes his own decisions.' Joe was confident Liverpool had been left in safe hands and felt no need to make further contact with Dalglish after the Arsenal match. 'Joe would always have been welcome and him dropping by would never have been a problem,' says Dalglish. 'It would have been great for me if he could have come back as a coach. I knew he was always there if I needed to talk to him, but he was a bit shy about coming up to the ground. It was a matter of showing respect. He didn't want to step on anyone's toes.'

Bob Paisley had gone back to work as an advisor to Dalglish. A more involved role than the odd scouting trip was also open for Joe had he been willing to step back into the comfort of the Bootroom. Tempting as it would have been, Joe's personality made a comeback all but impossible. He would have seen his return as a distraction which could cause problems for Dalglish. It was far easier for him to slip away unnoticed. He also believed that there was a right time to move on and let others do their job. Though he missed his work, Joe never showed any sign that he regretted his decision.

Once he stepped outside the inner circle Joe felt less comfortable about returning. Throughout the managerial spells of Dalglish and Graeme Souness he watched a lot of games, often at the invitation of his good friend Peter Robinson. However, he would only go down for a drink and a chat in the Bootroom if Liverpool had won. It would never have been interpreted as such, but Joe did not want to risk the manager or the staff thinking that he was somehow rubbing their noses in it after a draw or a defeat, so he stayed away.

Despite no longer being associated with the club, Joe's legacy would extend into the next decade. Just twelve months after he stepped down, Liverpool completed the coveted League and FA Cup Double with a squad containing five players signed by Joe – Gary Gillespie, John Wark, Paul Walsh, Jan Molby and Kevin MacDonald, plus another in Jim Beglin who he had introduced into the first team. These players would be involved in further successes, right up until the club's FA Cup victory in 1992, in which Molby played.

When Bootroom protégée Roy Evans succeeded Souness as Liverpool manager in 1994, Joe began to visit Melwood on a more regular basis. Though he was never a frequent visitor, he wanted to be there if he could help in any way. He was not one to give out advice, but acted as a sounding board for the rookie manager. 'Over the years he had become my father in football,' Evans remembers. 'I don't say that lightly because my dad is still alive and he played football to a decent level. Joe was just one of those guys who always looked after you and pointed you in the right direction. When I took over as manager we spoke and he would come in every now and again.'

Evans's approach to the job was influenced greatly by his mentor. Having seen the straightforward approach work so well for Joe, Evans decided not to try and be too clever in his dealings with press and players and that honest approach reaped rewards. Unfortunately Evans's team did not possess the same wealth of world-class players that Joe had been able to call upon. A number of notable exceptions aside, the team inherited from Souness were distinctly average. Even so, Evans produced an attractive team who came very close to bringing back the glory days to Anfield.

Joe's Anfield visits became fewer over time. But on 30 April, 1994, he took one final bow before the fans for 'The Kop's Last Stand'. To commemorate the last game played before the famous terrace was pulled down and replaced by an all-seat stand, the club arranged for a host of former players and managers to parade on the pitch shortly before kick-off. It was a carnival atmosphere, tinged with emotion. One by one the legends walked out to rapturous receptions. But the loudest cheers were reserved until the end when Joe, flanked by Nessie Shankly and Jessie Paisley, made their way up from the players' tunnel and across the pitch to the centre circle. Nine years after he shuffled away from the game with his head bowed, but now with a smile as wide as the Mersey, Joe strode proudly back into the spotlight. At last the fans were able to give him the send-off he deserved.

By the mid-1990s English football had been transformed by BSkyB's satellite coverage and the arrival of the Premiership. Though he had trouble pronouncing the names of the raft of foreign imports, Joe was always an enthusiastic spectator. He had the *Football Echo* delivered to his house and would tune in to *Match of the Day* every Saturday evening. He did not particularly enjoy some of the over-the-top modern-day media analysis, and often lamented: 'It is a very simple game.' Watching on television, though, was no substitute for being there. 'Dad got Sky installed for the football, but I think he only had it for about two months,' recalls Stephen. 'He couldn't be bothered with it. Having been so actively involved in the game for all those years, watching it on the telly used to drive him bonkers.'

Would Joe have been as effective and successful had he worked in today's footballing climate? It's an interesting point. Players have certainly progressed: they are fitter, and have different approaches to diet and alcohol. But the game itself and the skills needed to coach and manage players successfully have not altered a great deal. Shankly, Paisley and Fagan were united in the view that football never really changes – the fundamentals are constant. Those who worked with him are unanimous that Joe's man-management skills and football nous would have been equally effective in the modern game. 'It would be a doddle for him to work in football now,' believes Ronnie Whelan. 'All the big-time Charlies would have been cut down straight away. Joe would have been the man who could sort it all out.' Alan Hansen agrees: 'If I became a manager tomorrow I would go back and implement the basics that Joe, Bob and Ronnie Moran preached. Football is still the same game. You would maybe change certain things, such as having fitness coaches. But Joe would have moved with the times. He was unbelievably flexible about everything, about the way the game changed during his time at Liverpool.'

In many ways Joe's was an early exponent of the scientific approach to football training lauded today (though he would have given the 'scientific' label short shrift). He recognised the importance of recording every training session, every injury, every minor detail. He understood that players needed to warm down slowly after training: they were packed on to a sweaty bus back to Anfield rather than showering at Melwood. He also knew that what they ate would affect performance. As Kenny Dalglish says: 'Clubs do the same things now and call it sports science; Joe would have called it common sense. Back then Liverpool were miles in front of everyone else.'

If Joe would have found it relatively easy to cope with the actual football nowadays, the glitz, glamour and greed would have been much more difficult for him to get used to. The game he knew was the people's game. He was surrounded by honest, trustworthy men, and the media interest was far less voracious than it is now. Corporate hospitality and sensationalist reporting would not have been to Joe's taste; mercenary players and their insidious agents even less so.

Retirement did not sit well with Joe. Having led such an active life, he became something of a caged lion in his senior years. Eager to keep busy but with little to fill his time, he found it difficult to adapt to a slower pace of life. He was happy to be able to give more time to his wife and children (and his expanding army of grandchildren), but he was never entirely comfortable with having so much spare time. While he struggled to adapt to the life of a normal person, he was bemused that people did not treat him as they would anyone else. 'He could never understand why people would stop in the supermarket and want to talk football with him or shake his hand,' remembers Stephen. 'In his mind he had nothing to do with football anymore, and he found it amazing that people still valued his opinion or even recognised him. As far as he was concerned he was just an ordinary Joe.'

Joe had a strong sense of community and never fell into the trap of thinking his job made him any different to anyone else. When people made demands of his time he would oblige where possible. He was always warm and polite to those who approached him. Many times unsuspecting Liverpool fans would knock on his door on match days and ask if they could park across the driveway as it was only a few minutes' walk from Anfield. The shock was obvious when the door was opened by a former Liverpool manager. 'No problem,' Joe would say. 'I'll keep an eye on the car until you get back.' He would also happily chat to fans on the doorstep when they plucked up the courage to knock. Though he found the situation a trifle embarrassing, he never looked at it negatively. In his retirement he was as happy living on Lynholme Road as he had been when he moved there in 1958. He would have chatted to anyone who approached him back then, so why would he not do the same forty years later?

As the years passed Joe's health deteriorated. He lived with Lil in the same house until he finally lost his battle with cancer on 30 June, 2001, coincidentally in the same week that fellow Liverpool legends Billy Liddell and Tom Saunders also passed away. Joe was eighty years old. His funeral at Anfield Crematorium was a simple and solemn occasion, attended by friends, family and former Liverpool players and staff. Many fans lined the streets in their red (and notably blue) shirts as the funeral procession made its way from the family home to the crematorium. It was a poignant illustration of the depth of feeling that the people of Liverpool had for one of their own.

Apart from anything else Joe should be remembered as a man who loved football. His diary entries soon after taking up the managerial position portrayed his almost childlike enthusiasm. On 19 July, 1983, he wrote: 'Played five-a-side with the youngsters. Won as usual!' The next day, he added: 'Hoped to go down and play again but was too busy – a real pity.' It is hard to imagine many of today's big-time managers relishing the opportunity to rush down from their office and play five-a-side with the youth team, but Joe did. He did not love football for the glory and the glamour that it provided. He loved football for the game itself, the friendships it built, the release it provided and the satisfaction of a job done well. He was a sportsman in every sense, always quick to accept and acknowledge when he had been beaten by a better team.

Joe was a major factor in Liverpool's era of dominance. It was an age in which English teams rose to the top of European club football. It was not only Liverpool who marched into Europe during the 1970s and 1980s to carry off the silverware: Nottingham Forest, Ipswich Town, Aston Villa, Everton and Tottenham Hotspur all enjoyed great success. But Liverpool had shown the way. Joe's role in this development in English football, the journey from amateur-professional days to today's slick spectacle, has never really been acknowledged. 'There were men at different clubs who had that same old-school mentality, kept everybody's feet on the ground, and kept things moving forward, but Joe was the main one for me,' Roy Evans says. 'It is difficult to gauge different coaches and managers now because of finances in football, but I think the likes of Joe were the great developers of the English game. His impact went far beyond statistics and trophies. He was the best.'

Tellingly, those within the game did afford Joe the respect and stature he had earned. From Bobby Robson, then England manager, who travelled with Joe's Liverpool to the European Cup semi-final of 1984, to Gerard Houllier, manager of Liverpool from the late

1990s, many coaches and managers sought out Joe to pick his brain. He was happy to share his methods with aspiring young coaches, regularly accepting their requests to visit Melwood and learn from the best in the business. Future England manager Sven-Göran Eriksson was one of many coaches to whom Joe extended a warm welcome. Richard Møller Nielson, the coach behind Denmark's 1992 European Championship triumph, was another.

Not once during the course of his long career did Joe's popularity within the game waver. This was never more evident to his family than during the first few months of his retirement when letters offering commiseration and best wishes flooded in from all over Europe. Maurice Lindley, chairman of Bradford City, a club who were also coming to terms with tragedy, wrote: 'Just a note to express my sympathy at the way in which things turned out for you and Liverpool in Brussels recently. I personally felt for you, Joe.' Graham Kelly, secretary of the Football League, was in touch to say: 'Good wishes and good health to one of the most generous and sporting managers in the game.' From his villa in Genoa, Graeme Souness penned his own moving tribute: 'I, like so many more, have a great deal to thank you for. Not only in the football sense but outside the game, too. You taught us the right ways in life. I know in the time I was at the club you were the one the players respected most as a man and the one the players felt closest to.'

Joe Fagan's achievements as a manager, in particular clinching the Treble in Rome, are difficult to put into context given how much the game has changed in the intervening years. In 2001, Gerard Houllier led Liverpool to another triple-trophy success, this time in the FA Cup, UEFA Cup and League Cup. Two years earlier, Sir Alex Ferguson's Manchester United completed their own Treble, substituting the FA Cup for Joe's League Cup. Historians can argue about which was the better achievement: did the League Cup carry more weight in the mid-1980s than the FA Cup at the turn of the century? And which was more difficult to win: the old European Cup or the Champions League? Whatever, Joe would have been uninterested in the debate. For what it is worth, Peter Robinson believes the class of 1984 has the edge. 'I think it was more difficult to win the European Cup in 1984, under the straight knockout system, than it was in 1999 when you could have lost games in the group phase but still gone through,' he says. 'Back then English clubs could not compete financially with the richest in Europe, the big teams in Spain and Italy. They were much wealthier than Liverpool and therefore had the pick of the world's greatest players. Joe won the European Cup with a squad made up almost entirely of British-based players.'

Some critics may suggest that Joe's Treble was merely a continuation of the work done by Paisley. But that is a claim that Ronnie Moran vehemently refutes. 'It was only when they were on a good run that people would come up and say, "That's Bob Paisley's team". It wouldn't be Bob Paisley's team when we were losing and it was the same for Bob when he took over from Shanks,' argues Moran. 'Of course, Joe would always stress that he couldn't have done it without the players. A lot of those players he did inherit from Bob, there's no denying that, but a big factor is how you deal with the players.' Bruce Grobbelaar, the only ever-present during Joe's tenure as manager, concurs: 'While it was a good team that he inherited he still had to put his own stamp on it. The principles remained the same, but it was a new era at the club and Joe had to get the best out of his players, which he invariably did.'

However, despite all he did for the club over more than a quarter of a century, and though the achievements of Bill Shankly and Bob Paisley have been acknowledged, there is no permanent memorial to Joe at Anfield. This lack of recognition irks some of those who worked with him. Among them is Graeme Souness, the man who lifted the European Cup for Joe in Rome. He says: 'Bill Shankly and Bob Paisley have both been honoured, and rightly so. But this man Joe Fagan played such an instrumental role under them both and went on to achieve his own piece of unique history, so it would be nice and fitting if he was remembered some way. Too many people have already forgotten about Joe and that's not right. If he'd been at any other club it would be different. But even though Joe won three trophies in one season he's always in the shadow of Bill Shankly and Bob Paisley because of what they achieved over a longer period of time. But Joe was Mr Liverpool during the club's golden age and his contribution should never be allowed to fade from the memory.'

Peter Robinson, the man who promoted the idea of erecting gates at Anfield named after Shankly and Paisley, believes that a tribute to Joe will one day join theirs. However, such a memorial will be of greater significance to others than it would have been to Joe. Rome, the Treble and his time as manager is what Joe ultimately will be remembered for, but the man himself would have been equally happy had he never taken on the top job. He would have carried on with his role in the background, and kept on making his crucial, yet publicly unrecognised contribution. And that would have suited him just fine.

ACKNOWLEDGEMENTS

THE IDEA FOR this book stemmed from a programme about Joe's life which first aired on LFC TV in 2008. The writing of the book has been a long but enjoyable process and one we believe has been worthwhile. Piecing together the life story of someone who is no longer with us is no easy task, but it helps that the subject was such a universally popular character. Everyone who was approached for an interview agreed without hesitation. Their names are listed in the bibliography and we cannot thank them enough, especially Roy Evans who wrote the foreword.

A huge debt of gratitude is also due to the Fagan family for their invaluable help : (in alphabetical order) John Fagan, Lil Fagan, Margaret Fagan, Michael Fagan, Roger Fagan (Andrew's father), Stephen Fagan, Joanne Yih and Honto Yih.

For helping us to shed further light on Joe's life before he joined Liverpool, our thanks go to Frank Carlyle (Merseyside historian); Tim Johnson (Liverpool schools football expert); Iain Munro (Liverpool County FA); Glynn Jones aka WillieBob on the LFC fans forum raotl.co.uk (Earlestown Bohemians); Mike Pavasovic (Hyde United); Janet Parr, Stephen Taylor, Leon Collins, Fred Eyre and Gary James (Manchester City); Andrew Spencer, Gary Broughton, Mike Keel and Alan Stuttard (Nelson); Blake Richardson, Tim Clapham, Brian Jones, Jim Meehan and Jim Carr (Bradford Park

Avenue); John Laidlar and Terry Rowley (Altrincham); Mark Wilbraham and Steve Phillipps (Rochdale).

For all other help and assistance, we thank Arnie Baldursson (lfchistory.net); Tony Barrett (*The Times*); Tony Chinn; Derek Dohren (creator of the bootroom.net); Eric Doig; Stephen Done (LFC Museum creator); Brian Durand; Tony Evans (*The Times*); Bill Shankly's granddaughter Karen Gill; Louise Goulding (LFC TV); Steve Hale, commissioning editor Sam Harrison (Aurum) for his patience and direction; Simon Hughes (LFC magazine and programme); Stephanie Jones (*Champions* magazine); John Keith (journalist, author and broadcaster); Ian Kennedy (BBC Radio Merseyside); Adrian Killen (LFC archivist); our agent David Luxton for having faith in the book; Chris McLoughlin (Kop magazine); Bob Paisley's son Graham Paisley; Ged Rea (LFC statistician); Brian Reade for helping us get the project off the ground; Claire Rourke (LFC TV); George Sephton; Gary Shaw (author and sports historian); and copy editor Martin Smith.

And last, but by no means least, we would, of course, like to thank our family and friends for putting up with us throughout the course of the writing process. In particular (from Andrew) Ellen, Roger and Judy; (from Mark) Lynda, Jack and Ella, Arthur and Marie.

STATISTICS

JOE FAGAN
Born: Liverpool, 12 March, 1921
Died: Liverpool, 30 June, 2001

CAREER RECORD
Earlestown Bohemians (player – 1937–38)
Manchester City (player – 1938–51)
Hyde United (player, Wartime guest, 1939–40)
Nelson (player-manager – 1951–53)
Bradford Park Avenue (player – 1953–54)
Altrincham (player – 1954–55)
Rochdale (coach – 1956–58)
Liverpool (assistant trainer/reserve-team coach – 1958–71)
Liverpool (first-team coach – 1971–79)
Liverpool (assistant manager – 1979–83)
Liverpool (manager – 1983–85)

HONOURS WON

PLAYER
George Mahon Cup (1937)
Cheshire League East Section (1940)
Second Division Championship (1947)

PLAYER-MANAGER
Lancashire Combination (1952)

RESERVE-TEAM COACH
Central League (1969, 1970 and 1971)

FIRST-TEAM COACH
Football League Championship (1973, 1976, 1977 and 1979)
UEFA Cup (1973 and 1976)
FA Cup (1974)
European Cup (1977 and 1978)
Charity Shield (1974, 1976 and 1977*)
European Super Cup (1977)
*shared

ASSISTANT MANAGER
Football League Championship (1979, 1980, 1982 and 1983)
European Cup (1981)
Football League Cup (1981, 1982 and 1983)
Charity Shield (1979, 1980 and 1982)

MANAGER
Football League Championship (1984)
European Cup (1984)
Football League (Milk) Cup (1984)
Manager of the Year (1984)

LIVERPOOL MANAGERIAL RECORD

	Pld	Won	Drawn	Lost	For	Against
League	84	44	25	15	141	67
FA Cup	9	5	2	2	23	7
League Cup	16	8	7	1	27	9
European Cup	18	14	2	2	34	8
European Super up	1	0	0	1	0	2
World Club Ch'ship	1	0	0	1	0	1
Charity Shield	2	0	0	2	0	3
Total	131	71	36	24	225	97

BIBLIOGRAPHY

A NOTE FROM THE AUTHORS ON SOURCES

T HIS BOOK WOULD not have been possible without the support of so many of Joe Fagan's former colleagues, in particular the numerous players he coached and managed during his time at Anfield. The following all consented to be interviewed during our research and have all been quoted in the foregoing text. We would like to offer our heartfelt thanks for their time and invaluable insights.

Banks, Alan (2 April, 2010)
Beglin, Jim (20 January, 2010)
Callaghan, Ian (19 March, 2009)
Clemence, Ray (24 November, 2008)
Dalglish, Kenny (12 December, 2008)
Evans, Roy (7 August, 2009)
Fairclough, David (19 November, 2008)
Gillespie, Gary (20 April, 2010)
Green, Brian (18 March, 2011)
Grobbelaar, Bruce (2 December, 2009)
Hall, Brian (12 November, 2008)

Hansen, Alan (20 November, 2008)
Hart, Johnny (8 May, 2010)
Hunt, Roger (7 August, 2009)
Johnston, Craig (17 February, 2010)
Keegan, Kevin (25 November, 2008)
Kennedy, Alan (21 October, 2009)
Lawrenson, Mark (4 December, 2008)
Molby, Jan (24 October, 2008)
Moran, Ronnie (16 November, 2008)
Neal, Phil (21 February, 2009)
Pile, Chris (24 January, 2011)
Robinson, Michael (7 October, 2008)
Robinson, Peter (11 November, 2008)
St John, Ian (2 November, 2008)
Scott, George (30 March, 2011)
Souness, Graeme (18 January, 2010)
Thompson, Phil (1 October, 2009)
Waiters, Tony (19 August, 2009)
Whelan, Ronnie (20 September, 2009)
Yeats, Ron (2 November, 2008)

BOOKS

A'Court, Alan with Hargreaves, Ian – *Alan A'Court, My Life In Football*, The Bluecoat Press, 2003.

Barwick, Brian & Sinstadt, Gerald – *Everton v Liverpool, The Great Derbies*, BBC Books, 1998.

Belchem, John – *Liverpool 800, Culture, Character & History*, Liverpool University Press, 2006.

Bowler, Dave – *Shanks, The Authorised Biography*, Orion Books, 1996.

Dalglish, Kenny – *Dalglish, My Autobiography*, Hodder & Stoughton, 1996.

Dalglish, Kenny – *My Liverpool Home*, Hodder & Stoughton, 2010.

Darby, Tom – *Talking Shankly, The Man, The Genius, The Legend*, Mainstream Publishing, 1998.

Dodd, Jegsy – *Here We Go Gathering Cups In May,* Canongate, 2007.

Dohren, Derek – *Ghost On The Wall, The Authorised Biography of Roy Evans,* Mainstream Publishing, 2004.

Du Noyer, Paul – *Liverpool: Wondrous Place, Music from the Cavern to the Coral,* Virgin Books, 2002.

Evans, Tony – *Far Foreign Land, Pride and Passion the Liverpool Way,* Naomi Roth Publishing, 2006.

Foot, John – *Calcio,* Harper Perennial, 2007.

Glanville, Brian – *Champions Of Europe, The History, Romance and Intrigue of the European Cup,* Guinness Publishing, 1991.

Goble, Ray with Ward, Andrew – *Manchester City, A Complete Record,* Breedon Books, 1993.

Grobbelaar, Bruce – *More Than Somewhat,* Collins Willow, 1986.

Hansen, Alan – *A Matter Of Opinion,* Partridge, 1999.

Hansen, Alan and Gallacher, Ken – *Tall, Dark And Hansen, Ten Years At Anfield,* Mainstream Publishing, 1998.

Hargreaves, Ian, Rogers, Ken and George, Ric – *Liverpool Club of the Century,* Liverpool Echo Publication, 1988.

Hughes, Simon – *Geoff Twentyman, Secret Diary of a Liverpool Scout,* Sport Media, 2009.

Inglis, Simon – *The Football Grounds of Europe,* Collins Willow, 1990.

James, Gary – *Manchester, A Football History,* James Ward, 2008.

James, Gary – *Farewell to Maine Road,* Polar Print, 2003.

Johnston, Craig and Jameson, Neil – *Walk Alone,* Fleetfoot Books, 1990.

Keith, John – *Bob Paisley, Manager of the Millennium,* Robson Books, 1999.

Keith, John – *The Essential Shankly,* Robson Books, 2001.

Kelly, Stephen F. – *Dalglish, The Biography,* Headline, 1992.

Kelly, Stephen F. – *The Bootroom Boys, Inside The Anfield Bootroom,* Collins Willow, 1999.

Kelly, Stephen F. – *Bill Shankly, It's Much More Important Than That,* Virgin Books, 1996.

Kelly, Stephen F. – *The Official Illustrated History of Liverpool FC, You'll Never Walk Alone*, Queen Anne Press, 1991.

Kendall, Howard and Ross, Ian – *Only The Best Is Good Enough, The Howard Kendall Story*, Mainstream Publishing, 1991.

Lawrenson, Mark – *Mark Lawrenson, The Autobiography*, Queen Anne Press, 1988.

Liddell, Billy – *Billy Liddell, My Soccer Story*, Stanley Paul, 1960.

Liverpool FC Official Yearbook – 1977, 1978, 1979, 1980, 1981, 1982, 1983, 1983–84, 1984–85, 1985–86.

Liversedge, Stan – *The Liverpool Job*, Soccer Book Publishing, 1996.

Marks, Eddie – *Eddie's Golden Years Scrapbooks, Liverpool FC Season 1959–60*, Marksport Publications, 1986.

Murphy, Alex and Doig, Eric – *The Essential History of Liverpool*, W.H. Smith, 2003.

Neal, Phil – *Life At The Kop*, Queen Anne Press, 1986.

Paisley, Bob – *Bob Paisley, An Autobiography*, Arthur Barker, 1983.

Pead, Brian – *Liverpool, A Complete Record*, Breedon Books, 1986.

Pead, Brian – *Liverpool, Champions of Champions*, Breedon Books, 1990.

Phillips, Steven – *Rochdale AFC, The Official History 1907–2001*, Yore Publications, 2001.

Platt, Mark – *Cup Kings 1965*, The Bluecoat Press, 2000.

Platt, Mark – *Cup Kings 1977*, The Bluecoat Press, 2003.

Ponting, Ivan – *Liverpool Player By Player*, The Crowood Press, 1990.

Ponting, Ivan – *Red And Raw, A Post-War History of Manchester United v Liverpool*, Andre Deutsch, 1999.

Ponting, Ivan and Hale, Steve – *Liverpool in Europe*, Guinness Publishing, 1992.

Ponting, Ivan and Hale, Steve – *Sir Roger, The Life And Times Of Roger Hunt, A Liverpool Legend*, The Bluecoat Press, 1995.

Ponting, Ivan and Hale, Steve – *The Bootroom, An Anfield Legend*, The Bluecoat Press, 1996.

Reade, Brian – *43 Years With The Same Bird, A Liverpudlian Love Affair*, MacMillan, 2008.

Rowland, Chris – *From Where I Was Standing*, GPRF Publishing, 2009.

Rush, Ian – *Rush, Ian Rush's Autobiography*, Grafton Books, 1986.

Shankly, Bill – *Shankly, My Story*, Arthur Barker, 1976.

Shaw, Gary and Platt, Mark – *At The End Of The Storm, The Remarkable Story of Liverpool FC's Greatest Ever League Title Triumph 1946–47*, Gary Shaw, 2009.

Smith, Tommy – *Anfield Iron*, Bantam Press, 2008.

Souness, Graeme – *No Half Measures*, Willow Books, 1985.

St John, Ian with Lawton, James – *The Saint, My Autobiography*, Hodder & Stoughton, 2005.

Taw, Thomas – *Football's War & Peace, The Tumultuous Season of 1946–47*, Desert Island Books, 2003.

Taylor, Rogan, Ward, Andrew and Williams, John – *Three Sides Of The Mersey, An Oral History of Everton, Liverpool and Tranmere Rovers*, Robson Books, 1993.

Thompson, Phil – *Stand Up Pinocchio, Thommo, From the Kop to the Top, My Life Inside Anfield*, Sport Media, 2005.

Thompson, Phil – *Shankly*, The Bluecoat Press, 1993.

Thompson, Phil and Hale, Steve – *The Shankly Years, A Revolution in Football, Liverpool FC 1959–1974*, Ebury Press, 1998.

Wark, John – *Wark On, The Autobiography of John Wark*, Know The Score, 2009.

Williams, John – *Red Men, Liverpool Football Club, The Biography*, Mainstream Publishing, 2010.

Williams, John, Hopkins, Stephen and Long, Cathy – *Passing Rhythms, Liverpool FC And The Transformation Of Football*, Berg, 2001.

Wilson, Jonathan – *Inverting The Pyramid*, Orion Books, 2008.

NEWSPAPERS AND MAGAZINES
Liverpool Echo
Liverpool Daily Post
Liverpool Evening Express
Manchester Evening News
Bradford Telegraph & Argus
Nelson Leader
The Times
Sunday Times
Daily Mirror
Daily Star
Daily Mail
Daily Express
Sunday Express
The Guardian
The Kop
Xtra Time
Charles Buchan's Football Monthly
Shoot
Match
FourFourTwo
LFC Weekly

Various match programmes involving Liverpool, Manchester City, Nelson and Rochdale

TELEVISION, VIDEOS AND DVDs
No Ordinary Joe, LFC TV, 2008.
Liverpool FC: The Official History, BBC Videos, 1987.
Home & Away, Granada, 1984.
Requiem For A Cup Final, Periscope Productions, 2005.
Paisley: Farewell to a Legend, Granada, 1983.

RADIO

I Don't Know What It Is But I Love It, BBC Radio Merseyside documentary, 2004.

WEBSITES

www.lfchistory.net
www.liverpoolfc.tv
www.bootroom.net

INDEX